ONLY JESUS

ONLY JESUS

✳ ✳ ✳

Luis M. Martínez, D.D.

Translated from the Spanish by
Sister Mary St. Daniel, B.V.M.

CLUNY
Providence, Rhode Island

CLUNY MEDIA EDITION, 2022

This Cluny edition is a republication of *Only Jesus*,
originally published in 1962 by B. Herder Book Co.,
and is a a translation of *Jesús*, 3rd ed.,
published in 1947 by Editorial La Cruz, Mexico City.

The Scripture quotations are from the translation of Monsignor Ronald Knox.
Copyright © 1944, 1948, 1950, Sheed and Ward, Inc., New York.

NIHIL OBSTAT: J. S. Considine, O.P., S.T.M., *Censor deputatus*

IMPRIMATUR: Albert Cardinal Meyer, *Archbishop of Chicago*
MAY 10, 1962

For more information regarding this title
or any other Cluny Media publication,
please write to info@clunymedia.com, or to
Cluny Media, P.O. Box 1664, Providence, RI, 02901

⊰ VISIT US ONLINE AT WWW.CLUNYMEDIA.COM ⊱

ISBN: 978-1950970780

Cover design by Clarke & Clarke
Cover image:
El Greco, *Christ Blessing* ("The Saviour of the World"),
1600, oil on canvas
Courtesy of Wikimedia Commons

CONTENTS

TRANSLATOR'S PREFACE

It was in Mexico City that the works of Archbishop Martínez in the original Spanish first came into my hands. To spread the spiritual doctrine of His Excellency seemed a challenging apostolate. Accordingly, the last book from the pen of the late Primate of Mexico, a volume entitled *Jesús*, was selected for translation into English. Six Spanish editions have been published either in Mexico or in Spain.

When the first edition of *Jesús* appeared in 1940, the Catholic periodical, *La Cruz*, acclaimed it as the author's masterpiece, comparable to the writings of Monsignor Gay, Père Lacordaire, and Dom Marmion in solid doctrine, penetrating unction, profound, authentic mysticism and elevated style; a book belonging to those works that never grow old and never die.

The personal notes of Archbishop Martínez reveal his own reaction to the book review. "Regarding my latest book, *Jesús*, *La Cruz* states that it is my masterpiece. This delights me, not on account of the praise, but since Jesus is the Beloved of my soul, it is a great satisfaction that what I have written of Him should be my masterpiece."

May a similar satisfaction be the portion of all who read this unworthy rendition of a master's work.

Sister Mary St. Daniel, B.V.M.

PART ONE

THE TEACHINGS OF JESUS

CHAPTER 1

⚜

Love's Vision

On the manger straw the celestial babe lay wrapped in the whitest of swaddling clothes. His sweet Mother contemplated Him in silence, her heart melted with tenderness, her soul absorbed in profound adoration. Jesus opened His eyes and from those two divine suns radiated His first look of love.

What was that look? What was it like, O Virgin Mary? It met your virginal eyes, captivating your most pure soul; it was for you. For whom else would it have been? Where would the divine light be reflected but in the immaculate mirror of your purity? And you keep it there in the depths of your soul like an inextinguishable light in the blue of your sky. May our glorified eyes see the splendor of that gaze when we behold your countenance on the day of never-ending intimacies. But the impatience of our love dares in our exile to dream of the mystery of that divine look.

OUR SOUL shines forth from our eyes. A look is an emanation of the divine within our being; therefore it is the look that best expresses our inner self. Purity and love, grief and heroism; what the word does not say, what the lips do not sing, and what is too subtle to be contained in the sweetness of a smile, escapes from the soul wrapped in the transparent veil of a look!

But out of the eyes of Jesus not only His soul, but the uncreated Light, the Word of God, shone forth. The Father engenders His Son with a single glance, infinite and eternal, and the Word, Light of light, is the living reflection of the eternal look of the Father. In the bosom of God, the Father and the Son behold each other and there springs forth from them, like an infinite flame of love, the Holy Spirit. The mystery of the Trinity is the mystery of an eternal and ineffable contemplation of love.

That divine look of the Word shines out of Jesus' eyes wrapped in the immaterial light of His soul and in the visible splendor of His lovely eyes. What was the first look of Jesus like, O Virgin Mary? Purer than the ray of light reflected on the stainless snow of a mountain height, purer than the transparent glance of a child, purer than your own eyes, O Virgin Immaculate! Because it is so pure, that look has in its purity a divine fire more intense than the burning of volcanoes, the passion of enamored hearts, the fervor of heavenly seraphim. And because God, in whom everything multiple is unified, looks forth in that gaze, its ardor is bound with a tenderness so sweet and delicate that it surpasses the tenderness of all mothers, including even the Mother of God. In the depth of the purity, tenderness and ardor in Jesus' look, there is something that can be neither described nor understood, a profound and enchanting impression that attracts souls, that penetrates even to the interior of our being like a two-edged sword. It is the divine that is hidden in Jesus; it is the eternal and invisible look of God that shines through the visible humanity of Christ. That divine look, upon passing through the heavy atmosphere of earth, takes on a deeply human shade—the noble sadness and the unspeakable sweetness that sorrow puts into a look.

JESUS, I would give everything, even life, for one look of Your eyes. Is there not condensed in the brightness of that look all that our soul longs for in the infinite eagerness of its desires? I hope to bask eternally in the splendor of Your gaze, to contemplate the Light in the light of Your eyes. Is heaven not an eternal gaze of love? But however short and fleeting life may be, heaven seems distant to the impatience of loving desire. Look at me now! Look at me in this sorrowful exile, so that in the midst of the shadows of this life, the memory of those longed-for eyes engraven in my heart may shine as a vision from the skies!

All the looks of Jesus are divine, but the first must have held a singular charm because every first thing on earth possesses a unique beauty. In heaven, everything is first because everything is eternal. There, nothing fades away because everything participates in the eternal youth of God, because all is realized in a single instant, full and unending from eternity. But on earth, where everything passes away, where everything changes, there is in every beginning thing a touch of witchery, an unfathomable freshness that is never forgotten. Noonday has more splendor but not more charm than the dawn. After spring, warm and fruitful days will come, but they will never have the fragrance and the joy of spring. No matter how many joys life may bring us, we always covet the pristine joys of youth.

O Jesus, Your look grows and swells up in the soul of man like the light of the aurora advancing until it reaches midday, but the soul never forgets Your first look of love and will long for it until enfolded in heaven by that incomparable gaze which expresses both the virginal charm of eternal newness and the rich plenitude of perfection.

Such, without doubt, was the first look of Jesus—fresh, virginal, unique in its divine charm—when His eyes, like two suns, opened to illumine the loveliest, the most heavenly sight ever presented upon this earth: the virginal countenance of Mary.

OTHER EYES, very gentle, very pure, very beautiful, awaited the look of Jesus to gather the inexpressible first fruits of infinite love and limitless pain that issued forth from that first glance. As the ray of light is reflected by the purest crystal, producing another ray that embraces it in one kiss of love, so that look of Jesus was reflected in the clear eyes and the immaculate soul of Mary, fusing itself with her virginal look in a mystery of purity and of love. After the gaze of the Father, what is more worthy of union with the look of Jesus than the look of Mary? Truly, they were made the one for the other! It was fitting that the first contemplation of Jesus upon earth should be the most similar to that eternal one—full of tenderness, peace and fecundity which envelops, pervades, and engenders the Divine Word in the everlasting splendors of eternity.

Many eyes will rest upon the Word made flesh: the holy eyes of Joseph, the ingenuous gaze of the shepherds and that longing search of the Magi. Afterwards, the cold stare of the indifferent, and the cruel, sacrilegious glare of His enemies will desecrate that countenance. Let the first looks, at least, be worthy of Jesus. Let the first, at least, tell an enamored God coming to visit us that He is regarded upon earth as He is in heaven! That first look of Mary! Pure, because she is the Virgin of virgins; tender, because she is the Mother of God; holy, because she is the holiest of creatures. The purity of earth receives the purity of heaven; love awaits love; sanctity by participation unites with sanctity by essence.

The Word does not look at the Father only, nor must the Father be seen only by the Son. Therefore, every glance at Jesus is the eternal look of the Word both hiding and revealing itself in the visible light of His eyes. In the same way, every gaze that centers upon the Word—the look of faith, of love, of contemplation—is in reality the look of the Father which both hides and reveals itself in the expressions of souls. But in no look is that of the Father revealed with so great perfection as in the eyes of Mary. Thus, as the Father communicated His fecundity to the gentle Virgin when the Holy

Spirit covered her with His shadow, so He desired to communicate to Mary a reflection of His eternal gaze. When Jesus, upon opening His divine eyes, met Mary's gaze, He was filled with ineffable complacency because He discovered the Father looking upon Him through the pure, mild, tender eyes of the Virgin Mary. And in this valley of tears, in the poor, humble cave of Bethlehem, He appeared before the wondering angels as a new revelation of the eternal mystery of the life of God. When the looks of Jesus and Mary were joined in the holy unity of love, heaven and earth were filled with the glory of God and with that true peace of which the angels sang on that blessed night.

The mystery of those two looks, unique in their perfection, continues to be reproduced throughout the centuries in different degrees. Jesus wants to look at souls as He looked at Mary, and He wants to be looked at by souls as Mary looked at Him. He came to earth for that purpose, so that by His looking at us and by our looking at Him, our hearts might be carried away to the heights of invisible things, to the bosom of the Trinity, to share in the mystery of the eternal contemplation of love. Thus, the Church sings in the Preface of Christmas: "And we are drawn to the love of things unseen through Him whom we acknowledge as God, now seen by men."

The first look of Jesus had something transitory about it as if subject to time, but it also had something immutable and permanent, divine and eternal. Out of the centuries there comes to each soul of good will the unspeakable delight of the first look of Jesus without the fading of its freshness, the abatement of its ardor, or the loss of its divine clarity. The soul that receives it ought to respond by reproducing Mary's look, pure, tender, exceedingly holy, a copy of the Father's look, created but exact. And in the littleness and misery of each soul—happy reproduction of Bethlehem—the Word sees the Father, and again the sacred mystery is reproduced upon earth, a sure hope, an infallible pledge that such a soul will enter one day into the perfect joy of the eternal sight of God.

CHAPTER 2

✼

Three Nights

There are three nights of immortal memory: the night of the Nativity, the night of the Agony, and the night of the Resurrection. The first is the night of gladness and of hope; the second, of love and of anguish; the third, of joy.

JOYFUL NIGHT of Bethlehem!

The skies are opened; the earth trembles; the echoes of the universe repeat canticles of glory and of peace! "Glory to God in high heaven, and peace on earth to men that are God's friends!" (Luke 2:14).

In the midst of the night, when everything is silent, the omnipotent Word descends from His royal abode. "There was a hush of silence all around, and night had but finished half her swift journey, when from Thy heavenly throne, Lord, down leaped Thy Word omnipotent" (Wis. 18:14–15).

O wonderful exchange! God becomes man to make us Godlike. He becomes poor to make us rich. He shares our griefs to give us happiness! This marvelous exchange constitutes the basis of Christianity. It is the sublime thesis of Scripture. It is the divine drama of history because it is the *mystery of Christ*. Bethlehem is the beginning. There God and man appear indissolubly united. Bethlehem is the beginning of God's sorrow, which must be consummated in agony. The beginning of man's glory will find its climax on the night of the Resurrection.

A Child has been given to us; a Son has been born to us, who bears upon His shoulders an empire—an empire formed with all the glories of heaven and all the sorrows of earth. His name is Admirable, God, Strong, Father of the World to come, Prince of peace. Men and centuries will follow in His retinue. From all the confines of the world they will come to Him, bringing symbolic gifts: gold, incense and myrrh. The night of Bethlehem is the night of joy. It is the dawn that awakens and rejoices nature with a kiss of softest light and a caress of fresh whiteness. It is the love that makes a delightful entrance into souls though they may not guess, in their pristine purity, what treasures of bitterness or abyss of happiness that longed-for and mysterious guest bears to them so hiddenly. It is the first kiss of God and of man, enclosing with its idyllic sweetness the ignominious tragedy of the Cross and the glorious manifestation of the Resurrection.

Let the earth be glad and let the heavens rejoice, because the Desired of the eternal hills has come! Now man can see with his eyes, hear with his ears and touch with his hands the Word of life. Glory to God in the highest and peace on earth to men of good will.

NIGHT OF tenderness and of grief! Night of the Cenacle and of Gethsemane! The last night that Jesus spent with His own! Who can comprehend your mysteries? As swirling torrents of water break through a dike, to be precipitated impetuously into the ocean, so the immense love and sorrow which had accumulated in the Heart of Christ since the night of Bethlehem, finally swept away all obstacles and overflowed this night in an ocean of tenderness and grief. Jesus had loved His own. He had loved them in Bethlehem, in Nazareth, in the desert, on Tabor, in all the places He had traveled, preaching peace, preaching goodness. He had loved them, illuminating them with His doctrine, enriching them with His riches, curing miseries and wiping away tears. But He reserved for the end the most exquisite fruits of His tenderness. "He still loved those who were His own, whom He was leaving in the world, and He would give them the uttermost proof of His love" (John 13:1).

11

Never until then had He knelt before His disciples to wash their feet. Never had He spoken as He spoke to them then, so clearly, so confidentially, so tenderly. Without doubt, on that immortal night His eyes looked with more tenderness, His lips smiled more sweetly, His voice took on a more celestial accent. The discourse at the Last Supper still preserves, after twenty centuries, the perfume of the melancholy and the love of a most tender farewell. In it, Christ opens His heart entirely to His disciples. In it is poured forth—like Mary's ointment—the charity of Christ into souls. In it there are phrases that soften our hearts with tenderness. What name does He give to His own? "My friends…My children" (John 15:14–15; 13:33). And Christ is speaking! Of what does He speak? Of love: "Live on, then, in My love" (John 15:9). What a sentence! The lips become mute upon hearing it; only the heart can comment. "This is My commandment, that you should love one another as I have loved you" (John 15:12). The kingdom of love begins; the kingdom that, founded in the heart of Christ, is completed in the bosom of God, who is love. "Now I am going back to Him who sent Me. None of you is asking Me, Where is it Thou art going, so full are your hearts with sorrow at My telling you this. And yet I can say truly that it is better for you that I should go away; He who is to befriend you will not come to you unless I do go, but if only I make My way there I will send Him to you" (John 16:5-7). The Holy Spirit, the substantial love of God, will come to consummate for us that union which is the supreme desire of love. That hour is

Christ's hour, the hour of love. "Jesus already knew that the time had come" (John 13:1). The hour of sorrow, that is Christ's hour. In the Cenacle, *love* overflowed; in Gethsemane, *sorrow*.

When two things are united, their properties are mutually communicated. God, who is love, felicity and glory, communicated all this to humanity when He celebrated the eternal nuptials with it in the womb of Mary. And man, what did he communicate to God? What do we have of our very own? Wretchedness, sorrow and sin. When the Word descended from heaven, He received that doleful inheritance of human lineage. He took upon Himself our miseries; He burdened Himself with the immense weight of our griefs. He who had not known sin, who is the complete and eternal negation of sin, because He is the infinite being, the highest sanctity, became sin for us. "Our weakness, and it was He who carried the weight of it, our miseries, and it was He who bore them" (Is. 53:4). "Christ never knew sin, and God made Him into sin for us" (2 Cor. 5:21).

All the sins of the world, all the abominations of the earth with their incalculable number, their infinite malice, their abysmal ingratitude, accumulated in the Heart of Christ, oppressing it and overflowing in torrents of bitterness and blood on that night in Gethsemane. Hear, listen: "My soul…is ready to die with sorrow" (Matt. 26:38). Look, contemplate: "His sweat fell to the ground like thick drops of blood" (Luke 22:44).

There are on earth inconsolable sorrows that one marvels at. The sorrow of God can neither be consoled nor marveled at; one adores in silence. The night of the Cenacle and Gethsemane is the night of sorrow and of love. It is Christ's hour and Christ wanted to make it boundless and immortal. How many times we should like an hour to last forever! The love of Christ, sweet as heaven and strong as death, took that hour and extended it to all places and perpetuated it throughout all ages. The Eucharist is the crystallization of that hour, of Christ's hour!

"Let us then, prostrate, adore so great a Sacrament."[1]

13

ALLELUIA! CHRIST has risen! Humanity, having lost its heritage of death on Calvary, received an inheritance of glory through the risen humanity of Christ. Alleluia! A night witnessed this mystery, a night brighter than day, a night illuminated by the splendors of the Eternal King!

"This is the night in which Christ, the conqueror, having destroyed the chains of death, arose from the tomb....

"O truly blessed night, which alone knew the time and the hour when Christ arose from the dead. Night of which it was written: With thee, the night shines clear as the day itself; light and dark are one (Ps. 138:11–12).

"Blessed night that despoiled the Egyptians and enriched the Hebrews, night in which the terrestrial was linked with the celestial and the divine and the human were united forever."[2]

> O night that was my guide!
> O night dearer than the morning's pride,
> O night that joined the lover
> To the beloved bride
> Transfiguring them each into the other.[3]

O heavenly night! Divine night! Glorious night! Night that beheld the day-star shine, "that morning star which knows no setting."[4] Night that made man divine, as the night of the agony had made God profoundly human! O heavenly night! Divine night! Glorious night! May the saints extol you! May the blessed enjoy you in the

---

1. Office for Corpus Christi.
2. Liturgy for Holy Saturday.
3. *Poems of St. John of the Cross*, trans. by Roy Campbell (New York: Pantheon Books, Inc., 1953).
4. Liturgy for Holy Saturday.

luminous day of eternity of which you were the beginning and the dawn. We can neither comprehend you nor attain your full enjoyment. Laden with misery, yet with hope, pilgrims in the night of this life, we sigh for you, for the clear light of our fatherland, and stealing the angel's canticle, we repeat without understanding it the glorious hymn that expresses thy praise: Alleluia! Alleluia! Alleluia!

CHAPTER 3

☙

Paths of Peace

When the angels announced to the world the incomparable, unprecedented joy of Jesus' birth, they made two promises: one in favor of heaven, the other in favor of earth; the former, the *glory of God*; the latter, *peace to men of good will*. Both of these pledges include and summarize the entire work of Jesus Christ in this world: to give glory to God and to bring peace to souls.

As it would not be possible to discuss within the compass of some few pages these two sublime objectives of Jesus' work, I shall confine my considerations to but one of them, *peace*. Peace is the gift that Jesus Christ brought us from heaven, *His* gift, the gift of God; a gift so beautiful, so profound, so all-embracing, so efficacious, that we shall never truly comprehend it.

We might say concerning peace what our Lord said of Himself to the Samaritan woman at Jacob's well: "If thou knewest what it is God gives" (John 4:10). Truly, if we but understood this God-given gift of peace, we could appreciate how it is the synthesis, the very climax, so to speak, of all the graces and heavenly blessings which we have received in Christ Jesus.

Peace is the seal of Christ. It is not just one of His many gifts; it is, in a certain way, His own gift. When Jesus appeared in the world on that unforgettable night in Bethlehem, the angels proclaimed peace. On another unforgettable night, the last that He spent on earth, the sweet night of the Cenacle and the Eucharist, Jesus left peace to His loved ones as a testament of His love: "Peace is My bequest to you" (John 14:27).

Our Lord's customary greeting to His apostles after His resurrection was this: "Peace be upon you!" Furthermore, He recommended that in pursuing their apostolic mission, they should always say these words upon arriving at any house: "Peace be upon you" (John 20:21, 26), and if the Son of peace dwelt there he should receive their peace; if not, their good wishes for peace should redound to themselves.

Holy Church, the perpetuation of Jesus Himself throughout the centuries, understands our Lord's spirit thoroughly. Adopting her Master's expression in her liturgy, she constantly invokes peace upon her children. While imparting peace to us, she disposes us to give peace to one another.

Almost all the sacramental rites terminate with an expression of peace. The newly baptized, the Christian strengthened by confirmation, the sinner purified in the sacrament of penance, all receive a message of peace: "Peace be with you" or "Go in peace."

The communication of our Lord's peace sometimes takes place in an external ceremony, full of tenderness. It may be an embrace, as in a Solemn Mass, between the celebrant and the assisting ministers; it may be a kiss of peace, as between the bishop and the priest whom he has just ordained. The entire liturgy is impregnated with this spirit of Christ; at every turn it echoes Jesus' word to His apostles after the resurrection: "Peace be upon you."

The life of the Church is nothing else than the triumphant march of peace throughout the world. Above the cradle of the Church, as above the manger of Bethlehem, angels could fittingly sing the same canticle: "Glory to God in the highest and peace on earth to men of good will," for the Church has done nothing else nor does she intend to do anything else than to give glory to God and peace to men of good will. She has no other mission.

OUR LORD'S peace has distinctive characteristics which call for at least a brief consideration. First, it is a peace *exclusively His own*; He has a monopoly on peace. On the eve of His passion, He said to His disciples: "I give you My peace, the peace that the world cannot give."

The world, which counterfeits everything, cannot counterfeit peace, however much it tries. It misrepresents joy; the world's happiness is always superficial and sometimes even bitter. The world counterfeits wisdom, dazzling the credulous with a showy but empty knowledge. It counterfeits love, giving this sacred name to brute passion or to vile egoism. The world, the offspring of Satan, father of lies, is essentially an impostor, falsifying everything. But it is powerless in counterfeiting one thing: peace. The world cannot give peace because peace is a divine thing; it is the seal of Jesus Christ.

A second characteristic of our Lord's peace is its *profundity*. It is not superficial, merely exterior, the peace of the tomb or the desert. Such is not really peace, but solitude, emptiness, desolation. The peace of God, on the other hand, reaches even to the depths of our hearts. It pervades our innermost being, penetrating it like an exquisite perfume. Peace is plenitude; it is life.

Thirdly, peace is *indestructible*. Nothing, no one, can force the peace of heaven out of a soul that has received this gift of God: neither the persecutions of tyrants, nor the snares of the devil, nor the vicissitudes of earth can disturb a soul in which God has established His peace.

On the eve of His passion, Jesus, having told His apostles that He gave them His joy, added: "And your gladness will be one which nobody can take away from you" (John 16:22). Precisely the same may be said of peace: "And nobody can take it away from you." Everything else may be taken away from us: our homes, our property, our liberty and even our life. In a certain sense, we can be deprived of happiness. It is true that perfect joy can be experienced precisely when the eyes weep and the heart bleeds, but such heights are characteristic of only very elevated, perfect souls. Consequently enemies may take from us, in some measure, even our joy. But they can never deprive us of peace when Jesus has given it to us. Peace can continue its reign in our hearts in spite of the miseries, sadness and bitterness of life.

Finally, the peace of Christ is a *rich* peace, full of sweetness and mildness. St. Paul describes it as "the peace of God, which surpasses all our thinking" (Phil. 4:7). This peace is the only form of happiness unparalleled upon the earth; it is the substance of heaven. Without the splendors of the beatific vision, without the overflowing happiness of that everlasting state, peace is the substance of what we hope to enjoy in heaven.

NINETEEN CENTURIES have passed since Jesus made this richest of gifts to humanity. Each Christmas He renews this heavenly gift in souls and the angels again sing: "Peace on earth to men of good will." Each Easter Jesus risen again greets the faithful with His favorite expression: "Peace be upon you," pouring into Christian hearts a veritable torrent of peace.

I am not referring at the moment to exterior, collective or international peace. On the contrary, I refer to interior peace, which wars and persecutions cannot disturb. Why, I insist, is peace so greatly lacking in souls? I understand that there are struggles and sufferings within the soul; but what seems difficult to comprehend, if one thinks deeply, is that peace should be lacking in the soul of a Christian.

We Christians have a claim on suffering, struggle, persecution, but we have no claim to the loss of our peace. The proper attitude

and natural atmosphere of the Christian should be one of peace, and
in the midst of all the vicissitudes of life he ought to preserve peace,
the seal of Jesus and the characteristic feature of the Christian.

Where God is, there is peace, and we carry God in our hearts.
Neither life nor death, neither the powers of heaven nor the forces
of hell, neither height nor depth, nor any created thing whatsoever
can draw out of our heart that God whom we possess. Then why is
not our whole life utterly filled with peace?

I am emphasizing this point because I maintain that souls
ought to preserve peace at all costs. To do this it is essential to discover the secret of peace.

Holy Scripture says: "Let peace be all thy quest and aim" (Ps.
33:15), thus pointing out to us that peace is not to be sought with
lukewarmness and negligence, but with ardor, with care. In war one
pursues the enemy, in peace one seeks happiness; in the same way
we ought constantly to seek and pursue peace.

But is it always possible to preserve peace of soul? Should our
hearts never be disturbed by anything at all? Are there safe, direct
routes to reach this most blessed goal? Undoubtedly there are. But
the strange thing is that souls lose peace so easily and then live in
turmoil. This is a real evil. But what of suffering, struggle, desolation? Let them come! But anxiety, disturbance—never! Sufferings
conceal sweet, celestial fruit under their bitter rind; anxiety and
disturbance never contain any good.

Our Lord never asks nor can He ask the sacrifice of peace even
of souls entrusted with a mission of suffering. He will ask them for
the sacrifice of all earthly goods; He will ask them for the painful,
life-long immolation of themselves; He will ask them for interior,
tormenting holocausts, but always in an atmosphere of peace.

It would be interesting to make an analysis of our anxieties,
but we would be ashamed of the ignorance, the egoism, the distrust
causing them. Rather than analyze the evil, I prefer to set forth the
means whereby the soul may preserve peace despite all obstacles.

FAITH

The first path to peace is faith. In fact, if we lived by faith, we should live in peace. We read in Scripture: "It is faith that brings life to the man whom I accept as justified" (Heb. 10:38). He who lives under the rule of faith lives in perfect peace; all faith's teachings tend to calm us.

Let us make a synthesis of the teachings of faith relative to the subject we are treating, to help us realize the facility with which we may attain peace when we live supernaturally.

Faith teaches that God loves us and that He loves us not as a group, but personally, individually: "He loved *me*!" Each one of us can make these words of the Apostle his own without fear of error. He knows my name, He has engraved my image in His heart. Still more, I can be assured that His heart is all mine because our Lord cannot love as we do, by halves; when He loves, He loves with His whole heart, infinitely.

Souls sometimes say, with a mixture of love and of ignorance: "I wish our Lord would love me more." But is that possible? Can He who loves infinitely love any more? If nothing else existed in the world except God and you, O soul who reads these lines, He would not love you more than He does right now. If you were the only object of His love, He would love you just as He loves you now.

God's love has all the characteristics of the love we idealize in our ardent dreams, for we all dream; it so becomes the human heart to dream. Yes, we want to be loved with a deep, tender, consuming love. Half measures do not satisfy us nor do they satisfy elect souls destined for intimate union with God, those souls tortured by the insatiable desires of love.

Now let me assure you of this: Jesus loves us more, infinitely more, than we desire, more than we dare to dream of. Sometimes our dreams seem bold, almost absurd; nevertheless, they are far below reality.

It is this very magnitude of God's love that so frequently disconcerts us. We think: "It is an exaggeration to say God loves me like that. If not even I can love myself that way, how is it possible that God does so? No, that is an excess."

Right, it is an excess; infinite love has to be so. The Incarnation, the manger, Nazareth, the Cenacle, Gethsemane, Calvary, each was an excess. And the Church and Pentecost are other tremendous excesses because they are the works of an infinite love. In comparison with our smallness, infinite love must necessarily be an excess. Yet, how difficult to convince souls that God so loves them. If they could be convinced, how many anxieties would be alleviated.

WE MAY go a step farther. God's love for us is not a sterile love, confined to heaven; it is an active love, provident, watchful, solicitous; it is a love that does not forget us one moment, that protects us unceasingly, that keeps arranging minutely all the events of our life from the most far-reaching to the most insignificant.

I am not exaggerating; Jesus Himself affirmed it: "No hair of your head shall perish" (Luke: 21:18). Some persons may consider this hyperbole. Perhaps, but at any rate it is a hyperbole expressive of the solicitude, the constancy, the minute care of God's love for us.

Consider a mother caring for her first babe, watching at his cradle, ever mindful of his needs, anxious lest he weep or become ill. The devotion of such a mother cannot match even remotely the constant, minute, tender solicitude of our Lord. If only we had the faith to understand this. Not for one moment does our Lord turn His eyes away from us, nor does His hand cease to guide us; at each instant of our lives His power protects us and His love enfolds us.

And if this is true, if God's solicitude for us is loving, unalterable, most tender, what reason have we to be disturbed? Can a child in his mother's arms be disturbed? Only in one way: only if he dreams that he is in danger and alone. His uneasiness would be the fruit of an illusion. If the child realizes that he is in the arms of the mother who loves and protects him, why should he be restless? Through what strange phenomenon, through what inexplicable illusion do we Christians disquiet ourselves, knowing with the certainty of faith that a loving God bears us in His arms and surrounds us with His divine tenderness?

Let us penetrate this mystery of love and of mercy a little farther. Let us see what are the sources of our own most frequent anxieties. Frequently we become disturbed by thoughts like these: "Could I have committed that fault? Shall I get rid of these temptations? Am I in a good state before God? Am I on the right road? Will my superiors change my place or my work? Have I lost the trust and esteem of my superiors?" If I am ill: "Shall I get well?" If I am well: "Shall I become ill?" I should never finish if I tried to make a complete list of all our worries; each reader may complete it on his own.

Ordinarily we concern ourselves about future events as well as those that are past. Well now, did all these disquieting events escape God's loving providence? Or could our Lord have been distracted when He determined that such a thing happen to us? Or was He unable to avert this event in spite of His attention and solicitude for us? Or did His love suffer an eclipse during which this misfortune befell us?

By no means. What does happen is that we forget that God arranges or permits all things, that nothing escapes His providence and that our Lord guides and governs our whole life. When we are disquieted it is usually through such forgetfulness or because the event is not according to our liking and we do not accept it with resignation, or because we want to know the consequences beforehand, whether for good or for ill. "Will this affair involve me in complications? Will it not be the first link in a chain of sufferings and contradictions?"

We forget that God regulates all things, that we are not alone but carried in the divine arms, those omnipotent arms which not only protect us but also direct the world and arrange all life's occurrences. Since we are in such hands, protected by such love, are we not foolish to be disturbed?

THE PEACE enjoyed by the saints intrigues us at times, but we wonder how they always remained tranquil in the midst of so many painful vicissitudes. To me it seems still more strange that Christians, who have the faith, are filled with anxiety, for to preserve peace, one single thing would suffice: to live by faith, especially to believe in the consoling dogma of the love of God and of His constant, solicitous providence. We should need nothing more.

"What will tomorrow bring? What will happen to me this year? Will it be better or worse than last year?" Idle questions, useless forebodings. I know only one thing: that today as yesterday, that tomorrow as today, that this year as last, God loves me, and He loves me as my heart yearns to be loved—no, much more than I dare aspire to. I know only that during this year as in the past I shall continue to live in the arms and in the Heart of Jesus, and that He, with incomparable solicitude, will rule over all things including each detail of my life, designing all for my good and for my happiness.

Since this is true, no one need wish me happiness in the new year; I carry happiness in my heart. If I become ill, if I am persecuted, if I am dying—incidents of no importance. In reality all these things will contribute to strengthen my peace and to increase my happiness. In utmost tranquility, therefore, I rest in the arms and in the Heart of Jesus. My heart echoes Bethlehem's hymn: "Glory to God in the highest and peace on earth to men of good will." My soul resounds with the tender accents of Jesus' farewell: "My peace I leave you."

Let us recall an anecdote about Julius Caesar. He was crossing a river in a boat. Suddenly the winds were unleashed and rough waves rose high. The boatsman hesitated, trembling. Julius Caesar haughtily rebuked him saying: "Why do you fear? You are carrying Caesar." As if Caesar had the power to chain the winds and to soothe the waves! But the story reminds us of another phrase more wonderful still. "Why do you fear? You are carried by Jesus! Jesus guides you, Jesus takes you in His arms, Jesus bears you in His heart."

A living faith, especially faith in the sweet, consoling dogma of our Lord's love for us, is one of the most direct and sure ways to achieve peace. If God loves me, if He cares for me constantly, if His heart's loving solicitude attends every event of my life, I can and I ought to live in peace.

BUT IT may be objected: Do the love of God and His providence really influence all the events of our life? Perhaps our liberty—that God-given gift at once glorious and terrible—may snatch our affairs and our destiny out of His hands, so to speak, and place upon them the seal of turmoil, changing them into means of affliction.

We readily agree that some of life's situations are arranged by God, that we are here or there, healthy or ill, in desolation or in consolation, but it is difficult to regard others in the same way. For example, persecution against the Church—is this also providential? Is this not out of harmony with the love of God?

And there is something still more difficult to reconcile with God's loving providence, namely, our failings, our sins. How is it possible to commit faults and go astray if we are in God's arms? Can one sin within the Heart of God? Why does our Lord permit falls, especially a certain kind of fall? We pass over some faults easily because they are slight or less humiliating or of little importance, but there are others that disconcert us, that seem to change our life. "Lord, how did You permit such a thing? Could that moment of my life possibly have eluded Your attention?"

St. Paul gives us a very concise, enlightening principle in this respect: "Everything helps to secure the good of those who love

God" (Rom. 8:28). Let us take that *everything* just as it sounds, without exceptions: certain temptations and circumstances seemingly unfavorable for our sanctification, our defects and especially our falls. We must make no exception where God makes none. *Everything* helps to secure our good; consequently, persecutions from without and struggles from within, dangers and temptations, our defects and our very falls. All things work together for the good of those who love God.

25

I am among those who love God; therefore, I absolutely should not be disturbed by anything that may happen to me. If I become ill, blessed be God; this infirmity will sanctify me; if I am well, blessed be God; health will be a means of doing good; if persecution oppresses me, blessed be God; it will jolt me out of my lukewarmness; if persecution ceases, blessed be God; I can now devote myself to my sanctification with greater liberty; if I am tempted, if I fall into sin, how good, O Lord, that Thou hast humbled me so that I may learn to know and despise myself. Let no one think that I am trying to give a lesson in artificial optimism, emphasizing the fair side of everything in order to ward off suffering. Much less am I proposing a system of ease. May God deliver me, when speaking in His name, from advancing a human system, however perfect and ingenious. No, I speak only the truth in Christ Jesus and I do nothing more than explain the doctrine contained in the Scriptures: "Everything helps to secure the good of those who love God."

From this it follows that the knowledge of events in store for me is a very secondary matter, because I already know that whatever their nature they will bring me to God. A traveler whose chief concern is to arrive safe at a certain distant country regards the mode of travel as of secondary importance. He reaches one station of the trip and asks: "How does one travel here?" "By train." And he takes the train. "And here?" "By automobile." "And here?" "By plane." "And here?" "By boat." It is a question of greater or less comfort, of greater or less speed, but for the one who seeks neither comfort nor speed, but who is intent only upon reaching the end of his journey, the means is a very secondary matter.

What does the journey matter provided one reaches sanctity? The main thing is to reach it. What does it matter whether we go to God through sickness or through health, through struggle or repose, through consolation or aridity? If we ourselves set about selecting the way, in all probability we would choose sweetness and ease—and the wrong route, whereas our Lord chooses for us what we need at any given moment. The worst thing that could happen to us would be to be given freedom of choice in selecting our own path to heaven, for our selection would be unwise; we would choose desolation when in need of consolation, and consolation when desolation would be more suitable; we would choose struggle when rest would be in order, and rest when effort would be necessary. We would never make the right selection because we are too shortsighted to know ourselves the designs of God or the paths to perfection. St. Paul says that we do not even know what we should ask for—so simple a thing—therefore the Holy Spirit asks for us: "The Spirit comes to the aid of our weakness; when we do not know what prayer to offer, to pray as we ought, the Spirit Himself intercedes for us" (Rom. 8:26).

A keen realization of this truth should convince us that the best thing for us at each step is what God sends. Frequently it is not to our taste, but what does it matter, provided we are sanctified? What means are at hand today for my sanctification? Whatever God sends me, whether it be sickness, temptation or aridity.

The fact is that we would like, in greater or lesser degree, to please ourselves; or rather, to please ourselves in a merely natural order rather than in a supernatural order. So we often would like one thing or another for our own comfort, through self-love; and if what God sends us is not to our taste, we are disturbed and even rebellious. In the spiritual order, too, we would like to satisfy our personal tastes. I do want to reach sanctity, but by *this* path, in imitation of my favorite saint; but no, our Lord knows better than we along what path and in what manner we must reach heaven.

On the other hand, we would like to have clear insight into all that happens to us and its contribution to our sanctification. And so when we understand that such a thing will sanctify us, we are content; but if we do not understand, we are disquieted. How can this suffering possibly sanctify me? The Cross is indeed the way to perfection, but there are crosses and crosses, and in this one I see no prospect of coming closer to God. How shall I become holy if our Lord places me in these conditions which seem opposed to my sanctification?

What blindness of heart! Do you not understand the ways of God? He loves you more than you love yourself, He loves you more than anyone else loves you, He is unceasingly solicitous for your good. If He sends you this cross, it is exactly what you need for your sanctification.

If we but understood these truths, what could make us lose peace? How calm our lives would be! Come this event or another, it makes no difference—in the depths of the soul, I mean, for not being of stone, I shall not fail to feel. Some events bring joy and others, suffering; yes, I shall suffer and weep and I may even complain, but deep in my heart I shall experience peace. "Lord, this instrument You are now using to sanctify me must be very precious since Your love sends it; yes, I recognize it but it pains me; allow me, then, to weep and to complain." And Jesus allows us to weep and to complain; but what He does not want is that we become disturbed; while we groan and weep He would have us preserve peace in our heart.

I insist that what I keep saying is not something artificial, it is unadulterated truth, although profound truth. Things seen superficially can disturb us, but if we regard them with the profundity of faith, nothing can make us lose peace.

One day St. Ignatius Loyola was asked if anything could alter his peace. The Saint replied: "Only one thing could disturb me, the suppression of the Society; but I believe that a few moments would suffice to calm that disturbance and to recover peace."

Then no difficulty exists; all things work together unto good for those who love God, for in the divine hands even hindrances are converted into helps.

BUT DOES moral evil, sin, also promote the spiritual welfare of those who love God? Yes; the Apostle excepts nothing and neither should we: *all*, even our failings, even our sins. But is it possible that sins work toward the good of those who love God? Some simple reflections will suffice to clarify this point.

The sacrifice of Jesus was the greatest event in human history, the most fruitful, the most efficacious, or to speak more accurately, the only efficacious sacrifice, since it is the source of all efficacy in the supernatural order. Did not the sacrifice of Jesus require as an instrument the greatest sins ever committed on earth? Does not Holy Church describe the very sin of Adam as "happy" because it gave occasion for Christ to come to redeem us? On Holy Saturday the Church sings: "O happy fault that merited such and so great a Redeemer! O truly necessary sin of Adam!" What audacity in the Church to speak thus! But it is the audacity of profound insight.

Since the time of Adam's fall, God has this invariable strategy both in the general history of the human race and in the history of each soul: to draw good out of evil, which thereby becomes an instrument to achieve good. History proves this perfectly. The cowardice of Pilate, the cunning of Caiaphas, the intriguing, haughty spirit of the priestly leaders and the Scribes and Pharisees were the ladder along which Jesus went to His sacrifice. Again, the obsession of the Jews was the occasion for the vocation of the Gentiles, the tyranny of the Caesars during the first three centuries of the Church gave rise to the multitude of glorious martyrs. The heretics, who continued the persecutions, gave occasion to that group of Fathers and Doctors of the Church. Thus, in the succession of events, God always draws good out of evil.

29

What God does on a large scale in history, He does on a small scale in each soul. One day in heaven we shall understand the important role played in our sanctification by our frailties and our sins. And even though we regret having offended God, after all, perhaps we should paraphrase the words of the Church: "O happy sins of mine that merited so great a Redeemer." O truly necessary faults, for our failings humiliate us by revealing to us our nothingness. This is one of the main purposes for which God permits them.

But let us be sincere. Are our faults repugnant to us and do they grieve us only and exclusively because they are offenses against God? Do not motives of shame frequently prevail, such as the blemish of these faults, the wound to self-love, and the like? Similarly, we do not want to be freed from temptations only to be less exposed to the danger of offending God, but also to avoid the annoyance of a struggle against them.

This being so, is it not true that it would be a very simple, efficacious and gentle procedure to sanctify ourselves by accepting each day what our Lord asks of us? We have absolute certainty that what God plans for us each day is most suitable and sanctifying.

Sometimes in the morning we are too far-seeing; we would like to take in from the first moment the whole course of the day: What shall I have to do? What am I going to suffer? What do I fear? What do I hope for? And we set up our program. The only program for me is God's program. Let this day come as it may, God sends it; He and no one else. Let it come as it may, we are sure that it comes wrapped in the love of our Lord and destined to sanctify us. We ought to say: "I will sanctify myself precisely by the events of this day because the loving providence of God has sent them to me. He is acquainted with my necessities, He knows what is most conducive to my sanctification." If we were to understand this, would not our soul be a veritable ocean of peace?

ONE FINAL objection: I acknowledge that by following God's plan and subjecting myself to His will, I walk in security and live in peace. But anxieties arise on this account, for by the abuse of my liberty I may resist the divine will, go astray and follow a crooked path. Is not this a reasonable cause for worry? No. It is a reasonable cause for repentance, for tears and a firm resolution, but not for the loss of peace. God does not cease being good because I am bad, nor does He cease seeking me because I go astray. Did He not reveal to us His own heart in the parable of the good shepherd who left the ninety-nine sheep while he ran after the one that was lost? Yes, I have absolute certainty that if I go astray, Jesus will seek me. I shall place myself in His omnipotent hands. I shall rest upon His shoulders and I shall return to the fold. Perhaps I must suffer to return to the right path, but blessed be the sufferings which atone for my fault and bring me back to my God.

Whatsoever our failings may be, whatsoever our wanderings, we have no right to lose either hope or peace. We are Christians and we Christians have received peace as a gift from heaven, as a seal of Christ, that peace which the world can neither give nor take away.

I shall suffer, I shall repent, I shall do penance, I shall sacrifice myself…everything, but with peace in my heart; for I know that here is someone who loves me in spite of my infidelities; someone who, when I wander, puts me back on the right path; who, when I fall, raises me up; who, when I sink into the mud, knows how to purify me. If we but knew Jesus, His love and His mercy! Then fear would disappear from our souls and on the wings of hope we would rise above the miseries of life, and peace would establish in our hearts the kingdom of God.

HOPE

Our frailty and our diffidence never cease to make objections. 31
We are so inclined to mistrust, to be anxious seems to us so natural
a thing that often we try to withdraw from the peace that God has
given us. We wonder if it can be an illusion, we scrutinize to see if
we may not have reason to be disturbed. Perhaps it occurs to us to
say: "How is it possible to live in peace, without uneasiness, in this
sad exile, so far from our blessed fatherland, exposed to the loss of
our happiness forever? Could the Israelites live without worry when
they were wandering over the desolate sands of the desert, so far
from the Promised Land and so exposed to the possibility of never
reaching that land overflowing with milk and honey? There are at
least two justifiable motives for anxiety. First, will that happy day
ever come in which the intense yearning of my soul for close union
with God will be satisfied? Or shall I remain like Moses, contemplating the Promised Land from Mount Nebo, without ever setting
foot thereon?"

A second apparently legitimate reason for anxiety is this: "If
God loves me, if I am in His arms, from this viewpoint I should
have no fear; but my frailty and my malice, which daily become
more evident to me, will they not withstand the holy security of
divine love? It is true that Jesus carries me in His arms, but do I
not have the unfortunate prerogative of extricating myself? Jesus
certainly loves me, but shall I also love Him? Shall I be faithful?"

Do both these causes of anxiety exist in reality? No. At first
sight they seem warranted, but our Lord placed in our soul some
gifts so rich (we might even say divine) that they of themselves
establish us in peace.

One of these gifts is the divine virtue of hope, a heavenly virtue,
yet a forgotten virtue. How few souls, even among those consecrated
to God, give this neglected virtue the importance that it deserves!
Practical minded, we are preoccupied with more human virtues,
more in touch with earth: mortification, humility, obedience. Some

persons look upon hope as an impractical virtue, almost useless; at least they know neither when nor how to practice it.

Nevertheless, hope is an eminently practical virtue; it is the virtue that drives far from our heart the spectre of discouragement, the most frequent dangerous temptation in the spiritual life. As the inseparable companion of suffering, it confirms and strengthens peace in our soul.

Another motive of uneasiness is the preoccupation with the question of our attaining the divine union in the world and everlasting happiness in the next. In support of our fears we hasten to quote certain Scriptural passages, such as St. Peter's admonition to work out our salvation with fear and trembling. Solicitude is not synonymous with fear, not even the fear of God. The gift of the fear of God, the beginning of wisdom, is not a servile fear; it is a filial fear, the fear of the soul lest it lose its Beloved; it is a form of love. Evidently, such a fear is perfectly compatible with peace; we may say that it is one of the foundations of peace.

We can be sure that we shall attain union with God and eternal happiness because we have God's promise, and the promises of God are realities.

Abraham received magnificent promises from God and, strange as it seems, none was to be fulfilled for four hundred years, after the patriarch's time. Nevertheless, those divine promises filled his life with peace and consolation; his strong faith and hope gave him to understand that a promise of God is a reality. Aware of man's insincerity and limitations, we do not always place credence in human promises. God's promise is reality. I have absolute certainty that what God has promised me will be fulfilled, because heaven and earth shall pass away but God's word shall never pass, because His name, as Scripture states, is "faithful and true." God has promised us eternal happiness, and to enable us to support the divine weight of that promise, He placed in our hearts the virtue of hope.

Divine hope is not like earthly hope. The latter is subject to disappointment, for however strong our security, it can either be realized or not realized. Who is the fortunate person who has seen all his hopes fulfilled in this world? But the theological virtue of hope is not subject to disappointment; it gives us the holy, invincible certainty that we shall obtain what God has promised.

St. Thomas, whose authority is indisputable in the Church, poses a problem when treating of this virtue of hope: If someone receives a revelation that he is to be condemned, what should he do? The Saint does not hesitate to answer: Let him not believe it, because such a revelation would be opposed to the virtue of hope, and even if an angel from heaven brought the message, the certainty given me by the divine virtue of hope is above all the angels of heaven. God has promised me eternal blessedness; that promise is as good as actual possession, for I enclose it within the confines of my impregnable hope. I do not base my hope on my liberty, so weak and fickle, nor on my limited strength, but upon the promise of God, His omnipotence and His goodness.

Yet, someone may object that God has promised beatitude under such and such conditions. The conditions may be reduced to a single one, which was proclaimed by the angels at Bethlehem: "Peace on earth to men of good will." They did not say "to men of character," nor "to men of genius," nor "to men of good deeds," nor "to men of great virtue," but "to men of good will." When St. Thomas Aquinas' sister asked him how to obtain salvation, he answered her with one phrase: "Will it." Nothing more is necessary. The promises of God demand from us only this one condition: *Will it!*

Do we not sometimes have inward experience of the good will the angels heralded in Bethlehem? It is true that our will is weak and vacillating, but the angels promised peace not to men of energetic, constant, or strong will, but to men of good will.

Believe me, it takes a lot to be condemned; so much so that at times I cannot explain the mystery to myself. It is not because

I have no experience of man's malice and ingratitude, nor because sin seems to me a rare occurrence; no. I know that is very easy and frequent, but to be condemned it does not suffice to have sinned[1]; to be condemned it is necessary to wrestle with the infinite mercy of God; to be condemned it is necessary to tear out of the heart the last vestige of good will. Therefore, hope gives us peace.

THE VIRTUE of hope has another important function in this life. Hope is the inseparable companion of suffering; suffering without hope is a bitter, insupportable burden. Suffering is sometimes debilitating, oppressive, crushing. It crushed Jesus Himself, the very strength of heaven. Did He not feel overwhelmed that night in Gethsemane? Did He not sweat blood? Was He not in agony? Did He not feel the weariness and sadness of death? Did He not exclaim: "If it be possible, let this chalice pass from Me"? But if suffering overwhelmed Jesus, why should it not crush our frailty? In the midst of our sufferings we need something that will succor us in our weakness, support us in our wretchedness, something that, without blunting the pain, will make us see joy and happiness in the future and thus make us capable of persevering endurance.

Jesus Christ, as St. Paul teaches, foresaw the divine joy of glorifying the Father and the joy of making us happy, and because that joy was set before Him He endured the Cross. The Cross is so beautiful, so fruitful, so very precious! But no one can support just the Cross alone. We can endure present suffering only so far as we can foresee future joy. It was thus that Jesus endured the Cross: "Jesus... who, to win His prize of blessedness, endured the cross and made light of its shame" (Heb. 12:2). Therefore hope, which holds out to us sweet joy and complete happiness, is the inseparable companion

---

1.   EDITOR'S NOTE (Spanish Edition): The meaning of this statement is easily understood. In the order of justice one single mortal sin merits hell and suffices for condemnation. It is not so in the order of mercy, which struggles with the sinner until the final instant of life.

of sorrow. Suffering without hope is a sad, desolate experience; suffering with hope is a wonderful combination.

Permit me to make a comparison, which though rather prosaic, seems suitable for clarifying my thought. Just as physicians blend certain substances so that one may counteract the effect of the other in the resultant medicine, so Jesus has made a happy combination of pain and of hope. Suffering is the potent medicine of the spiritual life, hope is added to pain, and with this combination we can travel in peace over the dismal desert of this world with eyes and heart fixed on the promised land of eternity. Let us note that hope gives us not only the assurance of beatitude, but also the certainty of all graces for our sanctification.

Sometimes we say to God: "Lord, I promise you such or such a thing, provided You give me Your grace." Again: "If our Lord grants me His grace, I shall do this or that." It seems to me a kind of spiritual pleonasm to place this condition, "If He gives me His grace," because such a thing is not conditional but absolute. I have at hand the graces necessary for my salvation, because I have at hand the divine promise. Never will God's grace be lacking to me, because God is faithful and has promised to give me all that I need for my soul's salvation.

Of course, if I begin to dream about something that God has not promised, I must include the condition, "If God wants it, if God gives me His grace." For example, if I ask God for martyrdom, then indeed I must say: "If He gives me His grace, I shall endure it." God has made the promise of martyrdom to no one; He knows whether I shall receive that grace or not. Although martyrdom is a form of sanctification, our Lord has not promised it to all. But God has promised me the salvation and sanctification of my soul, and His promises are realities.

But shall I correspond with God's grace? Shall I not be unfaithful? This is the last stand of the diffident and the discouraged. I am sure that God has promised me beatitude and that He has put into my hands the necessary graces, but shall I correspond? Shall I preserve until the end the good will that I now possess?

To destroy this last doubt of the mistrustful, I offer two invulnerable points. The first is that fidelity itself is a gift of God; He is able to give it to me and Scripture assures me that He does. St. Paul declares that God gives "both the will to do it and the accomplishment of that will" (Phil. 2:13). Since the will depends upon Him, it is not subject to the vicissitudes and the velleities of poor human frailty; therefore, I hold fast to hope, I possess my soul in peace.

Shall I persevere in the will to be faithful? Lord, into Your hands I place both my will and my fidelity. I hope from You not only Your promised graces but also the will which that promise includes.

Still another objection may need to be settled. Though my frailty is great and my amazing gift of liberty may snatch me from God's arms to cast me down the slope that leads to the abyss, I know that God loves me sufficiently either not to allow this or, if He should permit it, He will come to look for me. He will descend with His love and His omnipotence along the slope that leads to destruction and He will take me in His arms and, like a good shepherd, He will place me upon His shoulders and bring me back to the fold. No; I do not fear my weakness, for as St. Thérèse of the Child Jesus said: "I know upon what I am relying in the love and the mercy of my Savior."

If we understood these consoling truths, if we exercised and developed the virtue of hope within our own hearts, we would be established in peace, and the spectre of distrust would disappear.

CHARITY

One more path to peace remains, the loftiest, the most excellent, the most secure: *charity*, *love*.

Scripture teaches that perfect love drives out fear. In St. John we read: "Love drives out fear when it is perfect love" (1 John 4:18).

He does not say that it casts out anxiety because perfect love is not required for ridding ourselves of worry; genuine love is enough. Peace is the specific, delightful fruit of charity. Therefore St. Thomas states that the beatitude of peace is the beatitude of love. "Blessed are the peacemakers for they shall be called the children of God." The peacemakers are those who love, who have concentrated all their desires into one single desire: desire for God; those who have gathered their aspirations and tenderness of soul into one closely bound bundle: the sheaf of love.

True love which has reached its maturity is a deep, solid love; it is sure of itself. It is not to be supposed that the love which St. Paul described is exclusively his own. His words reveal to us the mystery of love: "Of this I am fully persuaded; neither death nor life, no angels or principalities or powers, neither what is present nor what is to come, no force whatever, neither the height above us nor the depth beneath us, nor any other creature, will be able to separate us from the love of God, which comes to us in Christ Jesus our Lord" (Rom. 8:39).

Upon reading these words we say: "What a daring apostle! Who else could have his assurance? Only one elevated to the third heaven, the recipient of superabundant graces could be permitted such boldness—but I?" No, St. Paul did not speak thus because he was St. Paul but because his heart was filled with the charity that the Holy Spirit pours into all our hearts. When this charity takes root in our soul, when it has reached maturity, we can say the same.

Love cannot possibly be taken away from us. Earthly despots and diabolical powers may take away everything else from us; but they cannot deprive us of the charity of God which is in Christ Jesus. Only we ourselves have that unfortunate endowment. But if we truly love, shall we be so foolish, so suicidal as to tear out of our heart the charity of God?

Solid, profound, true love is sure of itself. And when, to the certainty of God's love for us, we add the certainty of our love for

Him (though a poor, miserable, inadequate love), shall we not have found at last the blessed state of interior tranquility?

These are, then, the paths that lead to the summit of peace. These three ways, these three divine gifts which aid our ascent to that longed-for height, we carry in our heart: faith, hope, love. These three virtues give us peace, because through them we touch God, because through them we embrace Jesus who, as St. Paul says, is our peace. "He is our bond of peace" (Eph. 2:14).

Bound to Jesus by these divine virtues, indestructibly united with Him by hope and charity, we can pass tranquilly through the desolate sands of our exile, with eyes and heart fixed on that happy region where peace is converted into everlasting beatitude. With faith, hope and charity in our soul, we can endure every suffering, saying bravely and boldly with St. Paul: "I can do all things in Him who strengthens me." Thus, consoled by God's immortal promise, bearing these divine virtues in the fragile vessel of our flesh, we shall be able to live in peace, while there resounds in our souls the echo of a hope, Bethlehem's sweet song: "Glory to God in the highest and on earth peace to men of good will."

CHAPTER 4

The Silence of Jesus

One of the most admirable characteristics found in the life of Jesus Christ, our Master and our Model, is silence. All the mysteries of His mortal life and the ineffable mystery of His Eucharistic life have this mark: the divine seal of silence.

Holy Church tells us that Jesus came to this world in the midst of universal silence: "There was a hush of silence all around, and night had but finished half her swift journey, when from Thy heavenly throne, Lord, down leaped Thy Word omnipotent" (Wis. 18:14–15).

The first thirty years of the life of Jesus were wrapped in an impressive silence. Afterwards came the three years of His public life. This was the time for speaking, the time for communicating with men. Yet even this period contains marvels of silence. Silence is something so characteristic of Christ's passion that the prophet commented on it saying: "Sheep led away to the slaughter-house, lamb that stands dumb while it is shorn; no word from Him" (Is. 53:7).

And in His Eucharistic life, does not that unfathomable silence enveloping the Eucharist impress us profoundly and communicate itself to us when we approach?

Silence is not classified as a virtue, but it is the atmosphere in which virtues develop. At the same time it is a sign of their maturity. Thus, just as we know that when the golden spikes of wheat appear in the field, the grain is ripe, so also, when a virtue is tinted with silence, we perceive that it is reaching maturity. Let us make some reflections upon the silence of Jesus and try to reproduce it in our heart so that we can imitate it in our lives.

THE SILENCE OF THE HIDDEN LIFE

Let us consider the silence of Jesus during His hidden life, that is, the first thirty years of His life. This silence is truly inexplicable. If there had ever been a man with the right to speak, with all the gifts for attracting attention, with all the means to create a stir, that man was Jesus, because He was the Eternal Word of the Father, uncreated Wisdom, the Master whom men had awaited for so many centuries. Certainly, if there is any single event in history that merits a stir in its behalf, it is the coming of Christ to live among us. But instead, a hush shrouds His first thirty years.

The Gospel, speaking to us of these years, is restrained, almost mute. Many times we would like to know a little more of the mysteries of the infancy of Jesus to nourish our piety. But the Gospel makes only an occasional reference to the episodes of His first years. A few pages refer to the hidden life of our Lord, and each incident mentioned, like murmurs heard in quiet fields, emphasizes and accentuates the silence rather than destroys it: the adoration of the Magi, the flight into Egypt, the going up to the temple—three events that do not disturb the silence of the hidden life, but make it more evident.

We feel this silence in a special manner in the house of Nazareth. It is the "house of silence"; we cannot conceive of it in any other way. Its very mention enshrines our souls in silence. When we meditate on the mysteries enacted there, we feel that all who dwelled there were divinely silent. St. Joseph—not a single word of his has been preserved for us in the Gospel, and we cannot imagine him except as enraptured in silent contemplation of those mysteries taking place around him.

The most holy Virgin, silent too, with that silence of wonder and of love which the presence of Jesus produced in her; a silence augmented by His holy illumination and by the mysteries that she witnessed and in which she participated. The Gospel presents one mysterious statement that allows us to catch a glimmering view as it were, of the abyss of silence and contemplation in the heart of the most holy Virgin. Having narrated those mysteries, the Gospel adds: "His mother kept in her heart the memory of all this" (Luke 2:51). She did not discuss them with St. Joseph, but she preserved them and meditated upon them within her own soul.

And Jesus, especially working in St. Joseph's shop, must have led a silent life with His soul and heart absorbed in the heavenly Father, His soul and His heart united in prevision to ours, dreaming dreams of love and of pain, thinking about the glory He would give to His Father and the good He would do for souls. His spirit was absorbed in the mysteries of the kingdom of heaven. As I see it, this silence is the silence of contemplation, the silence of the interior life.

Silence, even naturally speaking, invites us to concentrate within ourselves and to think about serious, profound things. For example, when we are in the midst of a forest, upon the ocean or in a desert place, we experience the necessity of concentrating, of recollecting ourselves. Such is our psychological structure that noise forces us outside of ourselves, distracting us and scattering our powers; it forces our spirit to go skipping around through external things; but when silence prevails, we concentrate again; once more we live within.

In accordance with this law of our psychology, we need to live within to live with God, because we always find God in the interior of our soul. It is natural that exterior silence is not only an invitation to an interior life but a necessary condition for that life of intimate communication with God. The atmosphere of the interior life, of the contemplative life, is silence; hence, the masters of the spiritual life recommend it so highly. Therefore, it is one of the most fundamental observances of the religious life.

In order to live the contemplative life, in order to live the religious life in any of its forms, and even for all true interior life, exterior silence is indispensable. To realize its importance in living above and not below, in living a life of intimacy and union with God let us not lose sight of the fact that silence should not be treated as a mere disciplinary measure or as a means of order such as is found in a school or in a class, but as a necessary condition for living within and not living without.

AT FIRST glance one may think that speech is superior to silence and that we communicate with God by speaking and singing, because song, as someone has said, is the language of love. Is not heaven the eternal abode of contemplation and of love? And in heaven one sings without ceasing. Isaiah and St. John listened to the new canticle of glory: "Holy, holy, holy, Lord God of hosts," which the blessed never cease singing day or night. Well, now, is not the Christian life the prelude and the beginning of the life of glory? Why, then, is silence necessary upon earth in order to communicate with God?

The silence of which I speak, for which Jesus gave us the example in Nazareth, is not the absolute lack of words and spiritual canticles. Assuredly, Jesus must have lived during the thirty years of His hidden life in an intimate and uninterrupted conversation with His heavenly Father. When His lips were silent, His heart spoke in a manner more eloquent, more divine. Exterior silence is not silence with God but with creatures.

The contemplative life is an intimate affair; it is a loving conversation of man with God. But in order that God may speak to

the soul and the soul speak with God, it is necessary that there be
silence. Neither God nor our heart will be silent, but the earth and
created things must be hushed because everything worldly hinders
the intimate conversation of our soul with God.

This silence is not the silence of the desert nor of the tomb—a
negative silence, the lack or suspension of life. It is like the apparel
of a more interior life that one wears outside because inside he is
singing a love song. He does not speak with creatures, because he is
speaking with God; he does not listen to the noise of earth, so that
he may hear the harmonies of heaven.

As an audience maintains silence to hear better the voice of an
orator, as music lovers keep silence during a symphony to admire
its artistic beauty, so the silence of contemplation is nothing other
than the indispensable condition for hearing the voice of God and
addressing to Him our heartfelt words.

SILENCE IS not only the indispensable condition for the development of the interior life, but it is also, as I said at the beginning,
a sign of the maturity of virtue. When the interior life reaches
a certain degree of development, it is marked by silence. In the
beginning we have some difficulty in speaking with God, but as our
intimacy with God increases, our conversation with Him becomes
easier because His love provokes an inexhaustible source of loving
words in our innermost soul. If this love continues growing until it
reaches a certain degree, if our friendship with Jesus becomes more
intimate and perfect, then words begin to fail us because they seem
impotent to express the sentiments of our heart. Little by little,
words disappear and our communication with God becomes the
divine communication of silence.

Even in conversations among men we find these different
stages. When one person begins to communicate with another, if
either or both lack confidence, conversation is difficult. Afterwards,
when both have become friends, the difficulty disappears and the

conversation can be prolonged for hours. But if this friendship develops into a deep affection, a moment will come in which words do not suffice. Then speech gives way to silence. The great emotions of the heart, like profound sentiments of the soul, are not expressed with words but with silence.

Silence has two functions in the contemplative life. At the beginning and at all times it provides the environment for developing the spirit of contemplation. Silence quiets all creatures so that God may speak. It cuts the communication with outside affairs and puts us in intimate contact with God. It concentrates all our energy on our interior and makes our life a living prayer. Afterwards, when contemplation has reached a notable degree of maturity, silence is not only its guardian but its supreme expression and most intimate language.

How does one practice this silence of contemplation? I have nothing to say of exterior silence because its rules are well known. On the other hand, when exterior silence is not kept, ordinarily it is because there is no silence in the interior of the heart. Without doubt, exterior silence helps the interior, but exterior silence is not kept perfectly when it is not observed within. Therefore, let us speak of interior silence.

IN THE large cities campaigns against noise are being waged relentlessly and, naturally, the causes have been investigated. If we want to make a campaign for silence in the interior of our hearts, we ought to begin by investigating the causes of the clamor. Ordinarily there are two causes of interior noise: the imagination and the heart. The latter is the noisier of the two.

How often it happens that we enter the presence of Jesus to converse sweetly with Him, and then the imagination begins to skip around, carrying us hither and thither. Sometimes it is nothing definite that attracts us but simply the incessant mobility of that faculty of ours. We want to find it but it flits around like a butterfly, stopping here and there, tracing improbable curves in the interior of our soul. Thence comes the noise; it is the imagination that disturbs interior silence.

At other times the source of the din is in the heart. As I said before, the heart is the more noisy of the two. Except in cases of abnormal agitation, the imagination never produces the clamor that the heart produces. When we are under the stress of some particular emotion such as love, fear, desire or anger, we cannot compose our spirit; our soul seems like a city full of noise. One single passion often produces a greater clatter in the soul than that which jars our nerves in an industrial city. When a disturbance arises from the imagination, it is transitory; but when the heart is the source, how difficult to be recollected, and how tense is our whole soul!

When we suffer, pain produces a constant and monotonous noise; a single word is spoken to us but it is a word that disturbs our entire being. On the other hand, when we love intensely, that same word repeated to us completely satisfies our heart, but it rules out every other voice.

Consequently, in order that silence reign in our heart, it is necessary that the heart and the imagination be hushed, or at least that they make a sound suited to what we want to hear. That is what happens on a liturgical feast: the religious music, the liturgical hymns, the chiming of the bells raise us to God because there is harmony between what we hear exteriorly and what we hear interiorly. That same thing can happen in our soul, when our heart and our imagination are making the same sound that we must make to Jesus.

To quiet the imagination is difficult. But it is necessary to moderate it. It is not necessary to treat it with violence, nor to subject it by force, nor to chain it up. When the imagination is subjected to force, it becomes even more aroused. Such a procedure is comparable to chaining a dog and beating him to make him stop barking; instead of becoming silent he will bark more and his bark will become more intolerable. Tact is necessary to manage the imagination. When this faculty is aroused, it is wiser to direct its activity into channels that more closely correspond to our purpose, rather than to strive to quiet it.

If for physiological or psychological reasons I have an excited imagination and I want to approach Jesus to converse with Him, what shall I do? Take the imagination and enclose it in a prison? That is impossible. What shall I do, then? The same that one would do with a broken record. If we cannot make it play properly, we change the record. In place of worldly songs we shall introduce religious music that supports our purpose. This is the way to deal with the imagination; it is useless to attempt to shackle it because it will not be shackled. Let us "change the record," replacing it with one that is in harmony with God.

THE HEART is silent when all its affections are concentrated on the love of God; it is silent when there are no discordant, scattered notes, when all its tones rise toward Him.

The silence that we are discussing is the silence of the earthly and the human in order that the divine may resound in us. It is evident that as the heart empties itself of discordant sentiments and of affections out of harmony with the cry of the love of God, silence becomes orientated in our soul.

For interior silence one needs detachment. If we consider the matter well, the only thing that cries out within us is love. When the love of God possesses us completely, we bear within our heart a close resemblance to the eternal Trisagion, and in our exile we begin the prelude of the new canticle of the fatherland. But when there are other affections that are not those of Jesus, there is a cacophony that hinders us in our contemplation and our love. In order to keep interior silence, therefore, we must chain our passions and rid the heart of earthly affections.

There is another remedy. Have you not had the experience of

being in church at some religious function, and when the organ
stopped playing and the liturgical hymns ceased, you heard the
cries of vendors, the murmurs of passers-by and various other street
sounds? But suddenly, the organ resumes its powerful overtones,
voices again intone the sacred canticles, and you no longer heard
what was outside because the harmony within was too intense.
Thus, there is another way of establishing silence in our heart: by
making contemplation and love more intense than the external dis-
tractions. The silence that is asked of us is a relative silence; it is the
calming of exterior noise so that the new canticle of our love may
resound with increased harmony and intensity.

To manage our imagination prudently, to divest our heart of all
emotion that hampers the love of God and to make contemplation
and love more ardent in our souls, I give you here some efficacious
means, expressed in a general way, for waging an effective campaign
against interior noise and for creating silence in the depth of our
souls. Little by little we shall imitate the silence of the hidden life
and our heart will be a replica of that sweetest of mysteries, the
ineffable silence of Nazareth.

The Silence of the Apostolic Life

At first sight it seems that Jesus broke His divine silence during
the three years of His public life. It would not be strange; in fact,
Scripture affirms that there is a time to speak and a time to keep
silence. But I think that if our Lord interrupted that profound
silence of contemplation which characterized His life in Nazareth,
He did not fail to practice in an admirable manner, or it well may
be in a still more admirable way, the virtue of silence during the
agitated years of His apostolic life.

How much time during those three years our Lord dedicated
expressly to contemplation. Some passages in the Gospel give us
to understand that Jesus used to go at night to some solitary place,

frequently to the top of a mountain or hill, and there He would pass the night absorbed in silence and love.

Yet it is not precisely to our Lord's silence of contemplation in the midst of His public life that I wish to refer to now; but I do think that in the midst of His apostolic ministry our Lord practiced silence in a less obvious manner than He had done in Nazareth, but very difficult for us and in reality very perfect. I refer to the silence of discretion and of charity; not an absolute silence, but a relative silence; a silence that we also ought to practice constantly in our relations with our neighbor.

We know that many times Jesus must have desired to express what was in His heart, but He remained silent. Prudence, discretion, charity sealed His lips so that He practiced a costly silence.

How many things Jesus would pass over in silence! For example, when He spoke of the Eucharist in Capernaum, if He had followed the impulses of His heart, how much He would have said, since the Eucharist was the ideal, the dream that He had cherished during His whole life because it satisfied all the desires of His love here upon earth. But discretion indicated to Him what He ought to say and what He ought to leave unsaid. We know that in such cases it is more difficult to know how to keep silent than it is to speak.

Our Lord must have experienced often the necessity of reprimanding the multitudes and even the apostles themselves in order to restrain abuses and vulgarities that offended His most refined soul. Nevertheless, charity required that He remain silent.

I maintain that one of the greatest griefs that afflicted our Lord during His public life—if we except the interior sorrows that tormented Him during His entire life—was to have to deal with all those poor souls that were so far from Him. Even for us simple mortals how distressing it is to have to deal with persons of a different mentality, different education, or contrary temperament. Let us imagine what it would be like to live constantly with men of misguided ideas, with infidels, or with persons of complete moral

degradation. Without going to these extremes, how often it is a
true torment to deal with those who are more like ourselves but
on whose account we must make constant sacrifices in order to
live with them. With greater reason was this true in the case of the
sensitive soul of Jesus. Therefore I believe that because of their crass
ignorance, torpidity of spirit and coarseness of feelings, the persons
who surrounded Jesus must have been thorns piercing His Divine
Heart.

49

Of all the souls with whom Jesus had to deal, the apostles were
the best and most select; yet how slow they were to understand
His teachings, how imprudent in speaking when they should have
remained silent. On one occasion our Lord, attacking the scrupu-
lous and exaggerated practices of the Pharisees, had just explained
to the multitudes that to eat without washing the hands does not
defile a man: "It is not what goes into a man's mouth that makes
him unclean; what makes a man unclean is what comes out of his
mouth" (Matt. 15:11–12). And although the explanation was very
clear, the apostles did not understand and they made our Lord
explain still further. He does so, but one understands that He suffers on account of their limited intelligence.

Although it is true that on some occasions our Lord was obliged
to reprove His apostles in view of their spiritual formation—now
for the slowness of their minds in understanding His teachings,
again for the crude ambition which led them to dispute about the
first places, at another time for the imprudence of their impulsive
characters—nevertheless our Lord maintained silence on many
another provocative occasion.

This silence of discretion and of charity is much more costly
than the silence of contemplation. Doubtless it sometimes demands
effort to keep contemplative silence, but ordinarily this is not the
case. Silence in the midst of words, silence in communicating with
our neighbor is much more distressing. A thousand times we should
like to exteriorize that which we carry within, and thus unburden

ourselves. On a great many other occasions we have to conquer ourselves, enveloping ourselves in a silence of prudence and charity.

On the other hand, the Heart of Jesus was as human as ours, and consequently it must have experienced the urge to unburden griefs just as we do, especially when His heart was harboring deep secrets, immense griefs and great sorrows. Nevertheless, to have to repress the disclosure of His troubles, to have to hide His most intimate feelings, and to have to speak like the others as if He carried in His soul only what is lowly and ordinary, is not this an arduous and difficult silence?

It is also a perfect silence, that is to say, it presupposes a certain degree of perfection in virtue. The apostle, St. James, says that the one who knows how to restrain his tongue is a perfect man. Therefore, knowing how to restrain the tongue, that is, knowing how to speak when one ought to speak and knowing how to keep silent when one ought to keep silent, is a sign of perfection and sanctity. To possess the judgment and the discretion necessary to speak when one ought to speak and to keep silence when one ought to be silent, requires such an assemblage of virtues that the one who attains it is a perfect soul.

When the enemies of Jesus sent their spies to listen deceitfully to His preaching and to apprehend Him, they became frightened and did not touch Him. When asked why they had not carried out their orders, they answered: "Nobody has ever spoken as this man speaks" (John 7:46). And we might add, "and has known how to keep silence as no one else has known how to keep it." No one, in truth, has known how to keep the silence of prudence and charity like Jesus, and he who arrives at practicing all that charity and prudence demand in regard to silence is a perfect man. "*Hic perfectus est vir.*"

THE PRACTICE of this silence demands in a special manner the practice of two virtues: prudence and charity. Prudence is one of the most difficult virtues to acquire. When we consider all that one must remember, foresee and think of in order to act with prudence, we can understand that without the special assistance of grace it would be exceedingly difficult to practice this virtue.

On the other hand, it is not seldom that when we are most desirous of speaking, when we feel most eager to express ourselves, this is the time that prudence directs us to be silent. And if we do not heed this inspiration, we ourselves can verify the consequences of a single imprudent word. How many times we have repented of a fleeting word spoken without reflection! On the contrary, how many falls one avoids, how many anxieties one escapes, if he knows how to practice the surpassing science of silence. To know how to keep timely silence is the perfect work of prudence.

In order to govern our tongue, charity is united to prudence. The same apostle, St. James, teaches us that it is easier to steer a ship or to master an unruly colt than to manage our tongue, in spite of its being so small an organ. Therefore, to succeed, prudence and charity must join hands.

Doubtless, charity makes us speak many times, now to defend our neighbor unjustly defamed, again to make his good qualities evident, at another time to counsel him in his doubts and to console him in his griefs. But perhaps there are more occasions on which charity obliges us to maintain silence, for charity demands that we avoid every word, however insignificant, that may wound our neighbor. Charity is so exquisite, our neighbor is so sensitive, and so earnest is the desire of our Lord that we preserve this virtue unblemished, that we must constantly watch our tongue so that it never utters a word that would offend our neighbor and injure the sacred rights of charity.

How beautiful is the silence of charity! Our Lord gave us an outstanding example of this when, after His resurrection, appearing to His apostles singly or in groups, He did not reproach them in the least for having deserted Him in so cowardly a fashion. He did not utter a word to Peter himself about his denial, contenting

Himself with asking for a triple confession of his love. Is not this silence of Jesus affecting and admirable? Any one of us would have given in to the impulse of manifesting his feeling in some manner. We would at least have said to Peter in an injured tone: "Why did you abandon Me in the hour of trial? You especially, Peter, who in the Cenacle declared that you were ready to die with Me, why did you deny your Master? Nevertheless, I pardon you; peace be to you!" Our Lord did not say this; rather, it seems that His love and the sweetness of His words go to extremes: "Peace be to you.... Fear not.... It is I...." Oh, if we might imitate Jesus in this silence! If we really love our neighbor as Jesus loves us and as He asks us to love, we shall keep silent about our neighbor's defects and even about that which might embarrass him, although it is not properly a defect; we shall avoid all disclosures that may pain him, even when it satisfies our wounded self-love; we shall not set about investigating if this word wounds him much or little, because the charity that is disposed to avoid only serious offenses is a very immature charity; rather, we ought to avoid all that can even remotely offend him. Paraphrasing St. Paul, who said that if the fact that he ate a certain food would scandalize his neighbor, he would never eat, we ought to say: "If this word offends my neighbor, I will never say it."

I THINK that one of the ends of the religious life is to preserve the atmosphere, the fragrance, of those first communities of Christians described in the Acts of the Apostles, in which all possessed the same property, a common table, and above all, but one heart and soul. This is perfect Christianity, perfect according to the ideal of Jesus Christ. It is impossible that it could remain as it was originally after spreading throughout the entire world and running through all centuries. But the Church has formed those enclosed gardens of religious communities so that she might preserve in them this true, ideal and perfect Christianity. Therefore, here, rather than any place else, a faultless and delicate charity ought to reign so that all the members may have but one heart and one soul.

But because of the common life that is carried on in religious communities and because of the close association of the members and the diversity of their characters, charity is in greater jeopardy, friction is more constant and dangers of giving offense are more numerous. Hence, religious need in a special manner to practice the silence of charity, learning to keep silent when charity demands it, however much this silence may tax self-love. And in order to facilitate this practice, let us turn our eyes to Jesus, our Master and Model, and let us learn from Him to keep silent through prudence and charity.

The Silence of the Passion

In His most sacred passion, Jesus gave us an admirable example of a new form of silence: *silence in pain*. Sometimes it is exceedingly painful to keep silence; sometimes silence increases and revives the bitterness of grief. Our Lord gives us an example of these two forms of painful silence in His passion.

We see an illustration of the first when Jesus, appearing before the tribunal of the Roman pro-consul Pilate, was acquainted with all that was charged against Him. "Dost Thou not hear," Pilate questioned, "all the testimony they bring against Thee?" And the Evangelist adds: "Jesus would not answer any of their charges, so that the governor was full of astonishment" (Matt. 27:13–14).

How irritating this silence must have been for Jesus! When false testimonies were given, and calumnies uttered against Him, He must have experienced a burning impulse to speak, not so much to avoid death since He had already accepted it generously and determinedly for the love of His Father for our souls, but for the sake of justice, for His honor and for the justification of His holy conduct. With but one word Jesus would have been able to discredit the accusations and justify Himself, yet He kept silent. Is not this silence of Jesus heroic?

Many times we find ourselves in a situation which calls for imitation of Jesus in this silence. To keep still when with one word we could manifest our innocence and cancel out all charges against us is frustrating, is heroic, but how often it is necessary. To be quiet then, to choose not to excuse ourselves when we could, through love of humility, is a silence that imitates Jesus in His passion.

If we analyze the Gospel attentively, we find that sometimes Jesus defended Himself, sometimes He preferred to remain silent. For example, in the presence of Annas, when one of the guards gave Him a blow, Jesus justified Himself: "If there was harm in what I said...tell us what was harmful in it; if not, why dost thou strike Me?" (John 18:23). But before Pilate, as we saw, Jesus kept silence.

Our Lord's course of action on these occasions is nothing more than an application of the maxim in Scripture: "Silence kept, and silence ended" (Eccles. 3:7). In a general way it can be said that when it is for the honor of God or the good of our neighbor, we ought to speak. When it concerns only ourselves, it is almost always more perfect to keep silence, in imitation of our Lord in His passion.

IN THE passion of our Lord there is still another more heroic silence, the one Isaiah foretold when he said that Jesus would be carried as a sheep to the slaughter, without uttering a sound (Is. 53:7).

In order to understand this silence, one must ponder over the immense grief Christ bore within His soul. Every possible torture had been heaped upon His body, every ignominy poured into His soul. He was one incurable bleeding wound, as the prophets had foretold (Is. 1:6). His enemies did not spare Him one single humiliation, from parading Him in disgrace through the streets of Jerusalem to nailing Him, naked, on the infamous gibbet of the Cross, between two thieves and amidst the blasphemies of His foes. His sacred honor was mocked with a crowd's sneer.

In His heart He carried the "terror of the grave" (Ps. 17:6), far beyond our comprehension, but which some few souls have been privileged to perceive indistinctly as in a darkened glass.

If any one of us should have to suffer, not what Jesus suffered, for that is impossible, but even an exceedingly small part thereof, it would suffice to make us scream and grit our teeth with pain. And Jesus was silent! Like a sheep led to the slaughter, without a murmur, in a wondrous silence.

Only twice Jesus seems to have manifested His grief: once in Gethsemane, when He complained to His apostles because they could not watch even one hour with Him, and again, on Calvary, when He allowed to escape from His dying lips that poignant complaint: "My God, My God, why hast Thou forsaken Me?" But those two outpourings from His heart do not come as interruptions of His heroic silence because their purpose was to teach us two important lessons rather than to mitigate His grief.

First, He wished to show us that sometimes we can and ought to unburden our heart. He knew very well that there would be in our lives especially sorrowful moments in which, because of our weakness, we would experience the need of crying out. So that we might not be ashamed to do so at that time, He wanted to manifest the heaviness of His heart by crying out, not for His comfort but for our consolation. Second, He wanted to give us a fleeting vision of the profound sorrows of His heart. If He had not complained, we would not have found any testimony of them in the Gospel.

There are souls to whom God has given as a special vocation to know, venerate and love the interior cross of the Heart of Christ, that is to say, His innermost griefs—what might be called the "passion of the heart and the heart of the Passion."[1] These souls needed a revelation, the testimony of the Gospel concerning those sorrows which, like a flash of lightning, reveal a little of the sorrowful

---

1.   Charles Gay, *Entretiens sur les mystéres du Rosaire.*

mystery of the Heart of Christ. With the exception of these two disclosures, Jesus was silent during His passion.

Let us admire that silence in sorrow and try to imitate it. Alas, how many times sorrow indiscreetly manifested to others dissipates its fragrance and loses all its perfume. For sorrow resembles those delicate perfumes that evaporate quickly and therefore need to be kept in hermetically sealed urns. Grief is an exquisite perfume, precious in the eyes of God. For this reason we ought to guard it with the greatest care in the vase of our heart, so that its fragrance will not dissipate.

Without doubt it is most painful to keep the vase of our suffering closed. To share our suffering with others alleviates our heart's cruel pain, but it diminishes the value of suffering. Silence in sorrow, that is to say, suffering without lament, gives to our grief its highest value and rarest perfume. This does not mean that we should never manifest our sufferings. Jesus Himself manifested His on two occasions, in Gethsemane and on Calvary, to teach us that we, too, in certain circumstances and with discretion, should reveal ours. Sometimes we need to express ourselves, because if we did not, sorrow would suffocate us. Weak, limited in capacity for suffering as for everything else, we must allow a little of grief's perfume to escape so that we may be able to suffer more, so that suffering may not overwhelm us with its oppressive weight. Sometimes we need to disclose our griefs for just and holy purposes, such as asking for light, direction or a rule of conduct to be followed. But with the exception of those cases, the perfection of sorrow lies in silence.

Did we not say that silence is for many virtues the sign of maturity? When love is very intense, it expresses itself in silence; when sorrow has attained its perfection, it shares in the triumphant silence with which Jesus endured the inexpressible pangs of His passion and death.

The Silence of the Eucharist

But I have yet to speak of another august silence of Jesus: the
silence of love, the silence of the Eucharist. Few things impress us so
much in this incomparable sacrament as the silence that has enveloped it for twenty centuries. The quiet of the tabernacle impresses
us even physically when we approach it and, with greater reason,
when we concentrate on the mystery of the Eucharist, contemplating therein the silent Christ.

Because the very state in which Jesus is found in the most holy
Sacrament is a state of silence. According to the theologians, He
cannot speak nor can He make use of His senses without a miracle.
St. Alphonsus Liguori says that He is deprived in such a way of the
use of His senses and is so impotent for all things else that it seems
that here He has only one free activity, the activity of the heart; that
He placed Himself in that state that He might have nothing else to
do but to love.

And so it is in very truth. Jesus in the Sacred Host does not
speak; He knows only how to love. In an evil hour His enemies
come and profane the Sacrament of His love, but Jesus is silent.
Sacrilegiously they open their stained lips to receive Him, but Jesus
is silent. He does not take a whip as in the temple of Jerusalem to
punish the profaners. He does not throw into their teeth their sac-
rilege as He did the hypocrisy of the Pharisees. Jesus is silent, and
for twenty centuries that sacred, unfathomable silence has endured.
Simply because He loves, love has bound His lips and His hands.
Love has reduced Him to silence.

But is not that silence the most eloquent proof of His immense
love? Oh, assuredly we feel the love of Jesus when we listen to Him
on the eve of His passion, speaking to us the profound words of
the discourse at the Last Supper. But perhaps we feel it more in the
Sacrament of His love, hushed and silent. We do not lament that
Jesus does not speak to us from the Sacred Host; His silence is more
eloquent and expressive!

Sometimes we, who do not understand sublime and lofty things, complain, saying: "What a pity that Jesus does not speak from the tabernacle; it would be so sweet to listen to His words!" I think that it is better that He does not speak, because with His silence He expresses perhaps better than with His words the love that He professes for us.

Let us not forget it; the summit of love is silence. Love that can still be expressed with words has not arrived at its perfection nor reached its culmination. Our words are too restricted, too feeble to express what is great and limitless. Have we not realized that the deepest impressions of our souls cannot be expressed with words? When grief reaches its climax, it becomes silent. When the friends of Job who had gone to visit him saw him oppressed by every evil and in a state of terrible pain, the Scripture states that they remained in silence for seven days and seven nights because their grief was too great to be expressed with words.

And thus it always happens to us; when we see a splendid spectacle of nature, we are silent. Ordinary sights, on the contrary, make us talk and we happily comment on them. Something sublime imposes silence. Therefore, admiration, sorrow, love, all the great sentiments of our heart, all the deep impressions of our soul are like this: when imperfect and limited they can be expressed with human speech; when they increase and reach their peak, they cannot be expressed by weak words. Their only language is silence.

In heaven love is not expressed in this way because another language—not of this earth—exists there. Here below the greatest love is silent love. Such is the love of Jesus in the Eucharist.

Happy are we if we love Jesus with that sublime silence! Many a time our love speaks, our love sings, our love expresses itself in diverse manners. But when love increases in our heart, it tends to become silent. The fact is that then it has reached maturity; it has become so intense, so deep that it cannot be expressed with our dull human language.

Let us understand the silence of the Eucharist and put ourselves in unison with Jesus in that wondrous stillness. Every day we
can enjoy that most sweet silence. Especially at midnight,[2] when
all around is still, have we not experienced in our heart the deepest
impression of the Eucharistic silence, have we not felt our souls
enfolded, as it were, in that silence of love?

That silence teaches us more than words and it tells us how
much Jesus loves us. It is also contagious, for having possessed our
hearts, it soothes us, calms us and moves us to express our feelings,
with the same incomparable language of silence.

I do not mean by this that we always approach God in silence.
No! Love takes all forms and has all manifestations. Let us leave our
heart at liberty to speak, to sing, to be quiet. Especially, let us allow
ourselves to be guided by the Holy Spirit, where He wills and as He
wills. But what I am attempting to say is that there exists a sublime
silence of love, that there is a way of communicating with Jesus in
silence.

St. Thérèse of the Child Jesus used to say that our Lord is a
master who teaches without words. In fact, His silence is doctrine,
instruction, eloquence; His silence seems to penetrate even to the
core of our souls, teaching us great truths.

When we approach the tabernacle, let us not try to hear the
words of Jesus. Rather let us listen to His silence. Let us permit that
silence to envelop and penetrate us even to our innermost being,
and it will teach us more than all the words that we desire to hear.
"*Silentium loquetur!*"

FROM THIS rapid review of the different forms of Jesus' silence—
the silence of contemplation, the silence of prudence, the silence of

---

2.   EDITOR'S NOTE (Spanish Edition): These articles on silence are arranged from
     shorthand notes of conferences given by His Excellency, Archbishop Martínez,
     to the Religious of the Cross who adore the Most Holy Sacrament day and night.
     Hence the allusion to nocturnal adoration.

pain, the silence of love—how many lessons we can draw forth to our soul's advantage. We have already noted some of them. Jesus spent the first thirty years of His life wrapped in contemplative silence. His public life was spent in the silence of charity and prudence. His passion was bound up in a sorrowful silence and He lives the Eucharistic life in a silence of love. We ought to copy all these types of silence in our lives and reproduce them in our hearts.

We should live in an atmosphere of silence so that the divine flower of contemplation may flourish therein. In dealing with our neighbor we must exercise many times, like Jesus, the silence of prudence and charity. And as victims we ought to offer ourselves, in union with Jesus, to the heavenly Father for souls.

Thus, in the midst of these holy forms of silence, our life will pass, preparing us for the true, eternal life where we shall intone a new canticle, a heavenly canticle. But it seems to me that even in heaven that canticle would be expressed in silence. Why? Because in heaven all is silent except God; all is silent; only the word of love resounds. Doubtless, here on earth we hear the voice of God and we pronounce the word of love, but the din of creatures disturbs us and many times we have to interrupt our song. Not so in heaven. There all is hushed; no noise of creatures breaks the grand silence. There is but one note, one word, the one that comes forth from the Heart of God and from our own hearts—the word of love.

But do not the blessed in heaven hear the clamor that rises from the earth? Certainly, but in heaven those words have another meaning. St. Paul says that on the final day of time, Jesus will triumph over all His enemies and the last of God's enemies to be destroyed will be death. Once His enemies have been defeated, our Lord will take all men and subject them to God in order that "God may be all in all" (1 Cor. 15:28). Inscrutable expression! What does it mean that God may be all in all things? No, we do not now comprehend the profound meaning of creation, or of history, or of the universe. We hear the noises of the earth in a superficial manner and therefore they disturb us. But then, "God will be all in all," and all the sounds that reach even to the skies will speak to us only of God.

Therefore, we can well say that there is not, nor will there ever be, a silence similar to the silence of eternity, to the silence of heaven, because there every creature is silent and there is heard only one sound: God; only one word: the word of love.

CHAPTER 5

☩

And Jesus Slept

T hrough the intuitions of love more than through the liveli-
ness of the imagination, we have often constructed interiorly
an arresting scene—the ominous sky, the wild winds, a little boat
tossed by the seething waves of Lake Tiberias, with Jesus asleep in
the stern.

What a contrast between the fury of the tempest and the sweet,
majestic peace of the divine slumber! The omnipotent, the Most
High, He who is infinite activity because He is infinite perfection
and unfailing felicity, surrendered to that sure sign of limitation and
misery—sleep. What would the sleeping Jesus be like? St. Thérèse of
the Child Jesus states that children please their parents just as well
asleep as awake. To souls enamored of Jesus, the Beloved is as beautiful in the silence of His sleep as in the zenith of His activity. Jesus
is always beautiful, always great, always divine, "*totus desiderabilis,*"
as the Canticle of Canticles declares. The gentle Virgin Mary often
contemplated the ineffable beauty of Jesus asleep. With the eyes of
a mother, a lover and an artist she enjoyed the celestial delight of
that marvelous divine beauty. What mildness in that incompara-
bly comely countenance! What harmony in that motionless body!

What majesty in that sweet repose! What radiations emanated from that Sacred Humanity quietly resting there.

Jesus was exceedingly beautiful when He spoke words of eternal life, accomplished wonders, looked with love, pardoned with mercy, and caressed with tenderness. But I should like to have seen Him while He was sleeping because I could have contemplated Him to my heart's content, without the fascination of His gaze distracting me, without the perfection of His beauty and the glory of His splendor dazzling my eyes and enrapturing my soul. The beauty of Jesus awake is too great for my smallness. Who could support it? I feel it more suited to me veiled by sleep, as the glory of the sun is more adapted to my eyes when I look at it through a translucent lens. Mary most holy must have watched the sleep of Jesus many times. Mary's ecstatic eyes would never tire of looking at her Divine Son. With holy liberty she covered Him with the kisses of her virginal lips as her immaculate hands caressed Him tenderly. If we had seen Jesus asleep, small and helpless as we are, we too would have dared to caress Him without reserve and to lull His mystical sleep with our timorous but ardent kisses.

Great artists striving to express the contrasts involved in the strength of repose have succeeded in producing the impression of an immobility filled with power, a calm of restrained activity, an activity which is its own mistress. Through the magic of art, incompatibles—majestic repose and animated activity—are united.

Through a divine art, this mighty contrast is realized in an indescribable manner in Jesus asleep. With the person of Jesus the phrase of the Canticle, "I lie asleep but my heart is wakeful" (Cant. 5:2), is not a figure of speech used in the language of love, but a profound reality of the divine order. His sleep was like ours is because He took on Himself our miseries. His exterior and interior senses during sleep had that mysterious ligature which wise men have not yet explained satisfactorily. Sleep was not for Him, as it is for us, a suspension of our active life mingled with an occasional flash or

mysterious phantasm of light and action. Though the lower part of
His most holy soul was plunged in shadows, the higher part opened
fully to the light of glory and the beatific vision far beyond the
need of bodily aid, nourished in the unfailing torrent of the divinity. The profound understanding of Jesus was flooded with celestial
splendor. Beatific love burned in His heart, enveloping with flames
of blessedness and glory that Sacred Heart ever alert for love, ever
living to make to His Father the holocaust of His tenderness, ever
active to pour into souls the treasures of His mercy. In the presence of that regal immobility and the divine silence of that most
comely body, could one guess the interior glory? Through the delicate, celestial veil of human sleep, could penetrating and loving
eyes like those of the Virgin discover the deep secret of the interior
joy of Jesus?

65

The apostles, with their narrow, human judgment, because they
had not yet received from the Paraclete the deep sense of the divine,
did not suspect on Tiberias the mystery of that heart which was
always watching. Frightened by the din of the storm, they awak-
ened Jesus to command the winds and the tempest. "Why are you
faint-hearted? Have you still no faith?" the Master asked them
(Mark 4:40). They did not yet have it in the plenitude they were to
receive in the Cenacle. They did not understand that even though
we need to be awake to exercise our limited activity, Jesus, even as
man, concealed under the mystery of His sleep the limitless power
of the beatific vision. Who can comprehend the sleep of Jesus? Who
can conceive the strikingly beautiful contrast between the summit
of that soul bathed in the light of glory and the lower part covered
with the shadows of sleep, like the earth immersed in the sun's glory
in one hemisphere and submerged in the calm of night in the other?

JESUS LIVES mystically in souls, reproducing in them all the mysteries of His mortal life. With the keen intuition of her love, St. Thérèse
of the Child Jesus understood the mystery of this mystical sleep,

expressing it with her inimitable language, full of ingenuous and truest poetry: "Jesus slept in my boat, as was His wont. But how rarely will souls allow Him to sleep in peace. Wearied with our continual advances, our good Master readily avails Himself of the repose I offer Him, and in all probability will sleep on till my great and everlasting retreat; this, however, rather rejoices than grieves me."[1]

Who else would have thought of interpreting the dark, painful chasm of spiritual desolation with such amiable, heavenly light? Almost all souls are disconcerted by desolation. They conclude that Jesus has gone away, that the sweet visits of former times, bright and fragrant as a spring garden, were a fleeting dream, an idyll interrupted through their own infidelity and ingratitude. They fear that the love so sweet, so deep, so sure, to which Jesus invited them, has been turned into hate, as happens to all love that meets with neglect. In their unspeakable agony, these poor souls hold the firm conviction that the Beloved has fled from them, perhaps not to return, bearing away with Him the entrancing perfumes of heaven, the divine clarity which illuminated life's pathway, and the holy consolations superior to all earthly joys.

These desolate souls surmise everything except that Jesus is only sleeping within them, just as He slept in the little bark on Tiberias while the wind roared and the tempest raged. Only the pure eyes of the gentle child of Lisieux, only her gaze of love could discover the secret of a lover. Jesus has not gone away nor will He ever leave, because love, strong as death, never departs and its divine ardor cannot be extinguished by the torrents of our ingratitude. Jesus continues to live in the soul to whom He pledged love because His name is *Faithful* and *True*. He sleeps sweetly in that soul which belongs to Him, because she surrendered herself to Him, attracted by His irresistible fragrance.

---

1. *Saint Thérèse of Lisieux, the Little Flower of Jesus* (New York: P. J. Kennedy & Sons, 1927), Chapter 8, p. 134.

Could that consoling idea of St. Thérèse of the Child Jesus be an effort of an ingenuous and charming optimism to cover with a veil of piety the blackness of a terrible pain in order to endure it, or is there hidden under a precious symbolism a profound reality concealed from the eyes of the wise and prudent and revealed only to the little ones? The exceedingly deep love of the Carmelite virgin for truth and her remarkable sanctity, attested to by the Church, shows unmistakably that the girl saw clearly and deeply into the divine mystery. Jesus needs to sleep in souls so that they may contemplate the exquisite beauty of His slumber, so that the Divine Heart which watches while He sleeps may accomplish in silence the prodigies of purity and love which Jesus ordinarily accomplishes only in the midst of tempests and in the mystery of His sleep.

LIKE THE apostles, souls want to awaken Jesus when the storm threatens. What will they do without Him? Passions that seem conquered rise with new vigor. A darkness like that of death covers the sky of the soul, once a bright blue. The whistling of a hurricane disturbs the soul with gloomy, desolate, despairing ideas that seem to come out of hell. The frail little bark of the soul is about to capsize and Jesus sleeps. "Master," the soul cries to Him, like the apostles on Lake Tiberias, "art Thou unconcerned? We are sinking" (Mark 4:39). And Jesus, when He does awake—the time of trial seems so prolonged—speaks to the soul as to the disciples in the little boat: "Why are you faint-hearted? Have you still no faith?" (Mark 4:40).

Just as it was unnecessary to awaken Jesus on Tiberias, it is not necessary that He be awake in souls to give them life. The words of the Canticle may also be applied to His mystical sleep: "I sleep but My heart watches." Yes, Jesus watches solicitously in the souls that love, even though they feel that He has abandoned them. Love does not abandon. Jesus is there in the depth of the soul. He seems to sleep because the soul does not hear His refreshing voice, because she does not enjoy His celestial consolations. But the Heart of Jesus

67

is always watching with His inextinguishable love, with His incessant actions, with His tender care more solicitous each day.

If only one might know the fecundity of Jesus in His mystical sleep! He works in the soul with the same efficacy as when awake—perhaps with greater efficacy. Divine consolations dilate the heart, calm the passions and quiet the soul, filling it with the mildest unction. Desolations also accomplish the work of God—a delicate, profound work of purity, strength and love. There are certain delicate and intimate operations which Jesus does not perform in souls except when He is sleeping. His mystical sleep is not from weariness but from love. He sleeps because He loves. He sleeps, because while He sleeps, His heart watches, transforming souls profoundly, though this transformation is imperceptible.

St. Thérèse of the Child Jesus saw secrets of the spiritual life with remarkable clarity, and in order to explain why she was not grieved by her aridity in prayer and her naps during her thanksgivings, she observed that doctors put their patients to sleep in order to perform operations. It is likewise necessary for Jesus to place souls under a holy sedative, into complete darkness, into absolute unconsciousness to accomplish in them divine operations. When this occurs, the soul thinks Jesus is sleeping.

How would souls be able to endure those awful sufferings which, like double-edged swords, penetrate even to the depths of their being, if Jesus were awake, if that sweetest of voices rebounded in them, if the fragrance of His life penetrated their spirit, if they experienced the divine action clearly and palpably? With Jesus manifest, one does not suffer. Looking at Him and receiving His caresses, the soul becomes a replica of paradise. When He shows Himself, sufferings are either dissipated like vapor before the heat of the sun, or are turned into a brilliant and beautiful vision. The soul needs to suffer in its innermost being, and to suffer for a long time, and to suffer without much consolation. In order that the soul may suffer in this way and thus receive special graces, Jesus sleeps.

THE GRACE of purifying and fruitful sorrow is assured by the sleep of Jesus in the soul. As the tempest on Tiberias coincided with the sleep of the Master, so in souls the hurricane rages when Jesus sleeps. Souls need to be tempered in the clamor of the storm. They must be shaken by the seething waves to learn the stability of love. The sky must be overcast so that in the midst of shadows they may catch sight of the mysterious light of faith. The very depths must be opened beneath their fragile bark, so they may know how to hope against all hope. The ancients believed that pearls were formed when the ocean was shaken by the storm. The precious pearl of divine love (the possession of which causes one to despise all earthly things) is formed within the spotless shell of the soul precisely at the dreadful but fecund hour of desolation.

Together with the grace of suffering, spiritual tempests bring the grace of humility, a new, deep humility which hollows out in the soul a void so immense that God fits into it. When Jesus is awake and shows Himself to the soul in all His celestial beauty, when His divine lips speak of love and life, and when His infinite action becomes a delight, she has neither eyes nor time nor desire to look at herself adorned with the precious jewels from her Beloved. But when He sleeps, the night which envelops the soul with its cold, sorrowful darkness, obliges the soul to gaze upon herself in astonishment, to experience her wretchedness, to feel her powerlessness, to be lost in the abyss of her nothingness. From the depths of that abyss, humility arises by divine magic, and the soul, even if it were elevated to the third heaven, will never forget the repulsive sight of her own misery which she contemplated, horror-stricken, in the sad night while Jesus slept and the tempest roared.

Incredible as it may seem, it is necessary that Jesus sleep in order to refine love and purify it. At first sight we might believe there is nothing better than divine consolation to inflame souls with love. Was it not consolation which made the soul turn her eyes toward Jesus in the first place? Was it not He, attractive, resplendent, loving, who passed near the soul like a vision of life and happiness, saying to her as to the apostles: "Come, follow Me," making the soul leave everything to run after Him "to the odor of His ointments?" Then let not that vision of heaven be fleeting. Let Jesus always show Himself to the soul. Let Him speak words of love to her. Let Him charm her with His radiant beauty. Let Him establish His dwelling within her. Upon the summit of radiant Tabor, the soul's love will be converted into fire, into passion, into heaven.

But this is not the way that love is purified. Love, purest gold from heaven, mixed with earthly dross, needs the fire of suffering to recover the limpidity and brilliance proper to its celestial origin. When Jesus is awake, He gives more than He receives. The soul can scarcely do anything else than receive the divine infusions. When night comes, when Jesus surrenders to sleep, He moves the soul to correspond to the love she has received, to give generously, to offer her bitter tears and her secret martyrdom with heroic fortitude.

This precious prerogative of love did not escape St. Thérèse of Lisieux. Nothing escapes the intuitions of love! "And now, dear Mother, what can I tell you about my thanksgivings after Communion, not only then but always? There is no time when I have less consolation—yet this is not to be wondered at, since it is not for my own satisfaction that I desire to receive our Lord but solely to give Him pleasure."[2]

Most souls in their recourse to God seek in Him their own satisfaction. They go after consolations and sweetness. They think about themselves, about giving themselves pleasure, and not about pleasing their Beloved. They have true love but it is imperfect. Blessed are the souls who, like St. Thérèse of the Child Jesus, await God's visit only to please Him. Blessed are the souls who know how to watch over the slumbers of Jesus and peacefully await His radiant awakening. Blessed are those who shower upon Him loving caresses

---

2. *Saint Thérèse of Lisieux, the Little Flower of Jesus*, p. 142.

while He sleeps, converting their tears into pearls of pure love and their bitterness into sweet consolation. The love that forgets itself to think about the Beloved, that suffers so that He may rejoice, that watches so He may sleep, that weeps in secret so He may rest in silence and peace, is love pure and undefiled, born only of suffering and desolation, despoiled of the gross dross of egoism.

71

OH, IF one could understand the value of desolation! If one could appreciate the austere but exquisite beauty of Jesus when He is sleeping! But suffering souls neither suspect the mystery they guard in their hearts, nor do they have the serenity to contemplate the extraordinary beauty of Him who sleeps within them, just as the apostles, worried by the storm and overcome by fear, did not enjoy the divine spectacle of Jesus asleep in the storm.

When Jesus sleeps in a soul, the enraptured angels must contemplate that mystery of fruitfulness and beauty, for desolation has its beauty just as the deep, arid ravines have their beauty, as do the sheer, gigantic cliffs, bare of verdure, to which only the soaring eagle has access.

But how to appreciate that beauty in the night of the soul, among the shadows guarding the sleep of Jesus? There is a subtle, penetrating light shining in the darkness. It is the light of faith. When it is living, when it is nourished by love, when it receives from the Holy Spirit an unknown divine penetration and mighty power, it manifests to souls, who allow Jesus to sleep, who watch His sleep and who suffer so He may rest, the hidden and mysterious spectacle of Jesus sleeping—a most beautiful contrast of silence, darkness and sadness.

O SOULS enamored of Jesus, offer Him your pure and loving hearts so that He may come to rest therein. Permit Him to sleep as much as He wants while you, silent and tender, watch His mystical slumber. Fear neither the silence nor the darkness which guard the mystery of that sleep. Do not awake the sweet Beloved because His heart is watching when He sleeps and the apparent inaction of that repose hides prodigies of productivity that will transform your life. Be quiet in the midst of your grief, so He may not awaken. Weep in silence, so that your tears may be pearls of love for Him. Cover Him with your tender caresses, with your timid but ardent kisses. Open your eyes, "the illuminated eyes of your heart," to contemplate the hidden beauty of Jesus asleep. One day—day of rejoicing, of light, of rapture—Jesus will awake, and upon seeing that you have offered Him the warm, silent, perfumed couch of your heart, and that you have watched tenderly and solicitously during this slumber of love, He will command the winds and the tempest so that the peace of heaven may reign in you, and in the depth of that most sweet peace the mystery of love will be realized, happy and never-ending.

CHAPTER 6

⚜

The Hidden God

T hou dost fill the universe with Thy majesty, history with Thy thought and action, souls with Thy presence, the Church with Thy word and Thy Eucharist. Thou art present everywhere and in innumerable ways. Thou dost surround, envelop and penetrate us; in Thee we live and move and have our being (Acts 17:28). Nevertheless, the greater part of mankind forgets Thee; very many offend Thee; many do not know Thee; many deny Thee. Truly, Thou art a God of hidden ways, everywhere present and everywhere hidden.

Present in the universe, yet hidden, the heavens sing Thy glory; the earth is filled with Thy majesty; the depths vibrate with Thy power. Creator, preserver and governor of men and of the universe, Thou dost live in every creature. Thy light doth shine in every created thing and Thy love burns within them. All creation is filled with Thee. Men study the universe and scarcely find Thee. They contemplate its beauty and do not discover Thine. They enjoy creatures and forget Thee. Truly, Thou art a hidden God.

History is the realization of Thy thought and the fruit of Thy action. Thou art more present to history than we ourselves. Nothing is fulfilled therein but what Thou dost will. In Thy hands are all the complicated threads of human events. Thy action, Thy designs are the background of history; men make history, write it and read it; but few are they who guess Thy presence. Still fewer in number are they who contemplate Thee in its pages. Who sees Thee in history such as Thou art? Truly Thou art a hidden God.

Thou art present in the Scriptures even more than in the universe and in history. Every page bespeaks and glorifies Thee. Thy word appears under the veil of human words. Thou art there. Thou art hidden under its narratives, its counsels, its promises and its mysteries. Our feeble intelligence scarcely touches the surface of the Scriptures. Thou art its essence; who has penetrated it? Who has completely found Thee, O God, hidden in the Scriptures? The man who would possess a true understanding of the Sacred Books would forget the world, would forget himself, because He would have found Thee. Thy mortal life is epitomized in these words: "Truly, Thou art a God of hidden ways." Hidden in Mary's womb, hidden in Bethlehem, hidden in Nazareth, in Capernaum and on Tiberias and in every place of Thy public life; hidden in Gethsemane and on Calvary, who can duly comprehend each one of these stages of Thy divine concealment?

Thy mystical life is also hidden. Thou livest in the Church and there Thou wilt live even to the end of time. Thou teachest through her mouth; Thou givest life through her actions; Thou dost suffer in her sorrows and triumph in her victories. The Church is Christ. Who can comprehend the mystery of Thy Church, hidden under human appearances, persecuted and triumphant, rejoicing and sorrowing, subject in a certain measure to the vicissitudes of time? Thy Church traverses the centuries like Thee, doing good. And as the world did not know Thee, so it does not know Thy Church. "There is one standing in your midst of whom you know nothing" (John 1:26), can be said to men and to nations. Even Christians themselves do not penetrate the mystery of the Church. Few know to what extent Thou dost live in her. Truly, Thou art a God of hidden ways.

Where art Thou more present than in the Eucharist? Only in heaven art Thou more perfectly present than in the Eucharist. The Eucharist is the epitome of all Thy presences, because it is the compendium of all Thy love's excesses. Here are all the remembrances of Christ's mortal life. Here is the substance of His mortal life. Here are all the treasures of His divine life. O God, O ever present God, Thou who dwellest in our tabernacles, rest upon my lips and make a heaven of my heart. Who would have dreamed of a God like Thee, who dost exceed the immensity of our desires, the audacity of our hope, the madness of our love? In the Eucharist we touch Thee, we eat Thee, we are changed into Thee. Thou art our possession, our food, our life. Canst Thou be more present to us than that? Nevertheless, nowhere art Thou more hidden than in the Eucharist. When I approach Thy tabernacle, my senses seek in vain for a sign of Thy sovereign presence, and I behold Thee there, silent as in Mary's womb, motionless as in the sepulcher, impotent and immolated as on the Cross. When I see Thee in the tabernacle, the words of Thomas Aquinas occur to me: "Upon the Cross only the Deity was hidden, but here Thy manhood, too." O God of love, O sacrificial Lamb, I see dimly the unfathomed mysteries of faith and love while my lips and my heart pronounce the mystic words: "Truly, Thou art a God of hidden ways" (Is. 45:15).

Even in heaven, Thy supreme and glorious Epiphany, Thou art a hidden God, not indeed for the angels who praise Thee, nor for those who enjoy Thee, but for us who wander through the desert of this world longing for Thee, seeking Thee in the dimness of holy hope. O God, ever present and ever hidden! Blessed are the souls who seek Thee. More blessed are those who find Thee and enjoy Thee in the secrecy of Thy benign presence.

BUT I feel the necessity of meditating upon something that concerns me so intimately. I am not a creature like the other creatures of the earth, since God placed in me a soul, the breath of His mouth—a soul purchased with the blood of Christ and beauti-fied with the gifts of the Holy Spirit. I have a special place in the thought of God; I occupy a post of honor in His heart; I am the unique object of His providence and His action. God is singularly present in my life and in my soul. God is for me a God present and hidden. Not for a single instant does the action of God fail to touch me—not only that power which preserves and moves all creatures, but more especially, that exceedingly gentle action which keeps guiding me along unknown paths toward my perfection and happiness.

I do not understand how much God loves me nor how immense, constant and active is the love He has for me. Not for one instant does He fail to draw me toward Himself with the force of His love of predilection. My life, with its alternations of joy and grief, of fear and hope, of activity and repose, my life, with its vari-able and innumerable circumstances, is God's work. It is the fruit of His love. There is nothing in my life which he does not foresee, direct and dispose for my good. Only when I separate myself from Him by sin does my life cease to be the fruit of His action. Yet God permits even my faults, then returns again to convert me and to repair the damage wrought by sin.

Beneath all external happenings, God is always present and hidden. Joy and sorrow are equally God's messengers coming to accomplish in my soul the work of His love. They are instruments of His action, veils which cover His presence. If only I would con-tinue to discover this God hidden in my own life! If I would always let myself be led by His gentle hand, my life would be His action; my soul, a temple; and I, a saint.

But there is still something deeper and dearer because it is more loving. God is hidden in my soul, in the center of my being, in the very core of my heart. Hidden as in His own temple, as in His own tabernacle. With a presence that is not ephemeral but, by its very nature, eternal.

Only one thing can put His presence to flight and disturb that
happiness: sin. While grace is in my soul, although it may be present in a lower degree, God is hidden in me, and that presence can
be increased every day. I can augment it each instant, as the sun,
visible at sunrise, becomes more and more brilliant until noon. "If
a man has any love for Me, he will be true to My word; and then he
will win My Father's love, and We will both come to him, and make
Our continual abode with him" (John 14:23). What a promise! If
we had faith that would flourish as a grain of mustard seed, it would
suffice to make us saints. If we understood this presence, our heart
would be a temple; more, it would be a heaven. Our souls are God's
true temples; the tabernacle is only a waiting place. Jesus is there
because He knows that we will come to seek Him. The tabernacles
that He seeks and longs for are the living sanctuaries of loving souls.
In them He establishes His dwelling and even His sacramental presence. True, this latter does not endure continuously in our souls,
but His presence of love and of grace, if we place no obstacle, is
eternal. O God, hidden in our souls!

God lives in us in a more intimate way than we are present to
ourselves. Why, then, do we ignore Thy presence? Why do we abandon Thee? Why do we not live with love and adoration in the innermost sanctuary of our soul? We search for God and all the while
we are carrying Him within us. We keep seeking happiness and
happiness lies within ourselves. If God is a hidden God, one must
seek Him as one seeks a treasure. Those who find Him find life, and
the life that contains all: light, purity, love, happiness, immortality.
If there are so few who find God, it is because very few seek Him.
Wisdom, says Holy Writ, allows herself to be seen readily by those
who love her and she is found by those who seek her (Prov. 8:17).

How few are those who seek God! To live in this world is to
seek, and to seek something hidden which our spirit anticipates and
covets. Heaven is the fatherland of possession. There, to possess is to
live. In exile one possesses very little and desires much. In exile, to

live is to seek. We are all seeking; some for riches; others for honors; these aspire to glory, those to knowledge; some crave pleasure, others dream of love, and all seek happiness. Who are they who truly seek Thee, O hidden God—Thou who art for him who finds Thee, infinite riches, perfect glory, unspeakable love, complete joy and ineffable happiness? All who seek, find; those who seek creatures, find them. That is, they find deception and misery. Those who seek themselves find themselves. They find emptiness and nothing because all creatures, ourselves included, are vanity. Thankless is the task of seeking nothingness, disturbing ourselves, tiring ourselves out, suffering and dying only to find phantoms and falsehood. Is not this the life of the majority of mankind? Rightly is humanity so unhappy. Men do not seek the hidden God, the fountain of living water, but they seek creatures or themselves—broken cisterns which can hold no water. "Will you never cease setting your heart on shadows, following a lie?" (Ps. 4:3).

Even when we think we are seeking God, we are seeking ourselves; even in prayer we look for consolation; even in mortifying ourselves we seek our own satisfaction; even in doing good works we seek vanity. Who really seeks the hidden God? Who finds Him? Let us cease searching for creatures; let us stop seeking ourselves and let us seek God, for we cannot live without seeking something. When we abandon creatures and ourselves, our hearts will orientate themselves toward God. We shall look for God, and He who seeks God finds Him.

BUT HOW can we seek the hidden God, the most high mysterious God, who inhabits light inaccessible? Neither the senses nor the imagination nor the feelings will ever find Him. God is spirit and only the spirit can touch Him. If the senses were to find Him, He would not be a hidden God; He would not be God. In the excess of His love, no doubt, He wanted our eyes to see, our ears to hear and our hands to touch the Word of life. But this is only the beginning of the way that leads to God. The Church sings in the Christmas Preface: "In order that knowing God under a visible form, we might be caught up by it to the love of invisible things."

It is true that sometimes God allows Himself to be possessed by us in a manner so perfect He shows Himself to us with such clarity. He lavishes His gifts upon us with such profusion, that even our senses partake of the abundance of the spirit. The heavenly rapture cannot be restrained within the soul, and like a liquid overflowing the brim of the vessel, celestial joy fills even our senses. One would say that even the lower part of the soul experiences God's presence. In us are fulfilled the Psalmist's words: "The living God! at His name my heart, my whole being thrills with joy" (Ps. 83:3). The senses can help us find God and they can receive the crumbs from the divine banquet, but they do not sit at the table of the hidden God nor can they by themselves find Him. God is spirit and only the higher part of the soul can find Him and approach Him.

How many times we do not find God because we attempt to find Him in a sensible manner. We want to feel His presence, to feel His love, to feel union with Him. Forgetting that our God is a God hidden from our senses, we fall into lamentable illusions. Do we feel something? We think we are near God. Do we feel nothing? We judge ourselves abandoned. No, it is not in this way one seeks and finds God. In the majority of cases the senses hamper us. Therefore, the masters of the spiritual life, especially St. John of the Cross, insist that souls who aspire to union with God must detach themselves from the things of sense.

Human wisdom cannot find this hidden God. Even in the natural order, how dull is our poor mind in discovering the evidences of God in the universe and in history. In the supernatural order, human wisdom is utterly incapable of discovering God. It has neither wings to ascend so high nor eyes to penetrate so deep. Christ praises the heavenly Father: "Thou hast hidden all this from the wise and the prudent, and revealed it to little children" (Matt.

11:25). It is neither the wise nor the prudent of this world who find God, but the little ones of whom the Book of Proverbs speaks: "Simple hearts...draw near me" (Prov. 9:4). With these the Lord converses. From their mouths, the mouths of children, God draws perfect praise to confound His enemies (Ps. 8:3). Blessed smallness that magnifies us! Blessed simplicity that makes us wise! Blessed infancy that bestows upon us the fullness of the age of Christ!

Like human wisdom, everything human is powerless to find God—all grandeur, activity, love. To find God it is necessary that the Holy Spirit impel us and that the Father draw us with His Son (John 6:44), and in the light of the Word we shall see light.

To find God it is necessary that there be in us something divine. God has planted in our souls all that we need to find Him: eyes to see Him, hands to touch Him, and a heart to love Him. The eyes which discover God hidden in the darkness of mystery are the eyes of faith. Their gaze penetrates and transforms all. It contemplates the Creator through the creatures of the universe; it recognizes divine providence in the events of history, and it discerns the divine word hidden beneath the veil of the Scriptures. It beholds Christ in the Church and under the Eucharistic accidents. It sees the divine reality thereby concealed, in the interior of our souls it recognizes the God of love who has placed His dwelling there. Faith penetrates all, and consequently it transforms everything, making it divine. To faith, the world is a temple; history, the epic of God's glory; the Church, Christ Himself; our heart, a tabernacle; the Eucharist, a heaven. Oh, if we had faith!

TRULY, THOU art a hidden God, the God of Israel, the Savior. But wherever Thou art, faith discovers Thee. Thou art compassed by divine darkness, but faith is the light that shines in the shadows until the day without sunset dawns and the morning star shines in our heart. To discover Thee in the midst of shadows is a happiness, but it is also a martyrdom. He who perceives Thee in the twilight

of time aspires to contemplate Thee in the full light of eternity. He
who glimpses Thy beauty longs to enjoy it face to face.

In the measure in which our faith grows, our desires also
increase, and the happiness of seeing Thee becomes a martyrdom
of not possessing Thee. O Beauty! O Happiness! O Love! When
will the veils be rent asunder so that we may be immersed in the
splendors of Thy countenance? When will the mist of mystery be
scattered so that Thy voice containing all sweetness may sound in
our ears? When shall I dwell with Thee in Thy eternal abode? My
God, My God, for Thee do I sigh at break of day! For Thee my soul
is parched with a burning thirst and even my body is inflamed with
that same glowing ardor.

The life of faith would be a torture if the fever of desire which
it produces were not alleviated with the soothing balm of hope.
What are the years of my life (however long and painful they may
be), what are the years of my exile but a swift and fleeting day that
scarcely exists because of the intensity of my hope? Tomorrow I
shall possess Thee, my God and my All, and while that morrow
which never delays is drawing near, I rest in Thy bosom in tranquil
sleep because Thou has established me in hope.

God, hidden in splendor, I touch Thee with the arms of my
unbounded hope! But there is something more illuminating than
faith, more inspiring than hope—love! Faith discerns Thee; hope
touches Thee; love possesses Thee, O hidden God! If we but knew
the gift of God (John 4:10), if we but understood the wonders of
love! Desire is impatient. Our hearts, pining away with longing,
wait not until the morrow of eternity. Not tomorrow but today;
not in heaven but on earth. Let us love each other here amidst the
vicissitudes of time. Let us love here in the shadows of faith. I shall
espouse myself to Thee in faith. I shall pledge myself to Thee forever
(Hos. 2:19-20). Tomorrow the nuptials of love will take place in
the joy and light of glory. Today, in sorrow and in faith. Love finds
Thee, O hidden God; love beholds Thee with the illumined gaze of

the heart. It embraces Thee with the arms of tenderness; it imprisons Thee with unbreakable chains. "We shall never have finished with charity" (1 Cor. 13:8). Love alone is immortal; it alone crosses the frontiers of time, heavenly and divine. He who loves Thee finds Thee, O God of love, and he can exclaim with the spouse of the Canticle: "All mine, my true love, and I all His" (Cant. 2:16).

But let us not treat the mystery of love unworthily. Be silent, be silent.

TRULY, THOU art a hidden God, the God of Israel, our Savior! Everywhere present and everywhere hidden! In Thee we live and move. Thou dost fill everything with Thy majesty and Thy love: the universe and history, Scripture and the Church, our life and our soul. Lord, that we may see Thee! Men forget, offend and deny Thee because they do not know Thee, because Thou art a hidden God. Let men seek Thee, O Lord, forgetting their vanities and ceasing to seek themselves. Let us find Thee, O Lord, that our faith may contemplate Thee, that our hope may touch Thee, that our love may possess Thee! Thou art a God hidden to the worldly, but familiar, intimate and present to all who bear Thee in their heart. Truly, Thou art a God of hidden ways!

CHAPTER 7

☙

Via Crucis

FIRST STATION

The sentence which men spoke against Jesus was unjust, but the sentence of eternal justice is most just, because God placed upon Him the iniquities of us all.

What shame and what grief for Jesus to feel Himself responsible for all the sins of the world!

What a satisfaction to His love to suffer for the whole human race and to pay our enormous debts!

What shame we ought to feel for our faults!

What gratitude we owe to the one who with such loving generosity took the weight of our iniquities!

Sometimes we think that we suffer unjustly, and perhaps we are right if we refer to the immediate causes of our pains. But if we consider our sufferings thoughtfully, how many ways the justice of God is evident in them!

It is just to suffer so that we may expiate our faults.

It is just, most just, to suffer so that we may make ourselves worthy to receive the gift of God. If justice consists in giving to each one what belongs to him, is it not just that Jesus, who is ours by so many titles, be given to us? But acceptance of suffering is an indispensable disposition for receiving Him.

According to divine justice, it is right that we suffer for others to save them and to obtain happiness for them, as Jesus suffered for the salvation and happiness of all.

Suffering is *expiation*; it is *love*; it is *fruitfulness*.

Second Station

Jesus receives the Cross. What is the Cross? The crushing weight of all the sins of the world.

Jesus' sorrow surpasses all bounds. But by virtue of the love of the Divine Heart, the Cross is changed into a torrent of all good, into an inexhaustible fountain of happiness. For us, the Cross is suffering, love and hope.

Cross-bearers should appreciate that treasure, love it, and embrace it with Christ.

Third Station

The Cross oppresses. Jesus fell under its weight.

There are three types of spiritual falls:

The irreparable—the bitterness of these overwhelmed the Divine Heart; they are unmitigated suffering.

Falls from which the love of Jesus raises souls—these are for Him both a cause of sorrow and an occasion of joy.

A third kind of fall has no relation to sin, but consists in humiliation and self-contempt—these fill the Heart of Jesus with joy.

He fell, crushed by the suffering of the first. He fell to make loving reparation for the second. He fell to reward the third.

Is it not a reward for the humiliated one to be thrown to the ground with Jesus, there to be embraced by Him in the very dust of the earth?

Fourth Station

Many compassionate Jesus in His passion and participate in it: the women with their tears, the Cyrenean carrying the Cross, Veronica wiping the divine countenance. Mary penetrated the ocean of her Son's grief deeply, silently. She participated in His suffering, in His love and in His fruitfulness.

Cross-bearers should participate in these three prerogatives: to suffer like Jesus—through a love similar to His—to save souls with that celestial combination of love and sorrow.

The supreme example of cross-bearers is Mary.

Fifth Station

Happy the man who helped the Divine Victim with the Cross! We can help Him too. There are three ways: interiorly, by entering into the mystery of the divine suffering and participating in it with the heart; by patiently bearing our cross which is always touched to that of Christ, or rather, which is a part of it; finally, since the Cross is the only instrument of salvation, we can relieve Christ by bringing it to souls in order to take those souls to Jesus.

These three participations correspond to the three aspects of the Cross: love, sorrow and fruitfulness.

Sixth Station

What exquisite delicacy in Veronica's compassion for Jesus and in her participation in His sacrifice! She can neither support the weight of the Cross like Simon nor can she plumb the mysterious depths of suffering like Mary. Neither does she fit in with the holy women in their weeping. Her sensitive woman's soul sees Jesus exhausted by fatigue and she perceives the hidden beauty of the sacred countenance. With her veil, she cleanses that most lovely face, refreshing it in its fatigue. As a reward she receives the immortal portrait.

Veronica is the type of tender soul in whom love, conquering natural apathy, gives Jesus the truest, most exquisite consolation.

The divine countenance was the loveliest and most engaging feature of His royal body. Chosen souls form Jesus' face in the mystical body. To cleanse Jesus' face is to guide these souls to a lofty perfection. To cleanse Jesus' face is to pray and to sacrifice oneself on behalf of priests.

Also, in a higher sense, to cleanse Jesus' face is to study and to feel His interior sufferings, for they conceal what is most excellent in Jesus' soul.

In one way or another, cross-bearers ought to cleanse the face Jesus. He who cleanses it always receives as a most sweet recompense a divine transformation.

Seventh Station

Jesus fell again, because there are many degrees in suffering, because the Cross does not always weigh the same nor does it oppress equally those who carry it. Neither are our falls the same.

Jesus abased Himself to the very earth. He was stretched in the dust to raise and exalt us. Souls also undergo abasements that are very productive of good for others. There are souls who belittle themselves so that others may rise. How unknown, how fruitful and how sublime is the apostolate of humiliation!

To humble ourselves for souls who do not humble themselves, to accept degradation—so appealing to the Heart of God to save others, and to humble ourselves before rebellious souls that we may win them like Jesus, who does not disdain to beg us, to knock at the door of our heart, to humble Himself before our wretchedness in order to win our soul—all these methods, and many others which charity inspires, form the hidden and exquisite apostolate of humility.

Eighth Station

Of all the ways of compassionating and consoling Jesus which we find on the *Via Dolorosa*, the least is, in my estimation, that of the women who wept for Jesus. But very lofty and perfect is the lesson which the Lord gave us when He said to the pious women: "Daughters of Jerusalem, weep not for Me, but weep for yourselves and for your children."

To forget our own sufferings to attend to those of others requires disinterested love, genuine sympathy and exquisite zeal. We are our own worst enemies. If we could but forget ourselves completely! Every egoistic look detours the look of love which goes direct to what we love. Suffering is something so pure and so delicate that a single look tarnishes it. In order that our suffering may not lose its brilliance, let no eyes but those of God see it, least of all our own eyes. The apostolate is the gift of ourselves and to look at ourselves, even to contemplate our sufferings, even to see what souls are costing us, hinders the plentitude of that fruitful donation.

Ninth Station

The third fall of Jesus is the symbol of the supreme oppression of the Cross; it is the suffering that overwhelms, the humiliation that plunges one into the abyss. It was necessary that Jesus fall three times that some souls might rise. There are irreparable falls that oppress the Divine Heart with pain. The third fall, more prolonged and terrible than the preceding, certainly merited for some souls the grace of perfect self-contempt, of complete forgetfulness of themselves and the reward of meeting Jesus in the depths to which they descend.

Tenth Station

Jesus despoiled of His garments is the love that by stripping itself of everything attains august nakedness. It is the suffering

which deprives itself of all consolation in order to shine with exquisite purity. It is the apostolic charity which spends everything and is
spent itself for souls to be divinely fruitful.

ELEVENTH STATION

In the Praetorium, Jesus Christ embraced the Cross; on the road
to Calvary, He carried it lovingly upon His shoulders; on the sacred
summit, He espoused it in an eternal and indissoluble manner.

Sweet nails which fastened the Beloved forever upon His Cross!
Neither anything nor anyone will ever separate that which eternal
love has joined together. Ever since the bloody and fruitful nuptials
of Calvary, he who seeks love must be nailed upon the Cross; he
who loves suffering must unite himself with Christ; and he who
desires spiritual fruitfulness must be transformed lovingly into Jesus
and offer himself with Jesus for immense suffering.

TWELFTH STATION

Jesus Christ crucified is love enthroned, suffering that darts
Victorious to heaven, fruitfulness which, by attracting all souls
upward, pours into them the life of heaven.

Everything is consummated on Calvary: the truth to which
Jesus came to give testimony, the fire which He came to bring to
the earth, the life for which souls await hopefully.

Who could guess that light would shine in the shadows of pain,
that life would rise from death, and that the fire of love would burn
among the ashes of sorrow and in the ice of death?

Rightly did St. Paul say that he wanted to know nothing else
than Jesus Christ and Him crucified. Is there, in fact, anything
worthy of knowledge and love outside of Christ? Can one attain
proficiency in this science and art without climbing to the top of
Calvary?

Thirteenth Station

Suffering ceases, but not ignominy. What a humiliation in the sacred despoliation of Jesus! No, suffering does not cease; the friends of Jesus take it to their heart and in them Jesus, enamored of suffering, continues to suffer mystically.

Mary holds the lifeless body in her arms; in her heart she keeps the immense sorrow of her Son, which He left her as a precious bequest.

Jesus loved profoundly His interior suffering, relinquishing it only with His last breath. His suffering is immortal, preserved in loving souls. He will choose the most select souls to guard the sacred fire of His suffering. The chain of love and suffering which formed His mortal life will continue upon earth. The final link of His soul will intertwine itself mysteriously with that first link which is the Immaculate Heart of Mary. Upon leaving her as a bequest to John, He left her the sorrow of His soul. Are we not His executioners? Are not our ingratitudes and our sins the mystical substance of the thorns surrounding His heart and the cross surmounting it? Perhaps St. John, Magdalen, Joseph, Nicodemus and the holy women also gathered something of that precious bequest.

At the foot of the blood-stained, solitary Cross, around the sacred, despoiled body that Mary holds in her maternal arms, while the faithful few contemplate the Holy Victim, the cross-bearers are born. They will be perpetuated in the world by preserving the divine inheritance of suffering and of love. Priests like John, virgins like Mary, holy men and pious women represent the inner court, the small flock, heirs of the divine treasure which they will guard with everlasting fidelity.

Fourteenth Station

The Cross is not the end of the triumphal march of love, suffering and fecundity. After the Cross comes the sepulcher, bringing forgetfulness, silence, incomprehensible abasement—the sepulcher from which glory and love will issue forth, from which the new humanity will arise, "a chosen race, a royal priesthood, a consecrated nation, a people God means to have for Himself" (1 Pet. 2:9).

To be buried in the sepulcher is the last word of love, the marvelous extremity of divine suffering, the law of fruitfulness whereby seed is placed into the earth to prepare a copious harvest. The mystery of the sepulcher is the forgetfulness of self, giving victory to a mighty love, the suffering which appears boundless so that eternal happiness may reign, the life that undergoes death to give life to us with His death. "Life suffered death and by that death gave life back to us."[1]

---

1.   Rev. Joseph Connolly, *Hymns of the Roman Liturgy* (Westminster, MD: Newman Press, 1954), p. 82.

CHAPTER 8

٭

Consolation for Jesus

When we reflect upon the sweet obligation of consoling our Lord, we are apt to imagine a group of devoted children sympathizing with a sorrow-stricken father, striving to alleviate his suffering by caresses and tender words. Loving souls feel that they ought to comfort Jesus in the same way to make Him forget the ingratitude of man. Moved to great generosity by this consideration, they courageously and cheerfully accept every sacrifice in reparation to the grief-laden Heart of Christ.[1] However beautiful this may seem, souls who stop here have but a superficial understanding of what it means to console Jesus. Our Lord asks something deeper, more far-reaching. Therefore, in the present chapter I wish, with the grace of God, to delve into this mystery of consoling Jesus, so that souls attracted to a life of reparation may better understand their vocation.

There are two ways of consoling: one is human, the other, divine. Human comfort is exterior, superficial, and consequently, imperfect. It is exterior because our demonstrations of affection and condolence can but rarely penetrate the heart of the one who is suffering. At times it seems that human consolations, surpassing their nature, reach the heart. But this is something rare and fleeting. Human comfort, moreover, is extremely powerless, especially in certain sorrows. What can we give to one who has lost an immense good? The little we are able to offer is all out of proportion to the good lost—a few pennies, as it were, to compensate for the loss of a valuable jewel.

Divine consolation is the only true consolation, for the Comforter *par excellence* is none other than the Holy Spirit. He is the supreme model. As He consoles, so must we try to comfort the Heart of Jesus. St. Margaret Mary Alacoque is a magnificent model of the soul dedicated to reparation, since our Lord Himself chose her for this mission. St. Thérèse of the Child Jesus is likewise an admirable pattern of loving compassion, for from the age of three, as she herself attests, she never denied our Lord any sacrifice. But far beyond all the saints, the most holy Virgin is the ideal of consolers. Yet the supreme model, I repeat, is the Holy Spirit, whom the liturgy calls "*Consolator optime*."

IN ORDER to know how we ought to comfort the Heart of Jesus, let us analyze divine consolation, striving to ascertain how the Holy Spirit consoles. Such analysis lies within our power because we ourselves, on some occasion or other, have experienced the solace of the Paraclete. The consolation of the Holy Spirit is not exterior, but interior. There is no need to use our external senses. On the contrary, we close our eyes and our ears and, concentrating within ourselves, we find divine comfort deep in our heart. That consolation is

---

1.   EDITOR's NOTE (Spanish Edition): During His mortal life, our Lord suffered as we do; now He suffers in the sense indicated by Sacred Scripture, which states that God was "smitten with indignation to the depths of His heart" (Gen. 6:6). Christ suffers in His mystical body. Furthermore, He suffered during His mortal life all that He would suffer now if He were in a possible state, because through His infinite knowledge He had that suffering present before Him then, just as He also had present before Him (for the same reason) the consolations we offer Him now.

never superficial; it is always deep. It is not ephemeral and fleeting, but constant and permanent.

93

But why is the Holy Spirit called the Comforter? From time to time He sends a ray of celestial light into our souls. He fills our heart with holy affections. He even seems to raise us from the earth to taste the blessedness of heaven. But I do not think that the Holy Spirit is called the Comforter exactly for these consolations, for they are essentially transitory. There are souls greatly beloved by God to whom He sends aridity for long periods of time. Consider St. Teresa of Avila. How many years the admirable virgin endured a dark, terrifying, absolute desolation! Did not the Holy Spirit console her? No, those are not the consolations for which the Holy Spirit is called the Comforter. There must be a fundamental consolation that He pours into all souls that possess Him.

The most poignant grief requiring consolation is that we do not possess God fully. As long as we live in exile, we feel the ardent desire to possess Him. Sometimes we try to distract ourselves with the things of earth so that we do not feel that deep pain of separation, but when the things which distract us disappear, when we realize our true situation, we are compelled to exclaim with the Psalmist: "Unhappy I, that am still doomed to exile" (Ps. 119:6). Or with St. Paul: "I long to have done with it and be with Christ" (Phil. 1:23). Or with St. Teresa of Jesus:

> I live, yet no true life I know,
> And, living thus expectantly,
> I die because I do not die.[2]

The sorrow for which we need consolation is that we are not in full possession of God. The Holy Spirit is our Comforter because

---

2. *The Complete Works of Saint Teresa of Jesus*, trans. E. Allison Peers (New York: Sheed and Ward, Inc.)

while our exile is prolonged, He gives God to us so far as we can receive and possess Him on this earth. He gives us "that which gives substance to our hopes" (Heb. 11:1), as the Apostle says. He builds a heaven in our heart while eternity draws near. Rightly is the Holy Spirit called the Comforter. His consolation is not only interior, but it is also constant and permanent, full and perfect. He gives us the very thing for which we yearn, and on His part the giving is definitive and everlasting. Though not with all the splendors of the world beyond, yet in substance, every soul living the supernatural life—especially the perfect life—already carries heaven within her.

SINCE THIS is the way the Holy Spirit consoles us, we ought to exert ourselves to console the Heart of Christ in like manner, "that is impossible," you say. "It is like entrusting a gigantic enterprise to a pygmy." You are mistaken. If we were not to count upon the Holy Spirit nor possess Him in our hearts, we could not possibly give one crumb of comfort to the Sacred Heart. We would have to abandon that enterprise as an absurd undertaking. But we do possess Him! Jesus Christ gave Him to us as the fruit of His passion and death on the day of Pentecost. And since that day, the Spirit is poured forth upon all flesh. He fills the whole earth and we bear Him within us as an inexhaustible fountain of grace (John 7:38–39). And he who possesses the Holy Spirit can console as He consoles.

Another approach, perhaps, will be of greater service. The only one who can console the Heart of Jesus is the Holy Spirit Himself. He was Christ's Paraclete, His Comforter during the thirty-three years of His mortal life. And He is still the only one who knows how to console our Lord and is able to do so. But through the boundless condescension of God's charity, the Holy Spirit desires to use souls as instruments to comfort the Sacred Heart. Considered in this light, is not such a mission possible? Of course! Imperfect instruments that we are, we can gradually lose a little of the impulse of the Holy Spirit, but He is so genial an artist that He overcomes our limitations with His skill. Let us not stop with generalities, however profound and illuminating. With the grace of God, we shall plumb this mystery more deeply.

95

To UNDERSTAND the nature of that comfort which we ought to offer our Lord, let us set about analyzing the idea of consolation. What is it to console? To console is to give some good as a substitute for what has been lost or is unobtained as yet. When the unpossessed good is of slight value, comfort is a simple matter. It is very easy to console a child, because ordinarily his loss is merely a trifle. But when a man loses his entire fortune, it is more difficult to comfort him although, after all, the riches of this world are also a small thing. We can console him, extending to him the hope or even the opportunity of acquiring new wealth, or giving him a spiritual good so that he may forget the material good he has lost. When one deals with more lofty goods, the difficulty of comforting increases in proportion. How difficult it is, for example, to console one who has lost his mother, for what is comparable to his great loss?

Consolation is in order, too, when one cannot obtain what he desires. He who loves suffers to the extent to which he does not obtain possession of the good he loves. The greater his love, the greater his suffering. In order that he may await the satisfaction of his desires with fortitude, we can console him by providing him with another good and by assuring him that he will attain what his heart desires. This being so, in what sense can we console Jesus? What good has He lost, or what can He desire that He does not already possess? Why is He in need of comfort? Because He has asked for it. He asked it of St. Margaret Mary Alacoque. Holy Church places upon His lips this phrase from Holy Scripture: "Naught else but shame and misery does My heart forbode; I look round for pity, where pity is none, for comfort, where there is no comfort to be found" (Ps. 68:21–22). Undoubtedly, Jesus asks us to console Him.

But, once more, what has He lost or what does He desire that

He seeks solace from us? Can it be that He sighs, like ourselves, for the everlasting Fatherland? No, He possesses it fully; He is seated at the right hand of the Father, crowned with honor and glory. Jesus needs nothing. He not only possesses God, but He is God. He is King of heaven and earth. At His name every knee bows in heaven, on earth and under the earth. All creation intones unceasingly that canticle of the Apocalypse: "Blessing and honor and glory and power, through endless ages, to Him who sits on the throne and to the Lamb" (Rev. 5:13).

But if Jesus possesses everything in heaven, much is lacking to Him upon earth because the desires of His heart are not satisfied. What is it that He desires? To complete His mystical body, to reach the fullness of His stature (Eph. 4:13). He desires that souls be united with Him, live His life, and adapt themselves to His sentiments so that He may present them to His heavenly Father as the trophy of His victory for the glory of the Father and the sanctification of souls. Holy Scripture depicts Jesus Christ as a mighty victor whose cortège is formed by the very ones He has conquered (Eph. 4:8), in accordance with the custom of ancient warriors.

In a certain sense this triumph is incomplete. It will advance toward completion until the final day of time when the last soul will be brought to heaven by its Redeemer. Jesus desires that all humanity be gathered under the egis of His love in a perfect vital union, so that the kingdom of God may be established and consummated upon the earth. As long as these desires are not satisfied, as long as these designs are not realized, Jesus awaits our comfort with divine impatience, with insatiable ardor, until His triumph is definitive and His happiness complete.

It is very common for souls to believe that Jesus needs comfort only for the insults He receives. They do not realize that He needs compensation also for His unsatisfied desires. Is not a deep, unsatisfied desire a piercing sorrow? Therefore Jesus needs to be consoled both for the insults He receives and for His unfilled desires.

THERE IS one consolation, a personal one, which we ought to offer our Lord, namely, our own sanctification. He desires vehemently that each one of us be intimately united with Him, without limits, without reserve. He wishes to possess our whole heart. Each soul that removes all obstacles and surrenders itself to Him is a consolation because it is a desire satisfied. To console Jesus means, in the first place, to surrender one's heart entirely to Him. This is the consolation of love.

In the world, how much a true lover suffers from unrequited love! What, then, must our Lord suffer since He loves us infinitely more than all earth's lovers? How He desires that we be one with Him as He and the Father are one in the unity of the Holy Spirit! But many obstacles beset our path. In the midst of our wretchedness, there are certain delightful moments when we feel that Jesus is near; a flood of light inundates the soul and a heavenly fire inflames the heart. Yet often we feel that this happiness is incomplete, that we cannot be united to Jesus as we should like, and as He desires, because there are so many hindrances. What does it matter that these impediments are not very great, if they prevent perfect union? In precision instruments, where adjustments and gearings must be perfect, a speck of dust suffices to hinder proper functioning. Our union with God is likewise something delicate and precise. A speck of dust, any attachment, however insignificant, can disturb it. Let us offer to Jesus this kind of consolation—surrendering our heart completely to Him, without reserve.

THE SECOND consolation that Jesus awaits from us is that we so enter into His views and designs that we engage in the same enterprise that He does, and that we sacrifice ourselves for the same ends for which He sacrifices Himself—the salvation and sanctification of souls. Even if the desire of Jesus for the sanctification of our own souls were satisfied, many other desires remain unsatisfied in His Divine Heart.

Let us imagine a king ambitious to achieve a mighty conquest, who suffers keenly as long as his aspirations are unrealized. Could not his faithful vassals best console their king by placing at his disposal their fortunes, their own persons and their very lives? Never in the heart of any warrior has there been the unbounded aspiration that consumes the Heart of Jesus—His burning desire to save and sanctify all men. What consolation for Him if each one of us would say: "Lord, I have caught a glimpse of Thy divine enterprise, and here I am to help Thee. Since souls may be purified and saved by suffering, I wish to be a victim with Thee, the Supreme Victim. Henceforth Thy destiny will be my destiny. I wish that the same lance transfix Thy heart and mine, that the same thorns pierce both hearts, and that one and the same cross surmount them. Here I am. In all my smallness unite myself to Thee in Thy colossal enterprise of saving the world."

THERE STILL remains another aspect of consolation, for many are the souls in whom the love of God either has been destroyed or will be destroyed. Our Lord saw this in Gethsemane, and what grief tortured His soul! Perhaps it was this suffering that drew from Him that anguished cry: "Father, if it be possible, let this chalice pass from Me." Yet, in spite of His sacrifice, in spite of His love, in spite of His divine efforts, many souls will have to be condemned. And Jesus bears in His heart that deep and apparently incurable wound. As to the souls that are saved, even from them Jesus has received the wound of sin and ingratitude. He does, indeed, have the divine satisfaction of blotting out sins with His blood, but that does not eliminate the fact that these sins were committed, militating against the glory of God, insulting His heavenly Father, staining souls and wounding His Divine Heart with ignoble ingratitude. How can those inconsolable sorrows be consoled? By sharing them, by suffering with Him who suffers, by mingling our tears with His tears. We cannot draw out the dart which wounds His heart nor dry His bitter tears, but we can, indeed, share His sufferings and distill into our heart at least a drop of the bitterness in His.

99

Thus, the consolation that lies within our power to offer our Lord has three aspects corresponding to the three aspects of Jesus' suffering, which we ought to relieve. To console Jesus means to surrender to Him one's own heart without reserve and forever. To console Jesus is to offer ourselves as victims with Him, to work in His enterprise and to help Him realize His desires for the salvation and sanctification of souls. To console Jesus is to share in His interior sufferings; it is to beg of Him a splinter of the cross which He carries fixed in His heart in order to nail it into ours. To console Jesus, then, is a sublime and arduous enterprise, noble, holy, divine and most appealing to the heart that loves Him.

CHAPTER 9

⚜

Love

L ove is unknown upon this earth. We speak of it admiringly, earnestly, believing that love is happiness; but we neither understand it nor know its laws. We falsify its concept. We have no true idea of its genuine character or its secret and delightful end. Love is unknown; blessed are they who have received the revelation of love!

The world, in its falsifying spirit, dresses what is precisely most opposed to love—egoism—in the celestial apparel of love. For the world, to love is to enjoy, not with the pure, disinterested joy proper to love, but with the despicable, egoistic pleasure characteristic of self-interest. The beloved object thus becomes an instrument of pleasure, something subordinated to the advantage and caprice of the lover. The worldling who thinks he loves does not try to please the beloved, but to be pleased himself. Such love does not go out of itself, but turns in to itself; it is not an ecstasy but a selfish concentration. Since the spirit of the world penetrates farther than we think, even among Christians and pious persons, the love for God that we profess is thoroughly mixed with egoism and self-interest unless it is purified and elevated by grace seconded by our own efforts.

We form for ourselves a false, or at best a narrow, concept of love. We think that love consists primarily in receiving, and because we are possessed of an egoistic eagerness to receive, we imagine that we are languishing with love. We want to receive consolation, to feel sensible impressions, which by a psychological illusion we confound with love. And when these fleeting illusions are dissipated, like all human things, we believe we have lost everything. Without vigor or hope, we lament and weep over the irreparable loss of love.

But this is not love. "Not death itself is so strong as love.... Love is a fire no waters avail to quench, no floods to drown" (Cant. 8:6, 7). Love does not merely consist in receiving, much less of receiving consolations and sweetness. Love, it is true, accepts whatever comes from the hands of the lover. The quality of the gifts signifies nothing. Joy or grief, smiles or tears, life or death are equal in the eyes of love, provided they come from the hands of the Beloved enveloped in His unmistakable celestial perfumes. Love consists in giving and receiving. It is an ebb and flow of gifts and of life which does not cease until the lovers, consummated in unity, have reciprocally given to each other all that can be given, and nothing further remains to them except to continue their eternity in the incomparable ecstasy of their mutual love. Love consists essentially in giving rather than receiving. It receives because its complement and perfection is reciprocity. It gives because it is love. It receives because it is loved. It gives because it loves.

GOD, WHO is love, gives without measure or limit; giving is His name, His essence and His cherished law. I shall not speak of those gifts of love which constitute the mystery of the interior life of God. "Kings have their counsel that must be kept" (Tob. 12:7). In all the divine acts which concern creatures, what has God done, what is He doing, what will He do eternally, but give? He gave the universe being and life, perfection and beauty. Communicating with men through the prophets, He gave us His word, which is spirit and life.

And when, in the excess of His love, the Divine Word appeared, what did He do but give Himself to us, as St. Thomas Aquinas sang in those immortal verses: "By His birth, He became man's companion; at this supper He became man's food; in His death He became man's price; in His kingdom He becomes man's prize."[1] Love is a gift. When the giving is imperfect, love is desire; when it is consummated, love is rest; when it is eternal, love is bliss.

To give is the essential function of love. Love gives without tiring, without counting its gifts, without feeling their loss, without attending to them except to impregnate them with love's aroma. Love lavishes its goods, gives whatever it possesses, and after giving all—or rather, by giving all—it gives and spends its own self without stint, without reserve, completely, forever. He who loves does not look to himself nor does he seek himself. To the lover, what matter his own well-being, his pleasure, his honor, his future, even his very life? He is totally preoccupied with the beloved. Let him rejoice although I suffer; let him be rich although I be poor; let him smile although I weep; let him live although I die! But is it possible to suffer and to weep if the beloved is happy? My joy is thy joy; my glory is thine; my happiness, thy happiness. When I love, the *I* disappears and dies, to let my beloved live and reign in me. He is my life, my I. Truly, love is both death and life—the most absolute death, the most blessed life. "Love is strong as death."

BUT WHAT can I give to God, if He is in Himself eternally rich, happy, the fount of love and ocean of beatitude? What can I give Him, if I receive everything from Him?

Lord, I feel the imperious need of loving Thee. It is my duty, my glory, my happiness. If I do not love Thee, my life has no reason for being. O God of love! If love consists in giving, how can I love Thee? And if I cannot love Thee, how can I live?

103

---

1. Connolly, *Hymns of the Roman Liturgy*, pp. 122, 124.

There is one thing I can give to God, only one: I can give Him glory. For the glory of God the universe was created; for the glory of God Christ lived and the Church exists. I ought to live for the glory of God. To love God is to give Him glory. The motto of St. Ignatius, "For the greater glory of God," is the supreme formula of love.

Nevertheless, every creature gives glory to God, but not every creature loves Him. There is the glory of love and the glory of justice; the glory of order which is consummated in heaven and the glory of disorder whose consummation is hell. To love God is to give Him the glory of order—that which has grace as its beginning and heaven as its end. How pleasing to God is the glory given Him by love! It is a spontaneous, free, amorous giving by the creature, a giving which returns to God what belongs to Him, but by a new title which moves the Heart of God. God has in Himself the sovereignty of power over every creature as well as the glory which proceeds therefrom. But the sovereignty of love and the glory following from it are given to God through us by an act of our liberty.

God, whose proper action is to give, has found in His wisdom and love the means of adapting to Himself the joy of receiving, a joy peculiar to the creature, and has granted to the latter the divine joy of giving, of giving himself to the Creator. Let us take an example from the world around us. A father has whatever he needs and even the present which his small son gives him is his own, for he himself gave it to the boy. Nevertheless, how much it pleases the father to receive from the child the insignificant gift of love. He esteems it more than all his property, however extensive it may be. What has the gift received upon passing through the hands of the son? Something that is worth more than all the earth's treasures, which is not bought with riches nor obtained through power; something that only his son can give him: love.

IN ORDER to obtain from His creatures that glory of love, God has rightly permitted even sin—sin, which is contempt, ingratitude, disorder, evil. If the creature is not free, he cannot love; if he is free, he can sin through his natural imperfection. Therefore God permits the outrage as a means of obtaining love. The glory that fills God with complacency exalts and divinizes the creature. When I give glory to God, I do a divine work. My action has as its end the same end as the action of God. I rise above all created things. I enter into the thoughts and desires of God. If it were known what the glory of God is, one would think of nothing else. One would love that glory as the saints have loved it, passionately, regarding as lost every action that did not have it as the end.

A merchant, who can double his capital in a secure business, would be foolish to be content with a small gain, and still more unwise if he merely saved what he had. We receive from God a very rich capital—the talents of which the Gospel speaks—which is the aggregate of the natural and supernatural goods with which the Lord has endowed us. At each instant we can multiply our talents. To raise our thoughts, affections and actions to a heavenly level, it suffices to perform them for the glory of God, to do them for love. Is it not madness to pull our life down to a natural plane, even to the brink of sin, by seeking ourselves and creatures? If only we knew what the glory of God means! Would that we understood the first petition of the *Our Father* which expresses the glory of God and begs for it: "Hallowed be Thy name."

The glory of God is the one necessity of which Jesus spoke to Martha of Bethany. Such is generous and disinterested love! My happiness is the effect of the glory of God in my soul. It is the reflection of this glory within me. My happiness arises from knowing that He is happy, that He is glorified by my knowledge of Him and my complacency in Him, that I contribute with my insignificance to His happiness and glory. Let my soul glorify the Lord and, as a natural result, my spirit will rejoice in God my Savior, as the most blessed of creatures has sung: "My soul doth magnify the Lord and my spirit hath rejoiced in God my Savior."

Thy glory, O Lord, Thy glory! Let Thy name be sanctified among us, and Thy kingdom will come to us, Thy kingdom which is our happiness because it is justice, joy and peace in the Holy Spirit! O Divine Master, listen to our plea, the unspeakable cry which Thy own Spirit utters within: "Hallowed be Thy name!"

HOW OFTEN in those delightful moments, when God visits our souls, bathing them in the effusions of His love, we feel the weight of life and we desire to remain there forever like Peter on Tabor. "Lord, it is well that we should be here" (Matt. 17:4). Why descend from the mountain of love and glory to the prosaic plain of ordinary life to work and fatigue ourselves, to talk with men and to live among earthly affairs? Why lose ourselves in the inextricable labyrinth of business and the cares of life, so low, so painful, so oppressive, when one has breathed the pure, living atmosphere of the heights?

In those moments there comes to our hearts and lips the cry for liberation which the Psalmist uttered: "Save me from the enemy's power" (Ps. 30:17). Then we understand why and how Mary had chosen the better part and we should like to live as she did, at the feet of Christ, doing nothing else but looking at Him and loving Him. Blessed are they who live in the house of the Lord, who have no other occupation or recreation, no other care or rest than to contemplate and love the Beloved of their soul. "Lord of hosts, how I love Thy dwelling place! For the courts of the Lord's house my soul faints with longing.... How blessed, Lord, are those who dwell in Thy house! They will be ever praising Thee" (Ps. 83:1–5). "Shall I never again make my pilgrimage into God's presence?" (Ps. 61:2). "Had I but wings, I cry, as a dove has wings, to fly away and find rest!" (Ps. 54:7).

Can it be possible to live on earth, as the elect live, in contemplation and love? Can so great a happiness be possible in this vale of tears? Love is strength. Love has powerful, white wings like a dove to support us in our wretchedness and to raise us to the regions of felicity.

Love is strong. It attempts all; it achieves all; it transforms all; it embellishes all; it sanctifies all. Love made God human. Can it not make man celestial and divine? Yes, God came to earth to change it into heaven. Jesus has given us the mysterious power of beginning in time the blessedness of eternity. It would suffice for Jesus to touch the earth and permeate it with the aroma of paradise. It would suffice that He leave us His Gospel and His Church. It would suffice that He leave us His image sketched within us. It would suffice that He remain loving and living in His Eucharist so that we might eventually dwell in heaven.

Heaven is the country of love, yet on earth one can burn with seraphic love. With Jesus and love, everywhere is heaven. There is one difference between the heaven of time and the heaven of eternity. No one will suffer in the latter. Here, suffering abounds. Does not this difference give a certain advantage to the earthly heaven? Is the value of suffering understood? Is its excellence esteemed? Is its beauty known? The only thing that the angels would envy us, were they capable of envy, would be suffering. God fell in love with this precious pearl hidden among life's miseries. He loved it, came and died from it. The angels cannot say to God: "I love Thee even to sacrifice, even to death"; only man can taste the delicacy of that phrase.

"LET US dwell in heaven."[2] I have read somewhere that a certain soul inflamed with the love of God said: "When at the end of my life, the Lord asks me: 'What hast thou done on earth?' I shall answer: 'I only loved.'" To do nothing else but love! Behold the true love, the life of heaven, the simplest, the holiest, the happiest life; the one which makes us most like God because God is love.

Unity is the stamp of perfection. Our life should have one

---

2.   Collect, Mass for the Feast of Ascension.

single goal, the glory of God; one single path, love. Let us live love; let us dwell in heaven. Is it possible to reduce our life to the divine simplicity of love? If we were only heart, our life could be only love; but we have intelligence, we have speech, we have a wealth of activities. What is the philosopher's stone that will transform everything into love? One does not love with the heart alone. "Thou shalt love the Lord thy God with the love of thy whole heart, and thy whole soul, and thy whole mind, and thy whole strength" (Mark 12:30), is the first of the commandments. Hence, one loves with the mind, with the soul and with all the powers of one's being. And if we must love God with all our heart and soul and strength and mind, if our whole heart and soul and strength must be employed in the love of God, what remains that could stifle love? What must our life be but all love, only love, always love?

Our Lord said to St. Angela de Foligno, "Look at Me; is there anything in Me that you may not love?" The supreme ideal of sanctity consists in being able to imitate the Lord by saying to Him: "Look at me; is there anything in me You may not love?" Doubtless, the Virgin Mary can say it with complete exactitude, and the rest of the saints can say something similar. St. Paul was right; love is the bond of perfection, the unifying element of a saintly life. Many elements form sanctity, many actions, many virtues, but the unity coordinating them is love.

IT IS necessary to delve into this secret. How can life be converted into love? I have already explained how: to love is to give; it is to give ourselves; love is a *total* donation, complete, irrevocable, eternal. Let our life be a gift and it will be love. Let our life be a liquor ever flowing so that God may drink it; a perfume unceasingly evaporated so that God may inhale it; a grain of ever-burning incense so that God may be pleased with the sweetness of the holocaust. Thus, we shall love God with our whole heart, with our whole mind, with all our strength and with our whole soul.

Love is essentially a function of the will. The heart first makes the entire gift of love, but the other faculties complete and consum- mate the loving donation of their queen. The will offers to the Lord the tree of our life; the other faculties gather the fruits and present them to their queen. The will is the queen who signs and completes the treaties of love with God. The other faculties are the subjects and treasurers who deliver to the Lord all the riches stipulated by their sovereign. All love because all give, but the essential act of love is the will, because to it belongs the essential giving.

What do I mean when in the silence of my soul I say to the Lord: "I love Thee"? I am Thine; I belong to Thee; I surrender myself to Thee; I give myself to Thee without reserve. And in this giving is my joy, my rest, my happiness. When the word of love has been pronounced, nothing remains, as Father Lacordaire says, but to continue repeating it always. It is evident that if I have made a complete offering of what I have, of what I am, I can no longer do anything but confirm and continue that gift, repeating the sublime words. I can do nothing else because upon saying, "I love Thee," I have surrendered myself, I have lost myself in the one I love. I have disappeared, and I have died so that He may live. O love, love, thou art surrender and possession; thou art supreme loss and highest gain; thou art death and true life!

LORD, IF I truly loved Thee, everything in me would unceasingly repeat that heavenly word. I would tell it to Thee by my thoughts raised up to Thee, by my affections in celestial transports, by my words of praise, by my body which is Thy temple, by my spirit which would be one with Thy spirit, by my works, the fruit of my love and the instruments of Thy glory. Oh, if I loved Thee, my life would be one living and indestructible "I love Thee." And my death would only add to this word two others that perpetuate and consummate it: "perfectly" and "forever." Is not this the way of life in heaven?

110 Do what Thou wilt, be where Thou wilt; I love Thee and I am secure in Thy love. In work and in rest, in vigils and in sleep, in joy and in sorrow, my life is always love. Love is a flower that lives in every clime except that of egoism and sin.

Simon Peter, do not wish to remain always on Tabor; one loves here below, as well. One loves on Tiberias and in the desert, in the Cenacle and in Gethsemane; one loves especially on Calvary. The one place necessary to live is love; from that height we ought, indeed, to say: "It is good to be here."

CHAPTER 10

✵

The Intimacy of Love

D ivine love so far excels human love in sweetness and strength, in delicacy and audacity, in abnegation and satisfaction, that a comparison between the two is scarcely fitting. Earthly love is, indeed, an imitation of eternal love, and as such it has something Godlike about it, corresponding to the divine in our soul. It is like a joyous expansion, though limited and deficient, of that immaterial breath which it pleased God to infuse into the material body. Supernatural and divine love is a participation in infinite love, which satisfies and exalts the divine that God placed in us when He created us, drawing it out from its sphere and communicating to it an undreamed-of perfection and a joy which our heart, notwithstanding its capacity for happiness, can scarcely contain.

A few features suffice to show the indisputable supremacy of divine love over the human. Love is intimacy; desire of intimacy when it is born, fruition of intimacy when it matures, perfection of intimacy when it is consummated. The soul feels that strong, secret craving for intimacy. It is the desire to be changed into something else, as intelligence is miraculously changed into thought. It is the desire to be transformed because it foresees that its happiness lies in such transformation, the soul being too great to accommodate itself to its limitations, too small to be sufficient for itself. Can it be that God made the soul so godlike that it is not content with less than imitating, within its capabilities, the ineffable secret of friendship which is the life and happiness of God?

Friendship with creatures can never be profound and perfect. Even when the soul, rising above the narrowness and egoism of the material, arrives at those lofty regions where the thoughts of both lovers are fused like two rays of light into a single beam, and the beating of two hearts forms but one rich and harmonious rhythm, the intimacy of souls is irremediably superficial. One can never reach the real core of the other's soul, the summit of the spirit in which happiness lies, that high region where the divinity has impressed upon souls the image of the Holy Trinity. We ourselves find it so arduous to reach that profound center of our own souls where God dwells.

God, indeed, reaches the center of the soul, or rather, He dwells there. His action penetrates us even to our innermost being; His being is diffused in us with incomprehensible intimacy, and we can live in Him, entering into His infinite profundities, because our soul, breath of the Most High by its creation and participant of the divine nature by grace, is made to live in God, to move in those immense regions, to breathe that divine atmosphere of light and love.

On earth those who love live for and with each other. God and the soul live in each other. As the Father lives in the Word and the Word in the Father in the ineffable unity of the Holy Spirit, so the happy soul united to God through the mighty work of love lives in the Word and the Word in her. Through that union with the Word she goes to the Father in the unity of the Holy Spirit and thus enters into the ineffable joy of the Trinity. Jesus asked this gift for His own on the night of His passion: "And I have given them the privilege which Thou gavest to Me, that they should all be one, as We are

one; that while Thou art in Me, I may be in them, and so they may
be perfectly made one. So let the world know that it is Thou who
hast sent Me, and that Thou hast bestowed Thy love upon them, as
Thou hast bestowed it upon Me" (John 17:22–23). Souls that have
attained this incomprehensible intimacy on earth scarcely discern
it; souls who enjoy it eternally in heaven will never exhaust it.

COULD HUMAN love ever dream of an intimacy such as this? Since
it is divine, this intimacy seems removed from the conditions of
time, as if it had commenced to participate in the unmoved eternity.
Human love, like all things of earth, dies; like all temporal things,
it passes away; it runs the magic cycle of its seasons, reborn in the
springtime only to be disdained by human inconstancy, dying at
last, never to be renewed.

The divine union is inamissable and unalterable. How unknown
is this truth! It is so difficult to know happiness—perhaps the most
difficult knowledge to attain upon this earth. Theologians, referring
to the humanity of Christ, tell us: "The Word will never be separated from that with which He was once united." Due proportion
kept, this law is applied to the loving union of the Word with souls
when they have attained that perfection which St. Bernard char-
acterizes with these delightful Words: *stringere inamissibiliter*, "to
embrace indissolubly." So faithful is the Word! So true is His love!
So definitive is His embrace! St. Paul alluded to this mystery when
he said triumphantly: "Of this I am fully persuaded; neither death
nor life, no angels or principalities or powers, neither what is present nor what is to come, no force whatever, neither the height above
us nor the depth beneath us, nor any other creature, will be able to
separate *us* from the love of God, which comes to us in Christ Jesus
our Lord" (Rom. 8:38–39).

The foundation of love is happiness, the last word of love is
joy. The soul may have on its surface sorrow, wretchedness, or any
other earthly feeling; in the depths it has only the intimacy of love,

happiness, the eternal. The words of Scripture come to my mind: "In the eyes of fools they seem to die but they are in peace." Yes, even in this life, souls transformed into God live in unalterable peace, which is substantially eternal peace.

Just as the ocean, its surface stirred up by the winds and agitated by the fury of the tempest, always preserves in its depths the majesty of peace, so the soul that has attained intimacy with God is subject on the surface to all of life's miseries, to all the vicissitudes of human affairs, but in its depths, in the sanctuary of its union with God, the divine majesty of peace is preserved changeless and intact. Divine union tolerates only one change: constant progress while life lasts. It does not have the immobility of the Fatherland; it still moves, but its movement is the mutual motion of love—God penetrating more profoundly into the soul, the soul plunging more deeply into the profundities of God. How many souls to whom this mystery has not been revealed are disquieting themselves by what passes upon the changing surface! How few are established in the depth of interior peace, enjoying His loving felicity in the midst of all the miseries and all the storms! Is not St. Thérèse of the Child Jesus a likely model of this deep, true activity?

Love has happiness as its end and as its fruit. But it is so difficult to know happiness! It is, perhaps, the most difficult knowledge to acquire upon this earth. Many souls possess the divine intimacy but they do not fully understand their happiness nor do they sound completely the abyss of the love of God.

CHAPTER 11

☩

Hidden in the Face of God

To be hidden in the face of God, what a singular grace! The face of God is His Word; it is His Christ, "the radiance of His Father's splendor and the full expression of His being" (Heb. 1:3). To be hidden in the face of God is to be hidden in Christ, concealed in His wounds, submerged in the ocean of His mercy, imprisoned in His heart: *in abscondito faciei tuae!* This hiding-place is none other than the interior of Christ's heart; it is the *arcanum* of His divinity. What more can we desire? This grace contains many graces and includes many favors.

THE GRACE OF PROTECTION

When anyone is persecuted, he looks for a secret, secure place to escape from his enemies; secret, so they may not find him; secure, so they may not harm him. David was the victim of a terrible persecution, but he placed his confidence in the Lord, and the Lord prepared for him a secret and secure place of refuge—His own face. This means that God turned His countenance toward David, that He had His eyes fixed on him, that He did not deny him protection.

We also are persecuted. To the terrible persecution of the demons is added in our times the visible persecution of men. But why fear? God protects us; He has prepared a secret and safe refuge for us: His Christ. "Blessed be the Lord; so wondrous is His mercy, so strong the wall of His protection" (Ps. 30:22). In the thick of our struggles and in the presence of our enemies, we shall rejoice in the mercy of the Lord because He has constituted Himself our protector and because His strong, tender heart is as a fortified city to guard us. "For me no refuge but the Lord. I will triumph and exult in Thy mercy" (Ps. 30:7–8).

When anyone wishes to please, he conceals everything wretched and contemptible; the poor, their poverty; the sick, their weakness; the ugly, their deformity. Since we are wretched and weak in the sight of God, He would look at us with repugnance if we were not clothed with Christ, if our miseries were not hidden under the celestial beauty of Jesus. In this way the Father does not discover our insignificance because it is hidden in Christ; He beholds only His most beloved Son, the object of His eternal complacency. Like Jacob, we are covered with the fragrant vesture of the firstborn. When we approach the heavenly Father, He does not perceive the offensive odor of our wretchedness, but rather the sweet odor of Christ. He is compelled to say with Isaac: "How it breathes about this son of mine, the fragrance of earth when the Lord's blessing is on it!" (Gen. 27:27). Therefore He loves us. Therefore He takes complacency in us; He takes complacency in His face, as He himself has said.

The Grace of Union

If we are hidden in Christ, we are united to Him. What a sweet thought! Can it be true? United to Christ, who is light, peace, love, felicity—all! That is to be in heaven. United through faith, hope, charity; united through the Eucharist. When fear overwhelms us, let us strengthen our union with Him. Let us embrace Him as a child embraces its mother when it foresees danger. Let us hide ourselves in Him. It is so sweet to rest in the Heart of Christ. And even when we do not experience fear, let us unite ourselves to Him. Our very life is union with Him. For us to live is to be hidden in Christ: "For me, life means Christ" (Phil. 1:21). "Your life is hidden away now with Christ in God" (Col. 3:3). The atmosphere which our soul breathes is Christ; the blood that vivifies us is Christ; the bread that nourishes us is Christ; the wine that stimulates us is Christ; in a word, our life is Christ.

Let us breathe, let us eat, let us drink, let us live Christ!

Blessed is the soul that has received from God the assurance of never being separated from Jesus. Blessed is the soul that can exclaim with the Apostle: "Who will separate us from the love of Christ? ... Of this I am fully persuaded; neither death nor life, no angels or principalities or powers, neither what is present nor what is to come, no force whatever, neither the height above us nor the depth beneath us, nor any other creature, will be able to separate us from the love of God, which comes to us in Christ Jesus our Lord" (Rom. 8:35, 38–39).

And I should repeat the same thing, alternating between fear and hope, "Never permit me to be separated from Thee," as I pour out before the Lord the weight of my poor desires. Love is secret by its very nature. Those who love one another sequester themselves in order to talk and enjoy their love. Love is secret; therefore it is always accompanied by modesty. Even in God, love is secret; the mystery of love is closely veiled. The three Divine Persons enjoy their inconceivable love in the most hidden place in existence—the bosom of God.

When divine love descended to earth, it came in the midst of universal silence: "There was a hush of silence all around" (Wis. 18:14). He came in secret; in secret He lived, and He still lives in secret. Does not that passage of Holy Scripture have this meaning among others: "Truly...Thou art a God of hidden ways" (Is. 45:15)? Must He not of necessity be a hidden God simply because He is a God of love?

All abodes of love are very secret: the tabernacle, the bosom of the Father. Even on Calvary, where love seems to be shown in all its splendor, there also it is hidden—hidden, perhaps, as in no place else, hidden under a sea of pain and ignominy. Love is hidden, and when God calls a soul to the delights of His love, He calls her to silence, to solitude, to secrecy. He hides her, He hides her in His face, He hides her in His Christ, He hides her in His Beloved. "It is but love's stratagem thus to lead her out into the wilderness" (Hos. 2:14), says the Lord in Hosea. And does not the Spouse of the Canticle invite the beloved of His heart with the sweetest words: "Rouse thee, and come, so beautiful, so well beloved, still hiding thyself as a dove hides in cleft rock or crannied wall" (Cant. 2:13–14). God loves her and unites her to Himself so that she may enjoy His divine love. Therefore He conceals her; He hides her in His face, in His Word, in His Christ. Most blessed secrecy, mystery of love! Only in that most profound secrecy of the bosom of God can divine affections be enjoyed. Here the Holy Spirit—incomprehensible mystery—covers the soul with His shadow in order that the mystery of love may be accomplished in secret.

CHAPTER 12

ᴥ

Jesus, Glory of the Father

S o tender was Jesus' expression when His eyes were raised toward His Father, so ardent the passion of His love, so vehement His desire to glorify Him, that one of the apostles, St. Philip, who had undoubtedly observed all this in his intimate dealing with the Master, said to Him on one occasion: "Lord, let us see the Father, that is all we ask" (John 14:8). And Jesus answered him: "Philip... whoever has seen Me, has seen the Father" (John 14:9). This profound expression reveals to us the divine physiognomy of Jesus. He who sees Jesus sees the Father, because Jesus is "the radiance of His Father's splendor and the full expression of His being" (Heb. 1:3). As the eternal Word, Jesus is the consubstantial Son of the Father, His infinite image; He has with the Father "one single divinity, equal glory and co-eternal majesty" (Athanasian Creed). As the Word Incarnate, He is the living revelation of the Father and His most perfect and supreme glorification.

Jesus received everything from the Father and returned all to Him with immense love, because the Father is the *alpha* and *omega*, the beginning and the end of all things. Jesus knew that "it was from God that He came, and to God that He went" (John 13:3), and with the utmost complacency He proclaimed that He received all from the Father. His doctrine is the Father's doctrine: "The learning which I impart is not My own, it comes from Him who sent Me" (John 7:16). His will is His Father's will: "What I do is always what pleases Him" (John 8:29). His interests are His Father's interests: "Could you not tell that I must needs be in the place which belongs to My Father?" (Luke 2:49). And the only glory Jesus seeks is that of His Father: "I reverence My Father…not that I am looking to My own reputation" (John 8:49–50).

The first word of Jesus in Mary's womb is for the Father, as the psalms taught prophetically and St. Paul declares as accomplished: "As Christ comes into the world, He says, no sacrifice, no offering was Thy demand; Thou hast endowed Me, instead, with a body. Thou hast not found any pleasure in burnt sacrifices, in sacrifices for sin. See then, I said, I am coming to fulfill what is written of Me, where the book lies unrolled; to do Thy will, O My God" (Heb. 10:5–7). And the last word of His agony was for His Father: "Father, into Thy hands I commend My spirit" (Luke 23:46).

If the ineffable could be defined, if all that Jesus is could be condensed into a single human phrase—all that His life was, the expression of His eyes, the beating of His heart, the yearning of His soul, the depths of His being, the treasures of His life—I think that comprehensive and divine statement would be this: Jesus is the supreme glorifier of the Father, or better, Jesus is the glory of the Father.

THE DIVINE physiognomy of Jesus, those interior lineaments which angels desire to contemplate, that physiognomy beyond human understanding, whose features shone through His sacred humanity when He appeared on earth, is the very image of the Father. It is the same majesty veiled in the form of a servant, the same sensitive tenderness in a heart of flesh shining in the clear crystal of His words on eternal life. It is His love revealed under the subtle, transparent

veil of His boundless suffering. Do you wish to look at the Father?
Look at Jesus. Follow the ray of light from His gaze and you will
catch a glimpse of eternal light. Relish the sweetness of His smile
and you will taste the savor of infinite life. Allow the music of His
words to penetrate even to the depths of your spirit and you will
perceive the echo of the Father's voice. Open your soul to the celestial perfume of Jesus, and the Father in His tenderness will enfold
you in His most pure arms.

In order to know Jesus, it is necessary to look at Him in the
Father. In order to understand His life, it is indispensable to envision that current of life which issued from the Father's bosom and
has been manifested to us, "that eternal life which ever abode with
the Father and has dawned now on us" (1 John 1:2), so that allowing Himself to see through our eyes, to hear through our ears and
to touch with our hands, He might attract our souls and bear them
with Him to the source from whence He issued, to the ineffable
bosom of the Father to contemplate His glory and share in His
eternal light. Begotten by the Father, in His holy image, bearing His
divine physiognomy, constituting His glory, Jesus yearns unspeak-
ably to attract and present all to His heavenly Father.

How He loved the Father! With what unparalleled tenderness
He elevated His eyes and His heart to Him! How His expression
was transformed when He permitted the light from His Father,
enveloping His soul, to become visible on His exterior! How His
soul, always serene, was affected, and His voice, always firm, trem-
bled when He spoke to men of His celestial Father! His passion was
the Father; His ideal, to glorify Him; His rule, to do the will of His
Father; His supreme joy, to offer Himself immaculate in the sacrifice of the Cross to glorify His Father.

His very love for souls, so ardent, delicate, tender, fecund, audacious, merciful, pure, sacrificial, is but a reflection of His love for
His Father. If He loves souls, it is because the image of the Father
shines in them. If He saved them at the cost of His blood, it is to

restore that adorable image. If He desires to carry them to the peak of perfection and felicity, it is because the perfections and happiness of souls is the glory of God. Oh, if we could penetrate into the inner sanctuary of Jesus, if we could comprehend the depth of His soul and discover the key of His actions and of His life, ecstatic with admiration and love, we would see how the Father fills Jesus with His glory and how Jesus is the glory of the Father.

The Incarnate Word, like a flower opening to the sun, has opened His entire being to receive the glory of the Father, to reflect it, pure and complete. Jesus receives not only the rays of the eternal sun but the Sun itself with its glorious light, its infinite fire, and its eternal life. Not for a single instant does He cease to be flooded by the glory of the Father in one eternal orientation toward the will of the Father.

Men often saw the eyes of Jesus raised to His Father in heaven, as when He multiplied the loaves in the desert, when He raised Lazarus from the tomb, and when He instituted the Eucharist. He even desired that this heavenward look be perpetuated throughout the centuries in all Masses through the eyes of priests who are other Christs in the solemnity of the mystery. But men did not see, do not see, nor will they see upon this earth the uninterrupted gaze of Jesus' soul toward the Father—the gaze which began in the Incarnation and will never end. In that gaze is expressed the great soul of Jesus with its heavenly light, its ineffable love, its boundless sorrow, its immaculate purity, its deep, gigantic desire of glorifying the Father.

Jesus is truly the Father's glory. His whole being and His whole life are condensed in these two unfathomable expressions which broke forth from His lips in His prayer to the Father before His passion: "I have exalted Thy glory on earth, by achieving the task which Thou gavest Me to do; now, Father, do Thou exalt Me at Thy own side in that glory which I had with Thee before the world began" (John 17:4–5). The intimate relations of Father and Son are an ebb and flow of glory. The Father has shed on His Son His whole glory. Jesus has reflected that same glory upon the Father. Rather, Jesus is the glory of the Father. It is the terse, profound declaration whose abyss only God can fathom.

If Jesus would deign to explain that divine profession in our poor language, He would say to us: "Never did I do anything on earth—work miracles, lavish favors or alleviate sufferings—without raising My eyes and My heart to My Father, doing all in Him and through Him and for Him. To prove My love for Him was My dominant passion on earth. I would refer everything to Him. My entire life was one single continuous act of loving gratitude to My heavenly Father. My food, My drink, My entire life, with all its labors, privations and sufferings, was only to glorify Him in Myself and souls by doing His will and finding My joy in that will, even though it appeared painful and sacrificial. The divine and adorable will of My Father was paramount with Me. Such a height did My Father's will attain in My soul that I even subordinated My own beloved Mother to it, declaring that those who did the will of My Father were My mother and brothers and sisters. This is My ideal; this is the most distinctive mark of My interior and exterior life, dedicated to the will of My Father. The divine will is the golden clasp with which I enclosed all My actions and all My ideals. It pleased Me to teach the *Our Father*, pouring out the sweet ardor with which My soul was inundated. The centuries repeat and will repeat that sublime hymn with which I desired to honor My Father, subjecting all human wills to His sovereign divine will."

CHAPTER 13

✻

Stay with Us, Lord

All the solemn, melancholy poetry of the evening of the Resurrection is comprehended in this phrase. The Church gathered it from the lips of the disciples of Emmaus, and when repeated in the evening Office during the Paschal season, it communicates to us indescribable accents of melancholy and of hope. "Stay with us, Lord, for it is evening and the day is now far spent!" Christ is the sun of souls. When He illuminates and warms them, the day is bright; when He departs from them, gigantic shadows arise and night approaches. Therefore, heaven is a perpetual midday; the blessed fearlessly relish and penetrate the charm and sweetness of this divine phrase: "Thou art always at my side" (Luke 15:31). Therefore, hell is the night without dawn. Christ has withdrawn from the accursed place without leaving the least hope of His return.

On earth we oscillate between day and night, between heaven and hell. Sometimes we seem to taste the gladness of the Fatherland, so intimately are we united with Jesus. Sometimes we think the endless night has begun for us, because not even the twilight brightness of the divine Sun reaches us. Therefore, between fear and hope we utter the phrase of Emmaus: "Stay with us, Lord, because it is toward evening." It is the cry of souls that have known Christ or have discerned Him. It is the ardent, urgent plea of exile. Remain with us, Lord! If Thou shouldst go away, where would our eyes seek light? Where would our heart find the living flame of love? Where would our bird of hope sing? Thy departure would be the ruin of our happiness, and in the sad evening of our life we would begin to feel the night enveloping us in its cold and horrible shades. Stay with us, Lord!

Oh, if we could detain Jesus! It would be to imprison love and hope and our only happiness.

Where is the secret of happiness? Let us interrogate our own hearts, made to the image and likeness of Christ. What is it that arrests and binds us and makes us enjoy the loss of our freedom? Love—strong, omnipotent love! When God wants to captivate us, He binds us with the ligatures of love, with the holy chains of charity. Our sense of duty weakens; our own interest succumbs before passion; only love triumphs, only love is immortal.

Since love has the same name in heaven and on earth, the same law, the same essence, let us bind Christ with the sweet, strong chains of love. Let us love Him greatly. Let us love Him always. Let us say to Him unceasingly with every heartbeat the sweetest of words: "Remain with us, Lord." And Jesus will invariably remain with us. Even though He should wish to go away, He cannot, for He is bound fast, imprisoned with the unbreakable chains of our love. He Himself has taught us the secret of detaining Him: "If a man has any love for Me, he will be true to My word; and then he will win My Father's love, and We will both come to him, and make Our continual abode with him" (John 14:23). Heaven and earth shall pass away; the words of Christ will not pass.

WHERE HAS Christ remained? Where has He placed His dwelling? In Nazareth, in Bethany and in the Church. He went about doing

good, but He did not fix His dwelling in all places. But He took
up His abode in Nazareth, where the love of a mother surrounded
Him; in Bethany, where the love of a friend retained Him; in the
Church, where the love of a spouse has imprisoned Him. Always
love! The love of Mary the Immaculate, the love of Mary the convert, the love of the Church, struggling yet victorious.

127

Never has Christ been loved as He was loved in Nazareth
because there has never beat a heart like Mary's. Thus, He remained
thirty years with her—thirty years of unparalleled love. Even if
Jesus should have desired to leave Nazareth, He could not have torn
Himself away from that abode of love. Only the voice of the Father,
which called Him to save the world, could draw Him from that
copy of heaven.

A sinner found Christ and loved Him. Upon His sacred feet she
lavished the precious ointment and the still more precious pearls
of her tears. With the soothing of the ointment and the eloquent
cry of those tears, she spoke to her Beloved the phrase of Emmaus,
the phrase irresistible when love pronounces it: "Remain with us,
Lord." Christ did remain with her, and Bethany was His retreat.
From there He departed to enter triumphantly into Jerusalem,
from there He left to establish the Eucharist and to agonize in
Gethsemane; and when, victorious, He arose from the tomb, the
first visit related in the Gospel was for her, for Mary Magdalen. The
meeting actually occurred on the morning of His resurrection, near
the glorious sepulcher. They saw each other, they loved each other,
and between them passed these two words, each of which is a poem:
"Mary!" "Master!"

Why is Jesus in the Church? Because He has there the seat of
His wisdom and the Bethany of His love. Why is He in the tabernacle, forgotten, abandoned, despised? Doubtless because He
loves, but also because He is loved. I believe that the day on which
the earth would lack a heart beating for Jesus, He would abandon
the world, taking away His doctrine and His love, taking away His

Eucharist. But the earth will never be so lacking. Until the end of time the Church is there detaining Christ upon the earth with the bonds of her immortal love.

When we feel that the night of sin is approaching, when the evening of lukewarmness advances, when, sad and desolate, we see the day of our consolation decline, let us multiply the entreaties of our heart. They will say to Christ in an eloquent language: "Stay with us, Lord!" Yes, Lord, stay with us because Thou art light, strength, hope, consolation. Remain with us; with Thee, what shall we fear?

When I feel myself abandoned, suffering within my soul the sorrows of death, I shall place my hand upon my breast, and if I feel beatings of love, I shall say that Thou art with me. Consoled and serene, I shall exclaim with the Psalmist: "As in honor pledged, by sure paths He leads me; what though I walk with the shadow of death all around me?" (Ps. 22:4).

PART TWO

TRANSFORMATION INTO JESUS

CHAPTER 14

✻

Transformation into Jesus for the Father

I t is upon Jesus alone that the contemplative gaze of the heavenly Father rests with full complacency. Just as we desire to see the image of one we love everywhere, so the Father desires to see Jesus reproduced in souls. What a prodigality of graces it requires to accomplish this loving design! How many wonders must be wrought to transform souls into Jesus!

On the other hand, the gratitude which souls ought to feel toward the Father, their desire to glorify Him and to manifest their affection, as well as the happiness of basking in His clear, fruitful and tender gaze, should impel them to become Jesus always and in everything for the heavenly Father's sake.

But how to achieve this transformation? First, by looking at the Father through Jesus' eyes or by permitting Jesus to look at the Father through the soul's eyes; second, by loving the Father as Jesus loves Him; third, by possessing, like Jesus, a passion for fulfilling the Father's will perfectly, at all times and in all things.

✳

THE LOOK OF JESUS

We, in our own way, can conceive of the mystery of the Trinity as a look of love between the Father and the Son. Jesus, the Word made Flesh, lives in the light of the Father's gaze while His soul responds to that infinite gaze with a constant, sweet gaze which seems to blend with the eternal gaze of the Word.

That ineffable gaze was the foundation of the interior life of Jesus. His corporal eyes were frequently raised toward heaven but the eyes of His soul were always fixed upon the Eternal Father. Jesus put His whole soul into that look, so expressive of contemplation— love, surrender, abandonment, desire to glorify the Father, and fathomless tenderness, together with strong, complete, loving adherence to His will. That intimate beholding was irradiated in Jesus' physiognomy and reflected in His wonderful works and words.

Jesus used to find divine traces of the Father in all creation, particularly in souls, since the image of the Trinity shines in them. When Jesus looked with love upon the young man of whom the Gospel speaks, He discerned in the depths of that unblemished soul the Father's image. When His glance moved St. Peter and converted Magdalen, the divine efficacy of those looks was due to the fact that, in order to find the image of His Father within those souls, Jesus banished the shadows of sin and misery cloaking the beloved image, just as the sun dissipates the clouds covering the earth to give a kiss of light to the little flowers of the field.

THE LOOK OF THE SOUL

The attitude of the soul should be a replica of that of Jesus toward His Father. That attentive perception must be the foundation of her interior life. The chief characteristic of the physiognomy is the expression of the eyes, for it would suffice to see the eyes of a loved one to recognize him, although we might not see his features. It seems to me that what the Father seeks primarily in souls, in order to know if they are Jesus, is that distinctive expression which He would recognize among thousands, that look which completely satisfies and pleases Him. What the Father seeks in souls is the physiognomy of Jesus and in that physiognomy He scrutinizes particularly the look.

Happy the souls in whom the Father always finds the gentle glance of Jesus: pure, reverent, worshipful, mildest of the mild. Those souls regard the Father unceasingly with a look of purity, adoration, surrender and abandonment. They put into it all that world of virtue and attractiveness which Jesus put into His indescribable gaze, or rather, they permit Jesus to behold the Father through the glance of their souls.

These souls always look at the Father in this same way, whether in gray days wrapped in the clouds of pain, desolation and dereliction, or in the serene and sunny hours of consolation. They behold Him through tears as well as through smiles. The holy glance of the soul raised heavenward passes beyond all shadows and clouds, because it is a look of penetrating faith and piercing love. Was not Jesus' expression unfailingly tender, gentle and noble, the same on Calvary as on Tabor, in the Cenacle as in Gethsemane? So it should be in souls. Sometimes their expression will be of joy and sometimes of sorrow. But both joy and sorrow are in reality love, which invests itself with all forms.

Let souls see the Father in every created thing: in the splendid sky, in the smiling meadow, in the mighty mountain, in the boundless ocean. Let them see Him especially in other souls, and Jesus will give to their glance the marvelous power of scattering shadows and of purifying souls to discover in their depths the beloved image.

The gaze of Jesus was pre-eminently sacerdotal, the look of one who loves and is immolated for the glory of the Father, of one who implores graces for souls, the look in which the priestly spirit of Jesus is manifest. He desired that look toward the Father to be perpetuated by priests in Holy Mass.[1] As He elevated His eyes toward the Father at each instant, so the Mass is celebrated at each moment in some part of the world.

Souls transformed into Jesus participate mystically in His priesthood, and so they ought to look at the Father with that priestly look, and since their sacrifice does not have a fixed time as does the Eucharistic sacrifice, but is taking place at every moment, that sacerdotal look should be constant, making amends for the imperfections of chosen souls and uniting with the holy gaze of all the saints.

LOVE OF JESUS FOR THE FATHER

The Heart of Jesus is all love, only love, always love for the heavenly Father, because His intense devotion to the Father, His unspeakable sufferings, and His divine virtues have their origin, center and life in love. The Heart of Jesus is an abyss of love for the Father. Who can peer into that immensity? That love is unique, perfect, eternal, disinterested, active, tender, selfless, purest of the pure. Each one of those characteristics contains inexhaustible treasures, but it is better to contemplate them with the vision of the heart than to try to explain them with human speech.

Jesus loved the Father for all souls who do not love Him. All souls were engrafted in Jesus because He is the Head of regenerated humanity, the new Adam in whom we are all incorporated spiritually. With what longing and intensity Jesus must have loved the Father for all the souls that will never love Him. What solicitude must have been His, lest one spark of love be lacking to the Father, offering Him the immensity of His love for the lack of love in souls. The love of Jesus for the Father has a sacerdotal love, that is, a

---

1. Allusion to the liturgical gesture which the priest makes before the Consecration when he raises his eyes, upon saying: "And having lifted up His eyes to heaven...."

glorifying, immolating, redeeming and saving love, a love crowned on Calvary and perpetuated in the Mass and in souls. All this because Jesus desired to fill the Father, earth and heaven, time and eternity with His love. Just as the perfume of Magdalen anointed His head and ran down over His hair, scenting His whole person, so the love of Jesus for the Father was poured out upon Him and ran through the whole mystical body, permeating the world and history with its heavenly fragrance.

137

LOVE OF SOULS FOR THE FATHER

Our feeble love is only the overflowing of that divine ointment that has reached our poor hearts.

Heavenly Father, our love is very small and imperfect, very deficient and inconstant. But Jesus loves Thee for us and this insignificant love of our hearts comes to Thee from the heart of Thy Son. Dost Thou not perceive its fragrance? Dost Thou not recognize that richest of scents belonging only to Jesus, like the perfume of a flowery field blessed by the Lord?

Souls ought to love the Father in the same way that Jesus loves Him, so that they may be transformed into Jesus. I say *in the same way*, not because the soul's love can ever equal in wealth, perfection and intensity the immense love of Jesus, which surpasses all love, even that of Mary most holy, but because the soul's love should have the same fragrance as Jesus' love, because it must be a faithful reproduction, though in miniature, of Jesus' love.

Therefore, the soul should be all love, always love, only love for the heavenly Father. All her affections and all the acts of her life should originate from that divine passion and blend into it. Her sufferings, especially, should have that incomparable love as their origin, center and life.

Her love, like that of Jesus, should be unique, perfect, eternal, ardent, most tender, disinterested and active. It must be characterized by self-abasement, adoration, abandonment and sacrifice. Imitating Jesus, she ought to love the Father on behalf of all souls, on behalf of those that love Him and those who do not love Him. Exerting herself to love Him for them all, she must strive eagerly lest one spark of creatures' love be lacking to the Father.

Above all, her love should be mystically sacerdotal, that is, a glorifying, immolating, redeeming and saving love. Her love, like that of Jesus, must find its culmination in the Cross, in the sacrifice of Christ offered mystically every moment and in the sacrifice of herself offered ceaselessly in union with that of Jesus. She ought to suffer constantly because she ought to love constantly. She must suffer for all because she must love all.

Happy the soul in whom the sacrifice of love and of suffering, the offering of the Word and of herself never ceases to rise to heaven in a sweet-smelling holocaust.

Zeal of Jesus for the Father's Will

The divine will constituted not only the sole norm of Jesus' life but also His joy and recompense. It was His very food. Upon entering into the world He said: "See, my God, I am coming to do Thy will" (Heb. 10:9). All thirty-three years of His life were the most faithful execution of His Father's decrees, a living poem dedicated to that most amiable will, while His sacrificial death was its full completion, since, as St. Paul teaches, the central point of the Father's will was the oblation of the body of Christ (Heb. 10:10).

Jesus' fulfillment of the Father's will was absolute, on Tabor as on Calvary, whether it glorified the Son or immolated Him. He always awaited the Father's hour with loving patience, although His heart burned to be sacrificed, to save souls, to finish His mission. Sometimes the Father's will opposed Christ's human will, as in Gethsemane. The bloody sweat scarcely expresses the interior agony of His will. Nevertheless, in the midst of that cruel struggle, these words broke forth from the lips and heart of Jesus, like a cry of His triumphant love: "Only as Thy will is, not as Mine is" (Luke 22:42). Perhaps the chalice that Jesus was loathe to drink was the martyrdom of knowing that many souls would be condemned in spite of His passion. He who discerns how Jesus loves souls and what it cost His most tender heart to see them lost will be able to form some idea of the heroism of His love for the Father by accepting that disposition of the divine will.

Jesus always complied with the will of His Father, in every act, at every instant of His life. He was never master of His acts nor of His life, because His love always bound Him affectionately and freely to His Father's will. Not only did Jesus do everything that His Father disposed, but He executed it as His Father had appointed, adapting Himself even to minute details with indescribable sensitivity. Commentators observe that all the temptations which the devil placed before Jesus tended to separate Him from the Father's will. With what fidelity and love He conquered them! I imagine Jesus consulting the will of the Father at each step, and anticipating that will, so to speak, not only in its fundamentals, but in its manner and least circumstance.

The supreme motive of all the acts of Jesus was the Father's will. Jesus knew the wisdom and the love of all the Father's designs, but even if He had not, the Father's desire would have moved Jesus to embrace it with His whole strength. The Father's will was His joy and His martyrdom.

It was His joy. To love someone is to desire his good, and God has only two goods: the essential, which is Himself, and the accidental or extrinsic, which is the fulfillment of His will. Jesus enjoyed the essential good of His Father with beatific happiness, and He took loving complacency in the fulfillment of His will. Jesus desired no other recompense for His efforts than to please His Father most perfectly and to do the divine will always and in everything. Yet that will was His martyrdom, interior and exterior, for He endured all

His sufferings not only because the Father desired it, but because the will of the Father was His nearest and dearest sacrificer.

That firm attachment to His Father's will, that divine ardor to fulfill it, was the basis of His role as victim and as priest. The psalms and St. Paul compare Jesus' fulfillment of the Father's will with the sacrifices and victims of the Old Dispensation. A victim is a being subjected to the Father's will through pure love, without condition or reservation. A priest is a man divinely anointed and destined to fulfill the entire will of the Father, utilizing sacrifice as the center of his act.

St. Paul teaches that we were all sanctified in the accomplishment of the Father's will by Jesus. It follows that the only way whereby souls may be saved is the working out of the Father's will, lovingly and with all manner of sacrifice.

ZEAL OF THE SOUL FOR THE FATHER'S WILL

In order that the soul may be Jesus, she needs to imitate Him in fulfilling the Father's will, loving it and embracing it with the passionate ardor of Jesus. "What I do is always what pleases Him," she ought to say like Jesus. Everything, because not a single act or a single instant must be anything else but the most faithful fulfillment of the Father's will. The soul must no longer be mistress of herself; she has transferred herself, surrendering self, like Jesus, to the will of the Father as the happy slave of love.

Then she must accept and love everything that the Father arranges for her: joy or sorrow, desolation or consolation, silence or speech, activity or inactivity. She should always live in peace, always happy, because at all times she must be doing the Father's will without interruption, without stint, without alternatives, without restrictions, as far as human weakness permits. All her life, like Jesus, she must fulfill the Father's will by accommodating herself with docility to the manner that He determines and by accomplishing with devoted fidelity all the least details He signifies. Like Jesus, she must raise her eyes to the Father to perceive His thought, to discover His will, so that her life may be but a faithful echo of that adorable will.

She ought to do all that the Father desires because He desires it. Over and above her duty as a creature—for that will is so wise, affectionate and beneficial—she must comply with it precisely because it is the Father's will, because He wishes it, because it pleases Him.

Fundamentally, our love has two indispensable acts: taking complacency in the essential, supreme goodness of God and experiencing delight in the fulfilling of His will. Therefore, the soul should have two fundamental joys (for joy is the satisfaction of love): the essential joy of God which she now shares imperfectly through grace and which she will share fully and eternally through glory, and the exceedingly satisfying joy of complying with the will of God.

That will, which is her joy, also becomes her martyrdom, not only because clinging to the divine will brings her sufferings to endure, but also because that will must often be her interior sacrificer. Not only must she accept, love and adore the Father's will in what is related directly to herself, but she has to accept and adore it for what pertains to all her loved ones, accepting every suffering and every sacrifice which the divine will imposes. Upon thinking that someone could be lost, she will participate interiorly in Jesus' agony, crying out to the Father: "All things are possible to Thee; take away this chalice from before me; only as Thy will is, not as mine is" (Mark 14:36–37). Such a complete, ardent acceptation of the Father's will places the soul in the state of victim, exposed and disposed to all that the Father might wish. It also places the soul in the state of mystical priesthood, to sacrifice to that will Jesus, who lives in her, and to sacrifice herself and all her loved ones.

In order to glorify the Father as Jesus did, one must love and fulfill His will even to sacrifice, even to the cross. In order to save souls, one must do exactly the same. Every immolation, every sacrifice, every cross is the perfect fulfillment of the Father's will. That will, then, is a martyrdom and a joy, a Calvary and a heaven, because it bears every sorrow and produces every joy. True happiness on earth consists in performing with heavenly gladness the Father's will, which both martyrs and immolates.

This joy of executing the Father's will is the holy, unutterable, divine joy of the Cross. The Cross is the supreme accomplishment of the Father's will. Therefore it is the highest martyrdom and the loftiest joy. The passion for fulfilling the Father's will nailed Jesus to the Cross, upon which He attached for all time to come the secret of sorrow and the secret of joy, blended in the priestly love of His Divine Heart. All priestly souls must have the same ardor as Jesus. This passion must nail them to the Cross, where they will find pain and joy in love.

CHAPTER 15

⚜

Transformation into Jesus for Souls

I n the preceding chapter we saw how the soul must become Jesus for the heavenly Father. Now let us see how she must become Jesus for souls. Not many considerations are necessary to appreciate what Jesus is for souls. It suffices that each soul evoke the sweet remembrances of her own life and, full of gratitude and love, discover in her own intimate experience what Jesus has been for her.

How Jesus has loved us! How indescribably delicate His dealing with our souls! How patiently He has supported our wretchedness! How solicitously He has watched over us! How tenderly He has led us, not by taking us by the hand, but by sheltering us in His arms and in His heart! What heavenly riches He has poured out into our souls! What refined kindness He has shown them! How lovingly He must have thought about each one of us in the days of His mortal life: in Bethlehem, in Nazareth, in the Cenacle, and especially on the Cross! With what tenderness He loved us, not only then, but from all eternity! How much He suffered to redeem us; how much our souls have cost Him!

He felt all our sufferings before we did, more keenly than we did, and upon pouring them out from His heart into ours, He affectionately sweetened them. Not a single ray of light has come into our soul, not a single spark of love has inflamed our heart, not a single virtue, a single gift, a single grace has enriched our souls which Jesus did not prepare for us with solicitous care, warmed with the tenderness of His heart and purchased with the wounds of His body and soul.

He is still revealing His love to us, He is still pouring into our souls the torrent of His tenderness and the inexhaustible wealth of His grace; but He will give us more, much more, on earth and in eternity. Only in heaven shall we know what Jesus has been, what He is, what He will be for pure souls.

Now, what Jesus has been for each one of us, we should be for others, with due proportion. He said to us: "Love one another as I have loved you" (John 15:12). As Jesus has loved us, so we ought to love souls. Such is the unlimited measure of love we should have for our neighbor. St. Thérèse of the Child Jesus points out that we could not fulfill perfectly the precept of charity toward our neighbor if Jesus did not love us and if He Himself did not love the neighbor within us.

But it is to be noted that, since Jesus does not love all souls in the same way, all souls need not love others with the same perfection. The more a soul is loved by Jesus, the more she must love others, since she is obliged to love them as Jesus has loved her.

St. Thomas teaches that the precept of God's love has no limit, but that however much we may love Him, we are always under the pleasing obligation of loving Him more. Something similar should be said of our love for souls: we ought always to love them more. He who is loved more by God must love souls more, for the measure of our love toward others is the love of Jesus for us. He has loved our souls with the same love with which He loves His Father and as the Father has loved Him: "I have bestowed My love upon you, just as My Father has bestowed His love upon Me" (John 15:9). Jesus has loved us to the point of redeeming and saving us at the cost of love and sacrifice. He has loved us in order to purify us, to sanctify us, to enrich us with heavenly gifts. We ought to love souls in the same way.

Through us Jesus wishes to continue loving souls. Within us He desires to continue His immolation for them, illuminating, wooing, purifying, sanctifying and beatifying them. How sublime our mission! How sacred our duties! How unspeakable our happiness!

The love of Jesus for souls is a priestly love. It is a love in which are realized those words of St. Paul: "Who offered Himself through the Holy Spirit as a victim unblemished in God's sight" (Heb. 9:14). Sacerdotal love has a divine origin, the Holy Spirit; a divine character, purity; a divine term, the Cross; a divine fruit, the sanctification of souls; a divine end, the glory of the Father.

Souls transformed into Jesus ought to love others with priestly love, with the holy ardor of St. Paul, who said that he bore his sons within his own heart and that he would gladly spend every thing and be spent himself for souls. Jesus communicates to His priests the paternity that He has in respect to all souls, and, in a sense, He communicates it also to souls transformed into Him. This divine fecundity, which comes from the Holy Spirit, consists in giving Jesus to souls, for Jesus is the life of souls. To possess spiritual fecundity souls need *purity*, which is its source; *love*, which is its essence; *suffering*, which is its activity.

Intimate relations with souls, and especially this one of spiritual fecundity, have one single foundation, one single bond: *Jesus*. It is the giving and receiving of Jesus that knits souls together. How beautiful it is to become Jesus for souls! One must feel intimately their sorrows and their joys, their progress and their deficiencies. "Does anyone feel a scruple? I share it," said St. Paul. "Is anyone's conscience hurt? I am ablaze with indignation" (2 Cor. 11:29).

Through the love of souls one's heart is ennobled, making it similar to Jesus' heart, mighty in love, magnanimous in suffering, dynamic in activity, victorious in conflict. Because love has something of the infinite, our heart is not sufficient for itself when it loves. How we should thank God that He has given us this ingenious way of loving Him with other hearts, of suffering with the sorrows of others, of glorifying Him with the glorification rendered Him by other souls. In truth, love of God would be a truncated thing were it not united always with love of neighbor. What desires of spiritual fertility possess those souls who have been touched by the fire of God's love! How they long to receive in the spiritual order that blessing bestowed on Abraham—the promise of descendants as numerous as the stars of heaven!

Souls mean to us joy and martyrdom, pain and rest, immolation and heaven, just as they were to Jesus. For Him, all sorrow and all joy were born from His twofold love: His Father and souls; yet these two loves are only one because the glory of the Father is the good of souls. Let us not wish to have any other joy or any other sorrow than that of Jesus!

For Jesus each soul is His only one. He loves her as if no other existed in the universe, and as such, He cares for her, gives Himself to her and sacrifices Himself for her. Such is the model of our charity. Each soul that God commits to us should be the only one, as it were, in our heart's love, in our solicitude and care, and in our immolation. Like St. Paul, we should become everything by turns to everybody (1 Cor. 9:22). One should not give to a soul a portion of his heart, but his entire heart; not one instant of life, but the whole life; not one drop of blood, but all that the veins contain, poured out with the utmost abnegation.

Our love for souls should have all the characteristics which St. Paul attributes to charity: "Charity is patient, is kind; charity feels no envy; charity is never perverse or proud, never insolent; has no selfish aims, cannot be provoked, does not brood over an injury; takes no pleasure in wrongdoing, but rejoices at the victory of truth; sustains, believes, hopes, endures, to the last" (1 Cor. 13:4–7).

In a special way we ought to treat souls with that unwearying patience of Jesus, with that delicacy which makes His love so engaging, with that gentleness which never wounds but which always heals and attracts the soul even while punishing, censuring and actually immolating her. Our love of souls must be like that of God, who at all times loves with His whole heart, but gives to each one the graces belonging to her according to His designs. God's love for souls furnishes the pattern for our love for them.

147

The theme is inexhaustible, and however much one might write upon it, one could never explain adequately the treasures of the love, sacrifice and holy fecundity enclosed in this profound formula: to love souls as Jesus has loved them; to be Jesus for them.

CHAPTER 16

࿇

Transformation into Jesus Crucified

E very transformed soul must be Jesus, but none can reproduce
Him in His surpassing plenitude. Yet, while resembling Him
in all essential features, each one possesses a dominating characteristic of Jesus: a mystery, a virtue, a trait, and it is precisely in this
singular method of reproducing Jesus that the mission of each soul
is assigned, with the precise way marked out and the place which
she occupies in the mystical body of Christ designated. The best
place falls to those destined to reproduce Jesus Crucified, that is,
Jesus in the most excellent of His mysteries, in the most sublime
phase of His mission, and in the most poignant aspect of His love.

But Jesus Crucified is an infinity of light, of life, of love and of
perfections which do not fit into any soul. I mean that although all
is given to souls, and although all is reproduced in them, still there
is room to imitate that Divine Model in the most diverse ways,
and although very many souls do reproduce Him, none reproduces
Him in His fullness, but each one reproduces Him in her own way.

✳

JESUS CRUCIFIED IS TEACHER

150   Jesus' Cross is His *cathedra*, the loftiest ever raised upon the earth. Although Jesus was always a teacher with divine pedagogy, He gradually revealed His heavenly doctrine, and in each mystery of His life He disclosed diverse facets of His unique teaching. In His latter days He imparted to us His final instruction, the loftiest, noblest and most profound lesson of all, one which constitutes the foundation of His doctrine. This lesson is the one He taught on Calvary; it is the doctrine of the Cross.

St. Paul alluded to that lesson when he said that he desired to know nothing else than Jesus Crucified. The Church has taught that saving dogma through twenty centuries, and thousands of saints—living commentaries upon the Gospel—have explained its various manifestations and searched into its unfathomable profundities.

In this new epoch of history when hell seems to mass all its forces against the Church in an attack that it judges definitive, when all heresies and errors have united to destroy the doctrine of the Church, when a new paganism has organized all vices and concupiscences, justifying and extolling them, glamorizing them with modern marvels and even divinizing them in a certain manner, it pleased God to send His Spirit, as on a new Pentecost, to present to souls the doctrine of the Cross. The heavenly doctrine, with all its appeal, with its divine efficacy and limitless transcendence, opposes the world's doctrine. The life of suffering and of love opposes modern paganism, and the army of the Cross formed by pure, loving and sacrificial souls opposes the phalanxes of hell. This blessed army with the eternal symbol of the Cross will achieve a victory more splendid and transcendental than that won by Constantine when the holy *labarum* appeared in the sky.

At the foot of the "cross of the apostolate" could be written this legend: "In this sign thou shalt conquer," and that new *labarum*, that unique and immortal standard whose force and riches God wants to reveal to the world today in a more perfect way, will give to the Church a new liberty, more perfect than Constantine's, because it will be more spiritual, more profound, more true. It is liberty for the sons of God brought by Jesus, a freedom originating in truth, purity, love and suffering.

The "masterpiece of the Cross," the new lesson that Jesus gives to souls, is perhaps the last lesson, or rather, the lesson "ever ancient and ever new." It is the same lesson He taught on Calvary, now clarified by the Holy Spirit with an effusion of His light, thus ravishing the Heart of Christ. It will be diffused in souls like a heavenly outburst, like blessed seed to be multiplied prodigiously through the efficacious fertilization emanating from the heavenly Father. The "masterpiece of the Cross" is a doctrine ever ancient and ever new, which Jesus draws, like a heavenly benediction, from His inexhaustible treasury where, as the Gospel says, there are things both ancient and new.

Souls transformed into Jesus Crucified not only reproduce Him by sharing His sorrows and renewing His sacerdotal love, but they are chosen by God to give to the world through their influence the final lesson of Jesus, the holy, life-giving, transforming lesson of Calvary.

Modern science has produced a wonderful apparatus to dispatch sound to great distances without loss of tone, accent or intensity. God wanted to broadcast into the world His "masterpiece of the Cross" so that there might be reproduced, amplified and dispatched that mute, living, eloquent and exceedingly efficacious lesson which He gave the world twenty centuries ago upon the lofty *cathedra* of the Cross.

But that lesson may be neither produced nor commented upon nor broadcast except in the way Jesus gave it, that is, with a blood-stained body, with a soul plunged into a chasm of bitterness, with a thorn-pierced heart burning with love, opened by a spear and crowned with a mysterious cross. The lesson of the Cross is illuminating, interesting, and efficacious only when it is living. Therefore, in order to convey this lesson, to comment on it and to diffuse it, one must truly be Jesus Crucified.

JESUS CRUCIFIED, FOUNTAIN OF LIFE

From His open wounds, from His lacerated breast, from the extreme suffering of His soul, from the holy efficacy of His blood, there issued forth the life, the truth, the eternal. When Jesus was raised on high, He drew all things to Himself. When His side was opened there issued forth the pure, immaculate, holy, fertile and immortal Church, as Eve had mysteriously come from the side of Adam.

Jesus wrought wonders in His mortal life, but all had to receive their completion, their life, on Calvary. He preached in His public life, but the light to understand that doctrine emanated from the Cross. In Nazareth He taught the mysteries of the interior life, and in Bethlehem the secrets of detachment. The key to understand these prodigies is the Cross.

During His mortal life, Jesus had all the charms of earth and heaven, and despite these, He attracted few souls. After His sacrifice He appeared transfigured, and those indescribable charms that passed unperceived by those who looked at Him with their mortal eyes are so living and irresistible for souls who have not seen Him that they have kindled a fire upon the earth. This fire produces such a zeal and passion in souls that, wrapped as they are in the shadows of faith, they still need to be veiled so that they will not die of love.

The fecundity of Jesus arises from the Cross. He who desires to be productive in the supernatural order, he who desires spiritual offspring, needs to go to Calvary, be nailed to the Cross and become Jesus Crucified.

JESUS CRUCIFIED IS PRIEST

Jesus Crucified is priest in the supreme act of His priesthood. The soul that is transformed into Jesus Crucified shares in some degree in His priesthood. All the acts of Jesus have a priestly character, but the essential act of His priesthood is His sacrifice. Jesus perpetuates this sacrifice in two ways: in the Eucharist and in souls. There are, consequently, two mystical sacrifices: the mystical immolation of the real body of Jesus in the Mass, and the real immolation of His mystical body in souls. To these two sacrifices correspond two priesthoods: the official priesthood properly so called, and the mystical priesthood, both of which are a participation in the unique priesthood of Jesus.

Every priestly sacrifice requires a priest, a victim, an altar. Jesus Himself, as the Church teaches, was all three of these elements in the sacrifice of the Cross. The same is true of the sacrifice of the Mass and of the interior sacrifice of souls, for we cannot be priest or victim or altar except through Jesus and in Jesus.

THE PRIEST

The priest has one single principle, *love*; one essence, *immolation*; one end, *the glory of God*. Therefore, the Holy Spirit, who is the Personal Love of God, is the source of the entire priesthood. The Holy Spirit communicates Himself to us priests in ordination and makes us priests by impressing upon our souls the sacerdotal character, which is a participation in the priesthood of Jesus. The Holy Spirit also infuses Himself into those souls who, without the sacramental character, share in the priesthood of Jesus in a mystical manner, for without Him no one can share in the priesthood of Jesus.

But if the source of the priesthood is the Holy Spirit, its essence is an intimate union with Jesus, a transformation into Him. This is in reality what the Holy Spirit does in forming a priest: it unites him in a special manner to the supreme and only Priest and transforms that soul into Him.

Through ordination we priests receive that fundamental union with Jesus, that transformation into Him, which does not depend upon our virtue, nor upon our correspondence with grace, because

God did not want to leave the essential priesthood to the hazard of our liberty. From this fact is deduced the fundamental obligation of the priest, namely, to make full and perfect, through love and sanctity, that transformation into Jesus whose germ and root we receive in ordination.

In the mystical priesthood, the Holy Spirit unites priestly souls to Jesus and transforms them into Him through love, light and suffering.

A priest, then, is a man anointed by the Holy Spirit and through Him united to Jesus for the purpose of renewing the sacrifice of Christ for the glory of the Father and the good of souls. The fruits of the sacrifice are always the good of souls and this good is the glorification of God.

A priestly soul is a soul possessed by the Holy Spirit and anointed by Him to unite her intimately to Jesus through love and suffering in order to offer and immolate Him for the glory of God and the good of souls.

Every priestly sacrifice must have three parts: the oblation, the immolation and the communion. It is Jesus who is offered, immolated, and communicated in every sacrifice.

Sacerdotal souls must offer the Word to the Father; it is the oblation, the continuous offertory of an interminable Mass. This offering may have a formula, but it consists in something more inward, in a wholly interior life. The interior life is the foundation of the relations of our soul with God. These relations in transformed souls should be priestly in the sense explained. That is to say, souls should allow themselves to be possessed by the Holy Spirit and, under His divine impulse, unite themselves to Jesus and offer Him to the heavenly Father for the glory of God and the good of souls.

It is not enough to offer Jesus; one must immolate Him. In the Holy Mass, the consecration and the immolation are simultaneous. In the mystical Mass, in order to immolate Jesus, one must be changed into Him. The Jesus that souls immolate is the Jesus who

lives in them. To immolate Jesus is to immolate themselves because
they are Jesus.

Let it not be thought that it is audacious to say that we are Jesus,
for is not the Church the mystical body of Jesus, Jesus perpetuating
Himself in the world? Are we not incorporated with Him, are we
not His members? And as the whole soul is in each member of the
human body, the whole Jesus is in each member of the mystical body.
We are members in relation with the entire body of the Church, but
each one of us is destined to be Jesus. "Wonder and rejoice," says St.
Augustine; "we have been changed into Christ." To immolate Jesus,
then, is to immolate ourselves, but self transformed into Jesus.

To the degree in which we are Jesus, our sacrifice will be perfect.
Our sufferings and our sacrifices in themselves are worth nothing,
but if Jesus lives in us and is immolated in us, He makes our small-
est sufferings precious and, in a certain sense, divine. Jesus offered
Himself through the Holy Spirit; He, immaculate, offered Himself
to the heavenly Father in the midst of untold sufferings. Priestly
souls should offer and immolate themselves with immense love.
They should offer themselves through the Holy Spirit. They should
immolate themselves in the likeness of Jesus and they should suffer
with Him and in Him for the glory of the Father. The perfection of
the sacrifice depends, then, upon the degree of love, the degree of
purity and on the perfection of the suffering. It depends upon the
degree of possession of the Holy Spirit, upon the degree of union
with Jesus, upon the glorification of the Father effected by the soul's
immolation.

Every sacrifice is consummated by the communion and in
every communion one receives Jesus, one participates with Him as
a victim. The first and supreme communion is that of the Father.
Therefore, in His bosom the sacrifice is consummated. This communion of the Father is the acceptance of the sacrifice which is
prayed for in the Mass with these words: "Humbly we beseech
Thee, God almighty; command these things to be carried by the

hands of Thy holy angel up to Thy altar on high, in the sight of Thy divine Majesty, so that those of us who by partaking in the sacrifice of this altar shall receive the sacred body and blood of Thy Son may be filled with every grace and heavenly benediction."

By the Holy Spirit the sacred Victim is carried to the sublime altar of heaven before the presence of the divine Majesty, and from there the fruits of the sacrifice descend upon the Church and upon souls.

Our communion is a consequence of that divine communion. The Father's communion is a communion of glory, and as a consequence of that glory, there is a copious diffusion of kindness and mercy for souls. The mystery of the Trinity is an ineffable communion, essential, eternal, realized in the bosom of God, but through the sacrifice souls begin to participate, in a certain way, in that divine communion. This mystery seems indicated in the doxology of the Canon: "Through Him and with Him and in Him is to Thee, God the Father almighty, all honor and glory, world without end."

That part of the Canon to which the communion of the faithful belongs is admirably linked with these words.

In the mystical sacrifice, the Father's communion of glory comes before any other. In that mystical sacrifice the Holy Spirit also bears the victim into the presence of the Father and from there the copious fruits of sacrifice descend upon souls.

After the Father, the first one to receive communion is the priest and this communion is indispensable in the sacrifice. Unfortunately, the priest's Eucharistic Communion is not always fruitful, but the mystical communion is always so. The sacrifice presupposes a transformation of the priest into Jesus which Communion renews and perfects. Therefore, the Eucharistic sacrifice should make the priest more perfectly Jesus, just as each mystical sacrifice should make the soul who offers it more perfectly Jesus. After the priest, the faithful receive Holy Communion and Jesus is diffused in souls like a divine dew, a heavenly rain, a holy radiation of light and love.

Souls also communicate with Jesus by participating in the mystical sacrifice. Therefore, priestly souls are fruitful. They possess the secret of diffusing Jesus around them. Transformed into Jesus, they are immolated with Him, and upon giving themselves, they give Jesus. Sublime mission! Perfect realization of the intimate longings of our soul! We feel a thirst to love, but what do we give if we are misery and nothingness? Through this divine transformation, through this mysterious sacrifice we give Jesus by giving ourselves. By the pouring out of ourselves, we pour out Jesus. In this way we satisfy the craving of our heart, the most ardent longing of the Sacred Heart and the desires of souls.

The Victim

The only victim pleasing to the Father is Jesus. Through Him, with Him and in Him we can and we should offer and immolate ourselves. Therefore, in the Eucharistic sacrifice the priest has the duty of being victim and of uniting himself to Jesus, although unfortunately, not all fulfill this sacred obligation. In the mystical sacrifice the priest is always the victim, for if he were not a victim he would not be a priest, since the Jesus whom he offers is the one who lives in him—Jesus, into whom he has been transformed. One would say that he is a priest because he is a victim. He who has received priestly ordination is a priest through the sacrament of holy orders and he ought to perfect his priesthood by voluntary and loving immolation of himself, because, since Jesus is priest, victim and altar, all who share in His priesthood must participate in the other two characteristics.

The qualities which a victim ought to have are evident: it must be pure, intimately united to the Great Victim, and it must participate in Jesus' priestly sufferings. It is not the suffering in itself which pleases the Father, but the suffering in love and in purity. A victim must be pure in itself, pure in love and pure in suffering.

The purity of a victim is measured by the degree of union with Jesus, who is Purity garbed in our flesh. The purity of love consists in lack of egoism and in adhesion to the divine will. The victim does not choose the way of immolation but abandons and surrenders itself to the will of the sacrificer, thus embracing in attitude and desire all possible martyrdoms. The victim should neither desire nor seek anything else in immolation than the glory of God, the manifestation of His attributes and the fulfillment of His will.

The purity of suffering can be measured by its origin, by the suffering itself and by its end. As for its origin, suffering is purer as its origin is holier and more generous. The true and only origin of pure suffering is the Holy Spirit, but that Divine Spirit can continually elevate the soul's motive for suffering. Priestly suffering is very pure because it springs from a generous and disinterested love. The priest does not suffer for himself, nor is he immolated for himself, but solely for the glory of God and the welfare of souls.

The soul that is both priest and victim can elevate all suffering to sacerdotal suffering, whatever may be its cause. Sufferings properly sacerdotal have as their motive the glory of God and the good of souls. The purest sacerdotal sufferings are those that, like the sorrows of Jesus, are endured not only for the glory of God and the good of souls, but also to rescue souls in danger of losing the beatific vision through their own rejection of God. What purity and generosity those priestly sorrows have that arise from the very offenses of those for whom they are offered! Such were the sorrows of the Divine Heart of Jesus. Their source was our own sins. That Heart was broken by them; they were its executioner.

When Jesus received all of our sins, the magnitude of this malice, once placed in contact with His infinite love, was transformed into an infinity of purifying and sanctifying sorrow, which in turn brought happiness to these souls. In the same way the heart of a priest is a victim, a transformer which by the power of love takes away malice with purifying pain. Is greater similarity to the Sacred Heart possible?

Suffering in itself is much more pure as it becomes less entan-
gled with consolation. The suffering of Jesus was most pure, because
it was a desolate sorrow, because He wished to feel at the peak of
His suffering even the mysterious abandonment by the heavenly
Father. Therefore, the interior sufferings of souls who feel abandoned by heaven and earth are so pure and effective.

The more divine the end of a sacrifice, the purer the sacrifice. It
is good and holy to suffer in expiation of the sins of others. Good
and holy it is to purchase graces for ourselves with sufferings, but it
is better and holier to buy them for others. To suffer for unknown
souls, to suffer for enemies, to suffer without even having the pleasure of applying the fruit of our sufferings, to leave all to God, to
suffer in conformity with the most holy purposes of His will and
according to His designs, to suffer by identifying our own will with
His, is to suffer with divine purity.

The mystical priest is destined to help the official priest in many
ways: purchasing vocations, cooperating in the sanctification of
priests, supplying for their deficiencies and expiating their faults.

The Altar

The altar is the place upon which the victim is immolated, the
fruits for the sacrifice are spread out, or the blood of the victim is
shed. Doubtless, an altar must be clean from stain, because it must
be anointed by the Holy Spirit, the Fountain of purity.

But for the sacrifice of Jesus, there could be nothing pure upon
the earth because all purity, including that of the Virgin Mary,
comes from that sacrifice. But for the Crucifixion, the world would
be a mud puddle upon which the Father's most holy gaze could not
rest, nor could the Holy Spirit repose there, as the dove sent by Noah
did not find a place to rest upon the earth inundated by the flood.

The first and only *essential* purity to appear upon this earth was
Jesus. Therefore, He Himself had to be the altar of His sacrifice.

Through His sacrifice Jesus has purified some souls and anointed them with His Spirit so that they may be altars where His sacrifice may be perpetuated. The material altars, purified and anointed by the Church, are figures of Jesus and symbols of the souls who are altars because they are Jesus. After Jesus there is no altar purer and holier than Mary. In her heart Jesus was mystically immolated. She was the purest altar because she was the Immaculate, and the holiest because she received the fullness of the Divine Spirit.

In order that a soul may be an altar, in order that Jesus may be immolated there, she needs to be empty of self and full of the Holy Spirit. An altar is like an oasis in the desert upon which the Father may fasten His gaze and upon which the Divine Dove may rest. In one word, an altar is Jesus. The intimate relations among these three are clear: *priest, victim, altar,* for there are various participations with Jesus which must be intimately united.

We priests must be victims by reason of our loving sacrifice; we must be altars by reason of our purity. The soul that shares in the mystical priesthood of Jesus must necessarily be priest, victim and altar, that is, that soul must be Jesus.

PART THREE

THE INTERIOR OF THE HEART OF JESUS

CHAPTER 17

⚜

Plenitude of Purity

There is no more worthy object of our contemplation and our love than Jesus. He Himself has said: "Eternal life is knowing Thee, who art the only true God, and Jesus Christ whom Thou hast sent" (John 17:3).

But the most intimate, appealing and beautiful aspect of Jesus— if in this divine entirety one may distinguish more and less—is His heart, summit of His being, center of His life, source of His marvelous fecundity. To glance into that Divine Heart is to glance into heaven; to penetrate that sanctuary is to touch beatitude; to live therein is to find happiness.

These pages have been written to nourish the piety of souls that aspire to such great happiness. Far from being a complete study of that sublime theme, they are merely simple notes, poor little seeds that may happily be fertilized in upright souls by the Holy Spirit.

ONLY THE Holy Spirit with His divine light can show us the interior of Jesus' heart, but since it pleases Him that we with our poor strength prepare His work, or at least contribute what we can to receive His gifts, let us begin to study that interior of the Divine Heart.

Let us approach that sanctuary with the silence and the prayer of one who approaches something sacred. As Moses put off his shoes to tread on holy ground and to contemplate the mysterious vision, let us despoil ourselves of all that is worldly in order to approach the Heart of Jesus. With St. Paul, let us "find our true home in heaven" (Phil. 3:20).

The first impression felt by the soul that enters into Jesus' heart is one of incomparable purity, like the fragrance of celestial lilies, like the luster of heavenly light. The Heart of Jesus is a sanctuary of divine purity. It is "the glow that radiates from eternal light... the untarnished mirror of God's majesty...the faithful echo of His goodness" (Wis. 7:26). Rather than comment upon these deep words, we should silently adore and lovingly contemplate the most holy reality contained within them.

We are accustomed to conceive of purity as something human, that is, under its negative aspect. Viewed from this aspect, purity is the absence of earthliness, or everything that is not God. How beautiful is a heart in which there is no stain, no selfishness! When we on earth have the joy and happiness of finding such a heart, it seems like a vision from heaven; we contemplate a spectacle beyond all the beauties of the world. It is an image of God; it is a likeness of sovereign beauty; it is something that captivated the spirit with an inexpressible impression that does not seem to fit within our narrow confines.

But, alas, the pure hearts that we can find are not so pure that their light is without shadows and their loveliness without imperfections. However clean a human heart may be, it always has some fine and subtle specks—dust from which, in the main, one can never be completely free. There is only one entirely human heart in which that fine dust is not found, the heart of Mary. What a heavenly impression one would receive on approaching that singular heart! What happiness to look into that ocean of purity! In the Heart of Jesus the plenitude of purity abides. No dust is there, no shadow, no imperfection, nothing earthly.

But purity has another aspect; it is something positive, something divine. What it lacks of earth must be completed by something of heaven, something of God—the purity of God Himself of its reflection in creatures.

167

In the Heart of Jesus there are two purities: one of God Himself because that Heart is divine, and the other is the most complete and splendid reflection of God.

Divine purity is unfathomable in its simplicity; it contains all perfection, all beauty; it is the infinite being of God; it is ineffable life. God is purity because He is God, because He is what He is. The most Holy Trinity is a mystery of living and fruitful purity. The Father is the purity of all purity, without beginning. The Son is purity engendered, the term of infinite fecundity, of infinite purity. The Holy Spirit is the purity of love, who proceeds from the Father and the Son as from one single principle of purity.

Infinite purity has been lavished without measure upon the Heart of Jesus; therefore, that Divine Heart is heaven. Of that Heart more truly than of Tabor one can say with St. Peter: "Master, it is well that we should be here" (Mark 9:4). Would that we could always live within that Sacred Heart! To live there and never leave it; to live in purity as bees in the chalice of a lily.

Divine purity is reflected perfectly in the Heart of Jesus inasmuch as it is human. As an exquisitely appointed drawing room reflected in the mirrors on its walls seems to multiply its beauties, so infinite purity is reflected in the clear crystal of Jesus' heart, purer than the Immaculate Heart of Mary. It is evident that divine purity is not multiplied in itself because the infinite cannot be increased, but it is certainly reflected in a glorious, indescribable manner. The human purity of Jesus is, for us, the means of glimpsing the divine purity, for the Incarnation, upon making the divinity perceptible to us, carries us to it and makes us penetrate its secrets as the Church proclaims in the Christmas Preface: "Through Him whom we behold as God made visible, we may be carried on to the love of things invisible."

The human purity of the Heart of Jesus, far from concealing His divine purity from us, gives us a faint glimpse of it, fitting it to our smallness and fashioning us to its greatness.

THESE TWO purities are ineffably united; they are one single purity through the oneness of the Person possessing them. This purity, both human and divine, charms us and attracts us to Jesus.

In that Heart there is nothing that is not divine—divine looks, divine feelings, divine throbbings. Consequently, everything in that Heart is purity of the highest order. Even the purity of Mary grows pale before the purity of Jesus' heart. Our soul never experiences a deeper and more captivating impression than when we hear the throbbings of that Heart in which everything is divine.

But in ordinary hearts the divine is neither constant nor perfect nor uniform. Sublime acts in the human heart are always something fleeting and progressive, like a harmony that keeps increasing and perfecting itself, reaching at one instant the sublime and then fading away gradually until it is lost, like a light that increases and dazzles, then slowly dims to a mere flicker. It seems that the divine passes through human hearts as the glory of God passes over the holy mountain.

In Jesus the divine neither passes away nor declines; it is constant, perfect, perpetual. The sublime in that Heart is not a lightning flash, but a perfect, serene day with neither clouds nor sunset. What must be the interior of Jesus' heart, always sublime and perfect in its purity, always divine, always beautiful. It cannot be compared with the loveliness of created things which can always be expressed with a curve that rises, reaches a peak and declines. It is a beauty always uniform, always equal, a peak without sides, the simplest and richest point, without a variety of lines, with full harmony, without cadence, one single note which neither dies nor develops, and which encloses in its unity a whole world of harmony. The sublime, the divine in human hearts brings with it a kind of strength.

It cannot have the naturalness, the simplicity, the facility of what is ordinary. When a man does something heroic, superhuman, we feel that some force has enabled him to surpass his own powers. In Jesus the superhuman is ordinary. He does not make an effort to produce divine sentiments. The effort He needs to make is to hide them, lest He overwhelm our smallness with His greatness.

YES, IT is good to live always in that Heart in which divine purity becomes little so that we may enjoy it and in which human purity is always preserved on the heights without effort, without change, without guile. The purity of the Sacred Heart is the source of all purity, since of its fullness we have all received. For it is not a purity that we simply contemplate, but one that unfolds itself, that penetrates us, that possesses us, that beautifies us although we might have all the stains and ugliness of earth.

Let us imagine a cloud that could contemplate the glorious sunlight. It would not only enjoy that vision, but it would itself be enwrapped in the torrents of light which it was contemplating. It would become luminous and beautiful by contemplating the splendor of the sunlight. So it happens with the purity of Jesus. The soul that contemplates it, loves it, and lives in it, is bathed in torrents of celestial beauty and thus it becomes pure, beautiful, resplendent and divine.

CHAPTER 18

⚜

Abyss of Divine Virtues

As stated previously, purity positively considered is the diviniza-
tion of the soul. The soul of Jesus was divinized, first, by the
hypostatic union—the ineffable communication of divine purity
with the Word of God; secondly, by the most bountiful effusion of
sanctifying grace with its cortège of virtues and gifts; and lastly, by a
third grace distinguished by theologians as belonging to Jesus in His
office as Head of regenerated humanity. He received graces in order
to infuse them into souls. Therefore St. John declares: "We have all
received something out of His abundance" (John 1:16).

Jesus purchased these graces with His merits. He produces
them as God. His most sacred humanity is the instrument for producing them, and He distributes them among the members of his
mystical body as the head exerts its influence on all the members of
the organism.

We can distinguish three classes of purity in Jesus and in the
interior of His heart, the center of His humanity: *divine purity*,
which He possesses through the hypostatic union; that which I have
called *human purity*, since it is of the same species as the purity
possessed by man, although it is supernatural and divine, having its

root in sanctifying grace; and *capital purity* which He possesses as Head of the Church.

THE FIRST is ineffable. Because of it His acts are not only divine in the same way as the acts of holy souls, but since He is God, His acts are all acts of the Word. Through this grace of union His heart is divine and His purity is the purity of God.

As I have already said, this divine purity in Jesus, far from being obscured by His human nature, becomes for us the more beautiful inasmuch as it is adapted to our littleness and by its sensible manifestation draws us to its invisible and divine reality.

It is this harmonious and inexpressible union of the divine and the human in the Heart of Jesus that attracts us so powerfully, if He were not human, or rather, if He did not become man, this purity would not be so adapted to us. If He were not divine, it would neither draw us, nor satisfy us, nor divinize us.

As mothers change solid food into milk so that they may nourish their infants, so through the mystery of Jesus, the highly substantial food of the Divinity becomes milk in order that we may partake of it and grow strong through this divine nutriment.

Blessed be the heavenly Father who has given us Jesus both divine and human. Let us eat this celestial food. Let us relish especially the exceedingly satisfying sustenance of Jesus' heart.

THE SECOND purity of Jesus is an incomprehensible plenitude; it is an immense ocean of grace and truth. "Full of grace and truth" (John 1:14), to quote St. John. It is full because it contains all degrees and shades of sanctity. St. Paul states that the blessed differ in brightness as the stars in the sky (1 Cor. 15:41). Jesus encompasses in His heart all splendors. He is not a star, He is the Sun.

Among the saints there are virginal hearts and heroic hearts, apostolic hearts and contemplative hearts, hearts that sing and hearts that weep. Who can enumerate the shades of sanctity and purity in souls? The Heart of Jesus unites them all in a marvelous harmony. That Heart is plenitude itself.

The purity of the Heart of Jesus is plenitude, because as the Church says, "He is the abyss of all virtues." The virtues are constituents of purity, traces of it, forms and shades belonging to it. The purity of Jesus contains all virtues, but in such a degree that each virtue is an infinity, and with such harmony that they are all one unfathomable depth.

Let us take a glance at the virtues of Jesus. Through the grace of union the Heart of Jesus possesses those virtues that St. Thomas calls exemplary and which are the very being of God, inasmuch as in Him is found the prototype of all virtue. These are precisely described by the term, *substantial virtues*. These virtues are the Word Himself to whose likeness our virtues have been conformed. He is Light, Love, Order, Purity, whom man's poor virtues, although they may be the admirable virtues of the most holy Virgin, merely imitate from afar. However precious the infused virtues may be, compared with God Himself, they are like photographs compared with the living person.

In God all the virtues are one single reality and they are infinite. They neither hamper nor limit one another as happens in a certain way in our souls. They are harmonized in an extraordinary manner so that when we shall see them through the beatific vision, we shall not discern which is the more excellent, their infinite intensity, their extensive variety or their perfect harmony. Rather, we shall then apprehend that what our limited intelligence distinguishes as three are fused into one single divine reality. These exemplary virtues are in the Heart of Jesus because of the hypostatic union. Rightly is that Heart called an abyss of all virtues. Who can plumb that profundity?

BESIDES THESE exemplary virtues, the Heart of Jesus possesses the virtues that accompany sanctifying grace, though most perfect in

degree, admirable in plenitude and harmonious in their unity—
veritable depths forming a single profound immensity.

Not long ago I heard an excellent symphony executed by an
equally excellent orchestra. What captivated me most was the unex-
plainable but deep impression of *unity*. What I heard seemed to
me only one entity present in all forms and shades, a creation alter-
nately showing and hiding itself, taking on gigantic proportions
that overwhelmed the spirit in one instant while in the next it was
commuted to the softest caress, bathing the soul in a sweet unction that seemed scarcely to touch the surface, but which nevertheless reached to the very depths. Yet it passed from one to the other
extreme with wonderful gentleness, with natural transitions that
made all the fibers of emotion vibrate. Overwhelming or gentle,
that harmony was only a single strain. It might be said that it was
not an aggregate of sounds but only one sound, full and rich, which
disclosed itself to the soul slowly and orderly, yet occasionally hid
itself without its fullness ever being either discovered or completely
obscured, so that one could not say which was the more enchanting, the crescendo or the diminuendo.

That symphony seemed to me an image—feeble and distant,
to be sure—of the abyss of virtues which is the Heart of Jesus. No
doubt, all virtues are in that Heart: humility, meekness, patience,
love. But they are so excellent, so divinely infused into indescribable harmony, that one perceives more clearly than in an array of
virtues a singular purity that runs the whole gamut of heroism,
serenity, delicacy, tenderness, pain. One perceives a unique, heavenly impression which at times is sublime indignation, holy anger
driving the sellers out of the temple with a whip, and at other times
the sweetness of love with which Jesus looked at the young man
desirous of obtaining eternal life. Sometimes that impression is a
deep sigh of distress (John 11:36), as St. John relates in the account
of the raising of Lazarus; sometimes it is the human, tender "*lacry-
matus est*" of the same narrative. On other occasions one senses the

glory of Tabor, and on others, the agony of Gethsemane again, the majesty with which He chained the tempests, or the humility with which He allowed Himself to be tied by the executioners; sometimes the courage with which He opposed the hypocrites. At times one perceives the delicate tenderness with which He allowed the beloved virginal disciple to rest upon His breast. But always it is an abyss of virtue, unique and immutable. His lips have the same accent when He rebukes and when He blesses. His eyes have the same depth when they flash angrily as when they allow the tenderness of His soul to shine forth. The Heart that suffers and the Heart that loves is the same Heart, the one that sends forth rays of glory in the Transfiguration and a sweat of blood in the Garden; the one that pardons and caresses, the one immolated, the one that promises heaven upon the Cross and gives itself in the Cenacle. It is the same divine reality that is revealed to us and is hidden from us, without our ever seeing it in its fullness, though it is never completely hidden from us. Were He to show Himself to us such as He is, His beauty would slay us. Were He to hide Himself from us completely, we would die from cold and darkness.

O JESUS, keep our souls ever aware of the divine symphony of Thy heart. Continue playing the celestial gamut of Thy innermost sentiments before our ravished spirit. Show and hide Thyself with divine art in our pitiable souls. Always live in them, Thou Thyself, ever divine, ever human, ever enrapturing hearts that love Thee.

Why do the virtues of Jesus have that wonderful unity? It is because they are most excellent, because they have a mighty plenitude. Imperfect things are complex; in proportion as they rise from perfection to perfection they become simplified and approach unity. In a mediocre orchestra the instruments are distinguishable; a masterful ensemble blends all into one. Rivers are multiple when they run toward the sea, but when they reach the mouth they form one single ocean. At night there are many lights, at noon there is only one splendid sun. The intelligence engages in many reasonings until intuition, a single glance, is developed. In creatures there are many ideas; in God there is only one thought: the Word. The heart perfects itself by pouring all its affections into one single love; there is no heart so one as the heart of the saints, because they have arrived at the perfection of love.

The virtues of the Heart of Jesus are the most similar to those exemplary virtues of God. They are, without doubt, those which St. Thomas calls "*iam purgati animi*," "proper to the soul already purified,"[1] and which are designated also as "perfect spiritual virtues," but with a heroism, a perfection, a divine shade that our language cannot express nor our intelligence conceive. They are virtues developed and ruled by the Holy Spirit through His gifts, but with such intensity and constancy on the part of the Sanctifier, and with such docility, perfection and purity on the part of the soul of Jesus that only in heaven shall we be able to catch even a glimmer of them. The Heart of Jesus is an abyss of virtues, but an abyss of divine virtues.

---

1. Cf. *Summa Theologiae* I-II, q. 61, a. 5.

CHAPTER 19

※

Fount of Holiness

The third purity we have considered in Jesus—the purity He has as Head of the Church—is diffused in souls, purifying, beautifying and deifying them. We have all received the fullness of His purity, yet that plenitude is never exhausted. What a happiness to receive all we have from Christ's superabundance! Graces can come to us from no other source. But if it were possible for graces to evolve from any other source, who would still not prefer to receive them from that most gracious Heart? Yes, let the graces that come to our souls come sprinkled with the perfume of Jesus, impregnated with His love, sealed with His blood and His suffering so that we can say of any grace: "Before this entered my soul, it resided in the most lovable Heart of Jesus."

Each grace our Lord gives us is a new bond of love, uniting us with Him. It is something of Himself that we receive. In truth, He makes us a present of Himself in all His gifts. By communicating His purity to us, in a certain sense He imparts to us His own purity just as an object reflected in a mirror is also in the mirror in a special way.

This sharing of the very purity of Jesus is realized most perfectly in the transforming union. Through that mysterious union the soul can exclaim with St. Paul: "With Christ I hang upon the cross, and yet I am alive; or rather, not I; it is Christ that lives in me" (Gal. 2:20). This is equivalent to saying: "I do not have my own purity, but I am clothed with that of Jesus. The Father sees me in His Son's virtue, and so do souls." Rightly did St. Paul say: "The one bread makes us one body" (1 Cor. 10:17), for this purity of Jesus that clothes souls unites them among themselves and makes them all one in Christ, one single mystical body. This is the Communion of Saints, this ebb and flow of Jesus' holiness in all the members of His mystical body. They are waves which descend from heaven to earth, from earth to purgatory and to heaven.

The Church, "all spotless and fair," adorned with the purity of Jesus is so beautiful; its center, the Divine Heart, spreads purity throughout the entire mystical body, as the heart in a living organism pumps the life-giving blood throughout the system.

We do not say that all graces of all souls are deposited in Jesus' heart, because this expression would seem to indicate that our graces are not His but that He holds them in deposit. This is not the case. Graces are ours because they are His. They are the vivifying influence of the Head that extends into the members. When will we understand that profound statement of the apostle: "We, though many in number, form one body in Christ" (Rom. 12:5)?

As God placed on Jesus "the guilt of us all" (Is. 53:6), so He placed on Him all our graces; rather, our graces are more His than our iniquities. O wonderful exchange! We deposit our faults in Jesus' heart; He reciprocates with His graces, erasing our iniquities.

It seems to me that the Heart of Jesus is like a marvelous transformer: by means of the divine workmanship of love and suffering in that most generous Heart, heinous sins that flow into it come forth as precious graces. Do we want to know how purity reacts in the divine alchemy of Jesus' heart? God puts into that Heart all our iniquities. Purest love reacts upon hate and filth. The first stage of that strange combination is an outburst of incredible pain, but love

changed into sorrow upon contact with evil destroys the latter and
then torrents of purity remain to cleanse the very souls that effected   *179*
the sin.

The supreme marvel of God's sublime strategy is profoundly
expressed by St. Augustine with these words: "He judged it better
to draw good out of evil than not to permit evil to exist." The key to
this extraordinary artifice is suffering, the magic wand love uses to
draw good out of evil. We attribute that marvelous transformation
to the Heart of Jesus, because, if it is certain that all His sufferings
contributed to that transforming process, the most precious and
efficacious among them were the innermost sorrows of His heart. In
truth, suffering would not be efficacious if it were not impregnated
with love, if it were not a form of love. The interior immolation
of Jesus' heart brought Him to the immolation of Calvary. Before
the redeeming and sanctifying blood flowed from His most sacred
wounds, that blood was in His heart and thence it drew its divine
efficacy.

Purity is not produced solely through the merit of Jesus' love
and sacrifice. Theologians teach that the humanity of Christ hypostatically united to the divinity, besides being the meritorious cause
of grace, is also the instrument of its production. In fact, the purity
of the creature has infinite purity for its source. "Who can cleanse
what is born of tainted stock, save Thou alone, who alone hast
being?" (Job 14:4). The Word of God, as St. Thomas teaches, chose
the most sacred humanity of Jesus as the instrument for the production of grace. In this precious instrument, the heart—symbol
of love and of suffering—has without doubt a mysterious and most
efficacious influence. Jesus purifies by loving; He purifies by suffering. The language of love would say that He purifies with His most
chaste kisses. With all propriety one may say that He cleanses with
His most Precious Blood. "By His bruises we were healed" (Is. 53:5).

Wherever purity appears, there is the hand of Jesus. There is the
influence of His heart, since each of the stages of our spiritual life

is an enrichment of innocence. In each step there is a new contact with Jesus, a new outpouring of love from His most Sacred Heart to wash our poor heart.

180

The first contact of Jesus with the soul is in baptism, when it is buried with Him to rise with Him to a new life of sinlessness and love. Baptism is a sacrament of purity, as its magnificent symbolism and the richness of its rite attest. In the early centuries, the neophytes, "a chosen race, a royal priesthood, a consecrated nation" (1 Pet. 2:9), were clothed during the entire Easter octave with white tunics, symbol of the immaculate whiteness of their souls.

Baptism has that inimitable and unique charm of all that is beginning, of dawn, of spring, of youth. And why not? It is, indeed, the first embrace of the soul with God, the first kiss of love, the first intimate caress, the first sweet possession that Eternal Love takes of the soul. It also has the charm of hope, the condensed richness of the seed that will develop into a fruit-bearing tree. "Therefore, whatever may be the degree of holiness to which that soul is eventually raised by God, whatever spiritual gifts may afterwards adorn it, these graces will only develop and confirm in it the pristine sanctity infused by the sacrament of baptism. As the tree is virtually contained in the seed, so baptism is the very life of the Christian soul."[1] It is as if God placed in the intensity of that first tender kiss the whole magnitude of His loving designs.

That kiss of love is not the only one nor is that effusion of purity the last one. It is the beginning of an interminable series of divine communications. In confirmation the Holy Spirit consummates in the soul the purity received in baptism, for if baptism is the beginning of Christian life, confirmation is the fullness of that life. The soul that has reached the plenitude of purity feeds upon the divine Eucharist, for, until the soul feasts in heaven upon the beatifying

---

1. Il defonso Cardinal Schuster, *Liber Sacramentorum*, trans. Arthur Levelis-Marke (London: Burns, Oates, & Washbourne, Ltd., 1924), vol. 1, chap. 2, p. 12.

Godhead in its divine essence, what could nourish pure souls except infinite purity hidden in the miraculous bread and in the wine? Should the soul become stained, Jesus will again open the refuge of His heart so that another torrent of purity may stream forth, the fruit of His inexhaustible love and His colossal sorrow. When the soul is about to leave this exile, the holy unction will pour out upon her the final surge of purity to dispose her for the eternal union. Nor are these the only communications between Jesus and the soul. At each instant the soul should receive the peerless pure contact of Jesus, His holy caresses, the gentle influence of His heart. The Christian life is not something intermittent; it is a continuous torrent of purity and of love that rushes forth from the Divine Heart and pours into the innermost recesses of the soul without any interruption other than those that are inevitable to human life and those which proceed from the negligence and infidelity of souls.

Jesus is a Head that does not cease to influence lovingly His mystical body; the Christian life is not an intermittent fountain but an inexhaustible spring flowing even unto eternal life.

CHAPTER 20

꙳

Like unto Jesus

We would not understand completely the third form of purity in the Heart of Jesus if we did not study the effusions of that virtue which abounds in souls by the divine method indicated in the preceding chapter. To make our study easier and more agreeable, let us fix our attention on the precious soul of Mary, upon her who placed no obstacle to the holy communications of Jesus and received them so abundantly. What could please our filial hearts more than to consider the Heart of Jesus beside that of Mary? Through the universal mediation of Mary the emanations of purity from Jesus' heart are diffused in a certain manner into souls.

The angel greeted Mary by calling her "full of grace," but that fullness proceeded from the supreme plenitude of Jesus. What treasures of purity are hidden in that "fullness" of the Immaculate Virgin!

WHEN THE Word became flesh, Jesus poured into the heart of His Mother the second form of purity which we have considered, the species produced in souls by sanctifying grace with its cortège of virtues and gifts. All these precious charisms, with which God adorns souls, form the different elements of a unique integrity, since all cleanse and deify the essence as well as the faculties of the soul, making it appear in the eyes of God attired in a lovely nuptial garment attracting the heart and gaze of the Spouse. Such is that regal vesture of gold, embroidered with wonderful variety, with which, according to the Psalmist, the queen appears at the right hand of Jesus.

Sanctifying grace is the profound deification of the soul, the sharing of the divine nature infused by the Holy Spirit into the very essence of the soul. The action of the creature is superficial; that of God is profound, penetrating even those secret recesses of the soul where none can reach but Him alone. "Bring a clean heart to birth within me" (Ps. 50:12), David exclaimed in his psalm of contrition and hope. This complete renewal is produced in all conversions, as it is in the first effusion of grace in baptism. The action of God is like a sharp two-edged sword that penetrates even to the essence of the soul and instills there that "new creation" (Gal. 6:15), as St. Paul declares, which purifies and renews our being from its deepest roots, placing in that depth a divine germ, the seed of God, according to the audacious and lofty expression of St. John: "So it is, when a man is born by the breath of the Spirit" (John 3:8).

From that prolific seed buds forth, like a heavenly flowering, the virtues and gifts that divinize all the faculties of the soul. Each virtue whitens and enhances a portion of the soul with the indescribable reflection of God. All the virtues joined to sanctifying grace—their root—effect a celestial cleanliness and beauty. As in a picture, each portion has its own light and coloring, yet all form one entity, portraying one idea, one beauty. In the purified soul each portion has its own divine reflection, but all the reflections together compose one single purity portraying the unique image of Jesus. Purity is the beauty of souls, and each virtue and each gift of God is like a feature of the spiritual physiognomy of the soul in which God's beauty shines forth.

The virtues are the elements of purity, but it is also true that the exquisite and perfect part of each virtue is purity. I mean that *185* purity is found in each virtue and each virtue is the more perfect as it is the more pure, the more divine. Faith is perfect when it is pure, when it lacks foreign elements, when it is pure light without losing its darkness, because it is an obscure light. Love is perfect when it lacks egoism, when it lacks all that is not love, when its beginning is more divine (if one may so speak) and when its cause, its end and its essence are divine. Suffering is perfect when it is pure; pure because of the love that feeds it, because of the purity of intention that motivates it and because of the purity of perfection with which it is endured. Similarly with the other virtues, they reach their perfection when they are changed into purity, as if all these, though distinguished and alienated one from another in the lower realms, upon rising to the heights are unified and mingled into purity. Below, each virtue may have its own color, but above, all will be tinted with the indescribable whiteness of purity. This has to be so, because the virtues, in proportion as they are perfected, become divine and approach God. God is purity, for St. John said: "God is Light" (1 John 1:6). It is this purity in virtues that is Godlike in them; they always partake of the divine, because they always include purity. If they did not have it, they would not be virtues. Upon reaching the summit they seem to be despoiled of all that is earthly, to be converted into what is divine in purity. The Holy Spirit is the source of purity and the more He directly influences a virtue, the purer it becomes. It becomes more divine and, therefore, virtues which have attained the maximum of purity are those which the Holy Spirit elevated through His gifts—the perfect spiritual virtues which are entirely produced under the influence of His gifts.

With these virtues Jesus is formed in transformed souls. Is not Jesus the purity of heaven? Upon this image of whiteness and of light the gaze of the Father rests with complacency.

INTO THE soul of Mary most holy, God poured a fullness of grace from which proceed the purest divine virtues. Therefore, the purity of Mary is unique and her comeliness is surpassed only by the ineffable beauty of Jesus. At the time of her immaculate conception, Mary received more copious graces than saints accumulate at the end of life. The foundations of Mary's sanctity were laid "amidst the inviolate hills" (Ps. 86:1). During her lifetime, Mary, City of God and Tabernacle of the Most High, received rivers of grace and purity poured forth by the Holy Spirit to fill her with joy (Ps. 45:5). We know that this Divine Spirit again infused Himself into Mary's soul in Nazareth to make her the Mother of God, and again in the Cenacle to make her the Mother of the Church, but we are ignorant of other intimate, copious and constant infusions which the Spirit of God was pleased to grant to the soul of His chosen Spouse. Was not Mary's life one unutterable infusion of eternal love into her soul—the holy radiation of a sun of love in a heaven of purity?

But if we do not know the secret graces which Mary received, the substantial grace given her for thirty-three years is manifest to our observation in the person of Jesus Christ our Lord, the fount of all grace and the supreme gift of God. Can we even surmise the torrents of grace that Mary received in her intimate and constant dealing with her divine Son? How thrilling it is to see Him, to hear Him, to touch Him, to serve Him, to receive His filial confidences, to enjoy His inexpressible charms, to perceive the indescribable fragrance of His adorable presence. All this without the veils which covered the souls of others who saw Jesus, but with eyes filled with light from heaven and with a heart inflamed with holy love!

How could Mary support the continual revelation of Jesus' charms? How could she abide the divine presence for thirty-three years? How could she see the sun without being dazzled, and live near the fire without being consumed? No one has penetrated into the Divine Heart as she has; no one has dwelt there as she has. Her eyes scrutinized the treasures hidden in that august sanctuary, and through the divine prism of that Most Sacred Heart, she saw all things. The fire of her heart, united intimately with that of Jesus' heart, formed but one flame that arose even to heaven, ravishing the heart of the Father and spreading throughout the earth, pouring forth purity and inflaming souls.

On account of Mary's perfect correspondence and her exquisite fidelity, the ocean of grace in her soul kept on increasing until it reached such a fullness at the end of her life that we cannot even estimate its extent. Rightly does the Church exalt the purity of Mary in the identical words with which the Scripture praises the purity of the Word of God: "She, the glow that radiates from eternal light, she, the untarnished mirror of God's majesty" (Wis. 7:26), in whom infinite purity is reflected.

Jesus communicated to Mary not only the purity of the grace of the virtues and the gifts which He communicates to all souls, but He placed in the virginal soul of His mother a ray of the grace of union, a resemblance to that unparalleled purity. He communicated to her a share in capital grace, making her the Mediatrix of all graces.

When an artist has completed his masterpiece, he can do no more than to reproduce it in all its forms; when a genius has spoken the final word of his wisdom, nothing remains for him but to develop and explain it. When a soul has pronounced the unsurpassable word of love, she can do nothing more than repeat it in all its tones and with all the accents of that sovereign word. Similarly, after God wrought the supreme marvel of the Incarnation, He does nothing more in the world of grace than reproduce it, although it may be with faint and imperfect imitations of the masterpiece of His omnipotence and His love. The best likeness of Jesus' grace of union is Mary's motherhood. On account of this extraordinary grace, Mary is above every other creature, touching, as she does, the order of the hypostatic union.

Through the Incarnation, Jesus is God. Through a singular

grace, Mary is the Mother of God. Through the grace of union, Jesus is the Son of the Father. Through her divine maternity, Mary participates in the fecundity of the Father. The plenitude of grace belongs to Jesus because He is God; to Mary, because she is the Mother of God, belongs a plenitude of grace lesser than that of her Son, but greater than that of every other creature.

Mary's divine maternity is an intimate and singular relation with God that unites them most closely and is also a source of copious graces and singular privileges for her. What a difference between ordinary grace and the august maternity of Mary! We are children, she is mother. We are sons by adoption; she is mother by nature. We are within the order of grace; she touches the order of the hypostatic union, for as far as a mere creature can participate in the grace of union, Mary was endowed richly with that singular grace.

FURTHERMORE, JESUS was pleased to communicate abundantly to His Mother the grace which belongs to Him as Head of redeemed humanity. Everything in God's works bears the stamp of unity and harmony. We separate the different mysteries of God because our feeble intelligence cannot grasp them all at one time and scarcely, indeed, do we even glimpse their admirable connection. But all these mysteries are links of the same chain. They are strophes of the same poem, flickerings of the same light, radiations from the same fire. They are the unique thoughts of God disclosed to men by dazzling them with His celestial brilliancy, the designs of one love, of one mercy, of one wisdom that continue revealing themselves before the astonished eyes of men who know how to meditate upon them.

The Incarnation, the Redemption and the economy of grace in the Church of God are one single divine reality which develops, grows and reaches full maturity. Together they are the root of Jesse, budding a celestial rod that produces a miraculous flower whereon rests the Spirit of the Lord. The surpassing perfume of this supernatural blossom impregnates the whole earth.

Since Mary cooperated in an admirable manner with the mystery of the Incarnation, the heavenly logic of harmony and unity
requires that she cooperate also in an equally admirable manner
with the mysteries of the Redemption and the diffusion of grace. If
in the Incarnation she was the Mother of God, in the Redemption
she was Co-redemptrix, and in the economy of grace, universal
Mediatrix. Mother, Co-redemptrix and Mediatrix are three links
in that heavenly chain which is Mary's unique and exceptional mission; they are three strophes in the poem of Mary's life, the most
sublime after the life of Jesus. Those two lives form a single heavenly
symphony in which each is a distinct melody. The one marvelously
harmonized with the other without discord to form an inimitable
harmony—the most beautiful hymn to the glory of God.

The Incarnation unites Mary to the grace of Jesus; the
Redemption associates her with His suffering; the role of Mediatrix
makes her sharer in the glory and fecundity of Jesus as Head of the
Church and Father of regenerated humanity.

To be Head of the Church belongs to Jesus as the Incarnate
Word, but with His Precious Blood He bought the graces that He
pours out into souls, and He distributes them in the Church. "Each
of us has received his own special grace" (Eph. 4:7), as the Apostle
expresses it. The deep root of all Mary's privileges is her divine
motherhood; but she was Co-redemptrix on account of her participation in the sacrifice of Jesus, and she is Mediatrix on account of
being Co-redemptrix. We might characterize these three stages of
the mission of Mary in Nazareth, on Calvary and in the Cenacle
thus: in Nazareth she was Mother; on Calvary, Co-redemptrix; in
the Cenacle, she consummated her office of Mediatrix.

On Calvary she was not a simple witness of the sublime mystery
of the sufferings of Jesus, nor was she only the loving Mother who
experienced in the depths of her soul the martyrdom of her Son,
but she was associated with the redeeming pain of Jesus. The blood

of the Son and the tears of the Mother mingled in the same chalice of salvation. The sorrow of Jesus' heart and that of Mary's heart were one sorrow, gushing forth from one common love and producing, as a delicate fruit, the singular innocence which is infused into souls. Mary, then, shares in Jesus' purity in all its forms. The heart of the Mother is the most faithful likeness, the most precious portrait of the Heart of the Son.

CHAPTER 21

☸

Ever Ancient, Ever New

One infers from all that has been said that the Heart of Jesus is a sanctuary of purity, which from its plenitude produces and diffuses that virtue throughout the world. Precisely because it is a sanctuary of purity, it is a shrine of love and of suffering, for these three have very close relationships.

Infinite love is infinite purity, and when that love came to the stained earth to cleanse it, it was changed into suffering so that from this store of pain, purity for souls might be born. God's purity is infinite love and joy, having no contact with either sin or suffering; Jesus' purity is love in contact with sin in order to destroy it with suffering; our purity is love sprung from the depths of sin upon divine contact with Jesus' suffering. The first purity is all love and all happiness; the second is sorrow born of love to produce purity in stained souls; the third is love which approaches happiness along the path of sorrow.

The Heart of Jesus is an unfathomable abyss. "God is love," said John (1 John 4:16). Blessed Angela de Foligno relates that on one occasion God said to her: "Look at Me well. Is there anything in Me that is not love?" All in Him is love, an inexhaustible, unique, eternal love. On account of our slight experience with love, we perceive faintly that it is something noble and heavenly, that it fulfills our aspirations and seals our felicity. But on earth love is limited because mere creatures cannot contain the infinite. If we wish to drink that heavenly draught in human hearts, sooner or later we drain all that earth's fragile, limited chalices contain of it. Our thirst is never satiated, because our capacity and our desires are infinite— our only infinite possession. The only fountain of love that is never exhausted is God, and that fountain is in the Divine Heart of Jesus. We can drink eternally from it without ever emptying it, because our soul's capacity makes our thirst for love infinite. The fountain of love in Jesus' heart is infinite, because it springs from the divine fullness. "Open thy mouth wide and thou shalt have thy fill," says the Scripture (Ps. 80:11). Open thy mouth, the mouth of desire with which thou dost drink love; open it wide and I shall fill it. Blessed are the souls who dwell in the interior of Jesus' heart! They will always drink from that sweet fountain without ever exhausting it.

An inexhaustible love! Who understands this mystery of happiness? Everything on earth runs out: joy and sorrow, fecundity and life itself. All created things, however beautiful, however perfect, have a limit, a measure, an end. We are so accustomed to things finished and used up that we do not comprehend the mystery of an inexhaustible love. In its interminable desire for love, our heart glimpses infinite love as one dimly glimpses the vast firmament when the spirit wanders from star to star in the night's immensity.

Who does not long for an endless love, a love ever ancient and ever new? Ancient because it has the charm of the familiar, redolent of the exquisite perfume of remembrance, but lacking the bitterness of dead memories. Ever ancient the love that smiled upon us like a delicate dawn in our innocent childhood; the same that illumined our youth with splendor and glory; the strong and fruitful love of our maturity; the love of our sorrows and our joys; the love that was mercy when we fell and a tender caress when we were faithful. Oh, we do not want only a love ever ancient, anterior to our existence, anterior to time, anterior to all that our intelligence can conceive as belonging to the past. We want to feel and to taste that divine expression: "With unchanging love I love thee" (Jer. 31:3). There has never been an instant in which we were not loved by that love.

At the same time that it is ancient—the love of yesterday, the love of all time—it is also eternally new. The particular impression that this love produces in my soul at each new instant is one that I have never felt before, although my soul may have delighted in the sweetness of that love. Things of earth lose their novelty and cause a tedium, but this love never wearies because it never loses its eternal novelty. It is a love which has the eternal charm of that which is beginning—of spring, of youth, of dawn, of the first love, of the first happiness—harmoniously united with that other charm, also inimitable, of what has become enriched with time, like sweet-smelling, centuries-old wine.

A love always new! Each day it seems to the soul that she is becoming acquainted with the love that is familiar to her; each of love's words sounds like the first word, filled with surprise and charm. Each look is the dawn that peeps into the soul. Each caress is the first fragrance of spring. Each holy kiss has the delightful thrill of love's first kiss.

THE SOUL who finds a love like this, feels that she has always loved, yet she is now beginning to love. She experiences the delight of being loved between two eternities equally unlimited by remembrance and hope because it is reality. Such is the love of Jesus. It is inexpressibly superior to what has been said or can be said, to what one dreams or can dream, to what one desires or can desire. Oh, let us live in the embrace of the inexhaustible love! And being inexhaustible, it is unique, containing all loves at the same time. Each earthly love has its own flavor, its own delightful tint. Maternal love is exceedingly tender; a father's love is strong and generous; the love of husband and wife is sweet and tender; the love of friendship is trustful even to full surrender.

Can all these loves be blended into one single love, like mixing all the perfumes of spring into one exquisite essence? That heavenly essence is truly found in the Heart of Jesus. For souls, it is sweet as a spouse, tender as a mother, magnanimous as a father, intimate as a friend of one's youth, considerate beyond anyone else upon this earth! In addition to all these familiar aspects of love, which in our Lord reach unutterable proportions, there is another new and unique joy which has no analogy with the pleasures of earth. It is something "that knows eternal life," as St. John of the Cross said, and which the same Saint expressed in these profound, obscure words: "And I know not what." The existence of this joy is not even suspected, much less known, by anyone who has not enjoyed it, even though he may have felt the happiness which it encloses. Man glories in not knowing it, because that sublime ignorance is a testimony of the inexhaustible, of the unique, of the divine in that love.

When that love has not been found, the poor heart born for unity is in the midst of a multiplicity of affections. Like Martha, she goes about anxious and disturbed about many things. But when she has found that love, which is "the one thing necessary" which Mary chose, the peace of heaven fills that happy heart. The love of Jesus suffices for her because it is one, and perfect love is like that. Being one, it includes the pleasure of all loves and makes all the fibers of the heart vibrate, filling the whole soul with heavenly enchantment.

That love is unique not only because, containing all loves, it excludes all the rest, but also because it is adapted perfectly to each soul and assumes in each one her own individual mold. Jesus is not the same for all souls, His love is not uniform for all, but He takes the color, the fragrance, the form of the vase that contains that heavenly liquor. He is ardent in Paul and sweet and tranquil in John. He is the repose of contemplation in Magdalen and the

thirst for martyrdom in Ignatius of Antioch. He is tenderness in
Francis of Assisi and exquisite delicacy in Thérèse of Lisieux. For
each soul that love is unique; He fashions Himself to her desires,
her attractions, her needs, her capacity and, I feel tempted to say, to
her caprices. I want Jesus to be my own. I yearn for love just for me.

That inexhaustible and complete love communicates to the
recipient the privilege of eternity. We can enjoy eternity without
fear of losing it, and the deeper we penetrate that ocean, the greater
our security.

"WHO WILL separate us from the love of Christ?" exclaimed St.
Paul (Rom. 8:35). In my judgment, that triumphant expression is
not only the testimony that gave the Apostle the consciousness of
his own stability, but it is the affirmation that divine love is of itself
unalterable and eternal. All can be taken away from us, even life,
but not love. On the part of God, His gifts are without repentance,
and if this were not so of the others, it would be true of love because
it is His first gift. On our part, the charity which the Holy Spirit
infuses into our hearts is of itself permanent, because it is a habit,
because it is eternal life. It is evident that it can be lost through
the frailty of the subject into which charity has been poured, but
only by wanting to do so can it be lost. Jesus can make us want
never to lose it and He desires precisely this. Holy hope gives us
the assurance that it will be so. He who truly loves and hopes feels
the holy boldness of St. Paul. In the measure in which love grows
and is established in the soul, the assurance that this love will be
eternal also increases, and when that love reaches perfection, fear is
dissipated, for St. John said: "Love drives out fear when it is perfect
love" (1 John 4:18).

He who truly loves thinks he will always love. Craven is the love
that fears to be quenched! Even earthly loves claim to be eternal
in the conviction and in the desires of those who love. In spite of
everything, they will die, but it is glorious for those who love not

to know the death of their love. It is proof that love in its essence is immortal. Here below, loves die because they are terrestrial, because they bear in their bosom foreign elements, such as egoism. But when they are extricated from their sediment, as happens when they are engrafted into the trunk of divine love, they do not die. Pure love is immortal because it is divine.

Be this as it may, the love of Jesus is eternal and it communicates to souls who love Him the privilege of eternity. Only this love realizes the ideal, the desire of all loves, for all who love feel the necessity of saying: "I love thee forever and do thou love me forever also."

CHAPTER 22

✵

Delights of Divine Love

I n the love of the Heart of Jesus, we can distinguish three aspects, just as we can in its purity: the divine, the human and the priestly.

The first love is ineffable; it is infinite gratuity, inexhaustible, plenitude of goodness, perfection and beauty. Touched by this love, our soul languishes with admiration and tenderness; wounded with love, it feels a burning thirst. The eye has not seen nor the ear heard nor can the mind ever conceive this singular love. One dreams about it, sighs for it, but without being able to express its sweetness, its ardor, its purity, its delicacy. "He passed through here," speaks the soul who has felt it, "I saw His sacred shadow projected against my smallness; but I could not catch a glimpse of His divine countenance. At His step the flowers bloomed in the desert of my spirit; the night of my mind was illumined with midday splendor; my heart burned as Sinai when the voice of the Lord sounded, and my whole being, stirred even to the depths, melted like wax when Love passed by."

The charm of the divine is to feel it without understanding it, to relish it without defining it precisely, to embrace it without encompassing it. The soul smitten by that divine love experiences a joy in a continuous spiritual development, though the soul never becomes adequate for the love that has touched it. There is no joy comparable to this unspeakable dilation (I cannot find a more fitting word). Boundless horizons open up before the eyes of the soul and as her gaze wanders along them, she is bathed in heavenly light. Her greatest happiness consists in not finding a limit, in not being able to clasp what she sees, in not being able to express what she contemplates. Were she to touch the boundary, clasp the final limits, or express what she sees, the indescribable charm would be lost, for she would not see the infinite, and the infinite is precisely the only thing that can satisfy her. As the gaze expands when it contemplates immensity—the desert, the ocean, the sky—the sweep of the soul's glance stretches to infinity when she contemplates the divine, as if she wished to become infinite. She struggles vehemently to embrace what she sees, and her highest exaltation, her deepest delight consists in her defeat, in feeling her impotence, and in possessing a capacity that constantly expands, yet is never satisfied.

The heart, too, enlarges in the ocean of infinite love; a new love, deep as the sea, boundless as the sky, breaks forth from the depths of the heart. Who would have thought that one could love like this? That love, so deeply interior, seems naught to the soul because in the light of the immense love that has captivated her, it is as nothing. She tries a new love. She feels the need of it, and she does not know which is sweeter, the new love that inflames her or the strange charm of feeling herself powerless to correspond to the older love that enfolds her.

Oh, the delights of divine love which surpass all the delights of earth! Oh, the glory of our love which feels the joy of being perpetually overcome by infinite love! Rightly did the spouse in the Canticle exclaim with the audacity of unrestrained love: "A kiss from those lips!" (Cant. 1:1). She was yearning for infinite love. She was dreaming of the happiness of that contact with the divine lips, swift and transient yet communicating to the soul the sweetness of

heaven. Of what importance is its brief duration the infinite fits
into the fragility of the instant? In exchange for that moment of
beatitude, she would suffer all the sorrows of earth. What is that
kiss? The soul can neither express it nor know it. The infinite is neither spoken nor known. One enjoys it in silence like an anticipation
of heaven.

THIS DIVINE love which can be neither defined nor expressed, this
love whose charm consists in being enjoyed without being understood, has been lavished upon the Heart of Jesus in its divine fullness in the hypostatic union. The supreme attraction of this Heart is
that it encloses the delights of heaven and earth. If this Heart were
not divine, it would not be what it is. It would not draw hearts and,
although most pure and most holy, it would not cut love's wound
so deeply, nor would it stir souls to their very cores as it does, totally
and forever.

When we place our eager lips to this most Sacred Heart, this
divine water of love fills us without satisfying us. It fills us because
it gives us the infinite, but does not satisfy us because we can never
exhaust the infinite draught. In order to satisfy our thirst for the
infinite, the love of God accommodated itself to our smallness by
enveloping itself in the human aspect of Jesus' love. If it were not
for Jesus, God would not kiss our souls, nor could our souls support
the divine kiss without dying. But Jesus enclosed what is divine
in love in the sheer, transparent cloth of human love. Across this
love—similar to our own—which is adapted to our weakness, we
catch a glimpse of eternal love, so that, without dying, we experience its inexpressible sweetness. We want such a love, divine and
human, because only the infinite fills us, because only when this
love is veiled by a human wrapping can we in this world withstand the divine. We want a love that revives souls as Lazarus was
revived, but by weeping at his tomb; a love that redeems the world,
but by feeling all its sorrows; a love that works the prodigy of the

Eucharist, but by permitting the beloved disciple to recline upon the Master's breast; a love that climbs Tabor, but also goes down to Gethsemane; a love that promises heaven, but from a cross; a love that pardons, purifies, transforms, beatifies, but one that also becomes weary, complains, weeps, suffers, dies.

We could not dream of a better gift than the love of Jesus, nor could the Father (pardon my presumption) give us a better gift. If there were no other reason for loving the Father, the thought that He has given Jesus to us is enough to make us die out of love for Him. Jesus suits our desires, our needs, our dreams in a marvelous measure. Great because of our aspirations and insignificant because of our miseries, we need Jesus, infinite because He is God, small because He is man; consubstantial with the Father, because He is the Word; our Brother because He is flesh of our flesh and bone of our bone.

Therefore, everything about Him attracts us: His look so mild that it does not wound us, so profound that it is unfathomable; His smile which allures and attracts us like an elaborate curtain which when half-opened discloses the sky; His hands, holy and venerable, as the Church says, that touch our wounds and fill us with blessings, that mold the clay and give it life; His most sacred feet that were covered with the dust of the road He traveled bearing tidings of peace; His words that sound sweetly in our ears of flesh and tell of eternal life for souls; His blood which runs upon the earth and cries to heaven, a purchase price upon the Cross and celestial wine in the Eucharist; His most sacred body replete with suffering on Calvary and containing all sweetness in the Sacred Host.

We want no other gift than Jesus; we yearn for no other love than His. Who is like Him? So tender in loving, so sweet in caressing, so selfless in suffering, so sensitive in appreciating, so delicate in directing, always faithful, always loving, peerless, without a counterpart in heaven or on earth.

B‌UT THE finest thing in that incomparable love, both human and divine, is its sacerdotal aspect. Christ's priestly love is His love in its plenitude, as the priesthood is the coronation of His mission. That sacerdotal love is an ardent and efficacious eagerness for the glory of the Father. Upon entering the world He said: "See then…I am coming to fulfill what is written of Me…to do Thy will, O My God" (Heb. 10:7). And this divine will which, according to St. Paul, has as its center the sacrifice of Calvary, was the moving force of His life, the impetus to His heart, the magnet of His soul, His food and drink, as He Himself deigned to reveal upon the brink of Jacob's well.

The glory of the Father was the fount of His joy and the source of His sorrow, the secret of His eloquence and the fire of His apostolate, the key of His life and the reason for His death. For that glory He offered His bloody sacrifice on the Cross; now upon the altar He offers His mystical sacrifice, and He will offer until the end of time the sacrifice of souls who are united to Him. For the glory of the Father He established His Church, endowing it with power and grace. For the glory of the Father He arranged that series of sufferings, honors, humiliations and marvels which is the life of His holy spouse. From the depth of that glorifying love broke forth, not a new love, but as a logical extension of that same love, His delicate, long-suffering, unquenchable and eternal tenderness toward souls.

How has Jesus loved us? He loved us when we were wallowing in sin; He loved us stained, perhaps hostile, displeasing and rebellious, hard-hearted and, without a doubt, egoistic and disdainful of His love. The abyss of our wickedness seems to deepen the abyss of His infinite charity. Why does that Heart seem to love with greater tenderness, with more sensitive compassion, with deeper anguish when we are more ungrateful and cruel toward Him? Through what incomprehensible delicacy does He change into graces the very sufferings we cause Him? How He seems to forget our faults when we are converted to Him, our ingratitudes when we love Him, and our infidelities when we approach Him!

He loved us when we were prostrate in our wretchedness. He loved us in order to raise us up to Himself, to unite us to His greatness in a binding embrace, to fuse our hearts with His, so that our souls might be His friends, His spouses, His children, His parents. He loves us in order to reveal His secrets to us, to share with us all that is His, to give us His spirit, to inebriate us with His love, to give us His own life and happiness.

To raise us from the dust and place us with the princes of His people, He traveled the paths of humiliation and grief. He suffered all that can be suffered on this earth—what He alone could suffer here, because no one on earth could experience sorrow so deep, so pure, so cruel, so fruitful as His sorrow. Yet His sorrow is not from heaven because no one suffers there; it is His own sorrow, the exclusive possession of that unique Heart, for His love is unique and exclusive.

How has Jesus loved us? In order to tell of that love, it would be necessary to penetrate the Gospels and to investigate the deep secrets hidden in history. It would be necessary to understand Bethlehem and Nazareth, Tabor and Gethsemane, Calvary and the Eucharist.

Ah, we cannot fathom even our own life. Were we to do so, the greatness of Jesus' love would overwhelm us. How He has loved each one of us! How many graces He has given us! How much has He suffered for us! With what delicacy, tenderness, ardor, patience and divine courtesy He has dealt with us!

Jesus, who loves like You?

CHAPTER 23

☫

Christ's Love for Priests

J esus knows how to love. His most Sacred Heart holds a tender, ardent, delicate, fecund and sacrificial love for all souls. But that love of Jesus, embracing all souls, is more tender and intimate for priestly souls, as the rays of the sun which bathe the whole earth are more splendid upon the snowy summits. We priests are summits in the supernatural order, because we are nearer to God, more united with the High Priest; summits because we ought to be filled with the glory of God and because from the heights of our dignity God's graces should be poured forth upon souls, as the life-giving waters which fertilize the valleys descend from the snowy peaks when the sun warms them.

Rightfully does Jesus love us so much, because in us He loves the Father, because in us He loves souls, because in our great littleness He loves Himself. St. Thomas says that from the viewpoint of the act of the will itself, God loves all souls equally in the sense that He loves all things by an act of the will which is simple, one, unchanging. God cannot love in any other way. But from the viewpoint of the good God wills, He loves some more than others, since He gives them greater graces, the cause of all goodness in things being God's love.[1]

Could Christ have given greater graces than He has given to us, His priests? To become glorifiers of the Father, instruments of the Holy Spirit, to become "another He," to place in our hands His richest treasures, the Eucharist and souls, to trust to us the fate of His Church and the eternal future of those He loves, to leave to our care His merits, which cost Him such great suffering, so that their lot may be left to our pleasure, to make His powers ours and His mission ours, to let His joys be our joys and His sorrows our sorrows, this is a great gift.

The Curé of Ars was right in saying: "Only in heaven shall we know what a priest is. If we were to know this on earth, we would die, not from grief but from love." God enlarged the capacity of our hearts on the day of our ordination so that He and all souls might fit into them, and He filled that immensity with the light of His wisdom, the sweetness of His love and the riches of His omnipotence. He filled it with Himself, with His own heart which is the source of our inheritance and of our chalice. That He loves me so much does not arrest my attention. What astonishes me, what ought to make me die of grief, is that we do not love Him more than other souls. What amazes me is that He loves us even stained, unfaithful, ungrateful, even traitors—O prodigy of love—so that His tenderness for us seems to deepen and increase when we drag our dignity in the mire and repay His love with perfidy, even turning His own gifts, the pledges of His love and the fruits of His sufferings, against Him and against souls.

But so it is. He loves us in this way, and whoever has any experience with priestly souls can give testimony that Jesus, always patient with souls, is more so with priests. Always generous, with priests He is so without measure, and whereas He has a treasury of tenderness for all souls, He has chasms of it for priests. It seems to me that Jesus has special norms for priests in trying to pardon

---

1.   Cf. *Summa Theologiae* I, q. 20, aa. 2–4.

and transform them. There are special graces, exquisite tenderness, incredible patience, exceptional condoning and a superabundant measure of graces for priests. I am expressing my own opinion in stating that under circumstances in which I would be tempted to despair of other souls, I do not despair of the soul of a priest.

We priests are both the glory and the shame of Jesus, His comfort and His martyrdom, His most intense happiness and His most cruel pain. We are His strength and His weakness, His hope and His fear. We are His martyrdom. Thou hast placed us, O Jesus, in Thy Divine Heart, and there we must be. We may be the burning flame of Thy charity or the piercing cross of Thy pain. How we should thank Thee for uniting us closely to Thee, thank Thee that Thy Divine Heart may be for us a permanent dwelling place, and that we may be a flame therein. Even more should we thank Thee that we may be a cross, although we should like never to be one. The most divine proof that Thou dost love us is that Thou hast desired that we be a cross within Thy heart when, by our ingratitude, we do not choose to be a flame of love.

THE HOLY Spirit has lavished upon souls a love that resembles the love of the Heart of Christ. The love that bursts forth at the first breath of the Holy Spirit is a distant copy, but a faithful one, of the divine love which is burning in the Heart of Jesus. This love has something of the infinite, because the fountain from which it leaps—the Holy Spirit—never runs dry. Jesus referred to the Holy Spirit when He said, "If a man believe in Me...fountains of living water shall flow from his bosom" (John 7:38).

This love is also *one*, because it absorbs and coordinates all the affections of the soul, channels her entire energy, and directs all to God. It comprehends all the affections, includes all pleasures. Through this love the soul loves God in the manner He desires—as a father or as a friend, as a spouse or as a son. Because that love is a living portrait of eternal love, it shares in the latter's qualities. It is friendship because it is ardent and fecund. It is maternal love because it is unselfish and gentle. It is something that surpasses all these aspects of love because it is divine, because "it knows eternal life," because it is the reflection and participation of the love with which the Father loves Jesus and Jesus loves the Father.

Furthermore, this love is a singular love, because each soul is for God "one beyond compare" (Cant. 6:8). To express myself in an inadequate manner, each soul gives to God a unique impression that no other gives Him, as each man his own physiognomy. The love of one soul for God can resemble that of another, but the two loves are not the same, for each soul has its own special character, an exclusive way of imitating infinite love. God created each soul precisely in that way, in order that each soul might give Him a special impression, in order that each soul might love Him with a love which is never duplicated. The duty, happiness, and glory of each soul is to give to God, her Master, that love, that honor which no other will give. We ought to exert ourselves to be what God wants us to be, to give Him what He is waiting to receive from us.

The divine element in that love which the Holy Spirit pours into our souls is enclosed in the human element of our heart. It is a heavenly refreshment which God drinks from the fragile chalice of our earthly heart, a divine pearl embedded in rough clay, an exquisite perfume in an unfired clay urn, a brilliant star veiled by an opaque cloud. I dare to express my thoughts on this point in the following way: in this contrast God finds (in our way of speaking) the fascination of our love. He wants the divine to be loved by a wretched creature. Our insignificance enhanced by divine love attracts Him. He takes a complacency in looking at His gifts, in beholding His own image in the frailty of our being. He wants to experience the satisfaction of descending even to the dust and depositing there a germ of His glory, to pour out into the immense trench of our nothingness the plenitude of His lavished love. But why continue? Can one perhaps penetrate the mystery of the innermost sentiments of God?

But the mystery exists; God must find a charm in our poor hearts, for He has told us: "My delight increasing with each day…with the sons of Adam for my play-fellows" (Prov. 8:30).

Philosophers have said that love makes those who love equal, although they may not have been so previously. That composite of the divine and the human proper to Jesus assimilates divine love, which is also composed of an element from heaven and another from earth. Our attraction toward Jesus lies in touching the divine through the human, to see the infinite in the terrestrial, to see greatness become small through love, and enamored majesty covered with misery. I suspect that the fascination of God is the same, but inverted to fill our emptiness with His plenitude, to see wretchedness raised even to heaven, and to see nothingness exalted even to the divine. Both loves have a mixture of the divine and the human. It was necessary that love descend from heaven so that earthly love might ascend. It was necessary that the infinite be brought low to divinize nothingness. In that blessed formula discovered by wisdom and love, both loves, one of heaven and one of earth, were established on a common plane, attaining as far as possible the equality love demands and, upon meeting, were affected the one by the other and were united and mingled in one embrace of love.

It is sweet and consoling to contemplate and to understand this truth: that God is pleased to be loved as we love Him, in the midst of darkness and wretchedness, with the timidity of one who is lowly, with the vicissitudes proper to earth, with the vacillation of the weak, with the eclipses of the transitory. In spite of those imperfections and out of consideration for the divine that the Sanctifier has placed in it, He accepts our poor love with the daring of its desires, the sublimity of its heroism, the force of its generosity, the purity of its disinterestedness, the ardor, the strength, the constancy and the immortality of the divine. How it must please God that we are clean in the midst of mire, faithful in dangers, loyal in struggle, loving in trials, steadfast in vicissitudes, and that in the midst of tears our love smiles up to

Him, and that by struggling through earth's miseries and against the weakness of our own heart, we bravely say to Him: "I love Thee in spite of everything; Thou knowest it, Thou canst be sure of my love!"

Jesus desires especially that souls participate in His priestly love. To all of us He said: "Your love for one another is to be like the love I have borne you" (John 13:34). Consequently, all Christians should bear in their hearts a copy of Jesus' love for souls.

But He wants some souls to share in that love in a special manner—priestly souls. The fruit of the priesthood is purity, its essence is sacrifice, but its beginning is love, a love forgetful of self, a generous love that realizes those words of Jesus: "I dedicate Myself for their sakes, that they too may be dedicated through the truth" (John 17:19). And those other words of St. Paul: "For my own part, I will gladly spend and be spent on your souls' behalf" (2 Cor. 12:15). It is a love eager to glorify the Father and to be sacrificed for souls.

This love is the characteristic virtue of priests, and it should also belong to souls who must exercise the mystical priesthood. All these souls ought to carry in their heart the pure, exquisite, priestly sentiments that Jesus bears in His heart. Like Him, they should be completely forgetful of themselves. Jesus did not seek His own glory; neither should they. Jesus had not a place to rest His head; neither should they. Having had joy set before Him, Jesus chose the Cross. "Let us fix our eyes on Jesus, the origin and the crown of all faith, who, to win His prize of blessedness, endured the Cross and made light of its shame" (Heb. 12:2). Sacerdotal souls should do likewise. Jesus, wearied, sat upon the edge of Jacob's well, forgetting to eat, content with the food and drink of His Father's will and sighing for laborers to reap the abundant harvest of souls that He foresaw down the centuries (John 4:21). This is what priestly souls should be—laborers for the harvest.

The priest does not live for himself alone, but for others, for souls. All his powers and all his graces are for them; for them should be his time, his prayers, his desires, his sacrifices, his life. He is the servant of his brothers, like the Son of Man who did not come to be served (Matt. 20:28).

In order to be a priest, to be a sacerdotal soul, one must be forgetful of self and fill one's heart with that immense love, so pure, disinterested and selfless, which fills the Heart of Jesus. Like Him, the priest ought to encompass in his heart all souls: those of the poor and of the rich, the wise and the ignorant, those that rejoice and those that suffer, the good and the bad, the select and the ordinary, all, even the defiled, the degraded, even those who seem to belong to Satan and his work of hatred.

Father Lacordaire used to say to the simple faithful: "It is not enough to say, 'I want to save myself,' but you must say, 'I want to save the world.'" It is the only horizon worthy of a Christian, because it is the horizon of charity. What should a priest say?

Universal in regard to the souls it embraces, priestly love should also be universal in regard to the sacrifices it imposes on itself. No sacrifice is outside the priestly orbit. A Christian can discriminate among sacrifices and put a limit to them. For a priest, there is no limit, nor is there place for discrimination. His heart is disposed for every sacrifice, because the Heart of Jesus was so disposed. Wealth, honor, well-being, time, tastes, health, life, all should be sacrificed for souls. Theologians may argue about what obliges and what does not oblige a priest as a strict duty. Priestly love does not argue; zeal does not examine into duty, because love has no measure, nor does it recognize limits. Its resemblance to Jesus' love is impressive.

Universal in embracing all souls and in desiring every sacrifice, sacerdotal love is also universal in regard to time. There is no moment of the priestly life that should not be steeped in zeal. The priest is not one intermittently but forever. He will be a priest eternally, and his love and zeal likewise ought not admit intermissions nor interruptions. He must love sacerdotally in vigils and in sleep, in labor and in rest, in activity and in contemplation, in sorrow and in joy, in failure and in success. At each instant his life should be a fire of love, an inextinguishable, devouring flame of zeal, a love that does not rest, a zeal that is never mitigated, a fire that is always burning, producing a flame that rises to heaven, like a longing for the glorification of God, like an uninterrupted supplication for souls, which spreads throughout the world eager to ignite all souls.

Sacerdotal love must also be universal in regard to the forms that it assumes to save souls. "I have been everything by turns to everybody, to bring everybody salvation," said St. Paul (1 Cor. 9:22). Love becomes all things. It becomes strength for the weak, comfort for those who suffer, a support for those who waver, a light for those who live in the shadows. It is a child with children, wise with the sage, simple with the ignorant, an artist with artists, a father to orphans, a friend to the friendless, generous with the needy, a teacher for those who seek the truth, a source of joy for souls thirsting for happiness; in a word, it lives in the atmosphere of each individual soul.

If in the priestly care of all souls, love establishes degrees and marks differences, they conform to the order of Jesus' love and His divine predilection, for the priest loves more what Jesus loved more. Jesus loved with a singular predilection priests, the lowly, and the needy. There is rank in love because love is ruled by wisdom, but this order neither flesh nor blood nor the will of man, much less caprice, marks out, but the Holy Spirit, who is the love that proceeds from the Father, the source of all order, and from the Word, who is order because He is wisdom begotten.

If the priest has preferences in the universality of sacrifices at his disposal, they are the same as those of Jesus. He prefers the most loving because they are the most efficacious, the most arduous because they are the most loving, and the most cruel because he thirsts to suffer.

Sacerdotal love is opportune, because at each instant it motivates the work of that moment—the one marked out by the most holy will of God.

How beautiful, how deep, how broad, how constant, how

well-ordered is priestly love! Like a reflection of Jesus' love, it has all its aspects without losing its divine unity. Though embracing all souls, it gives to each individual soul what is most suitable for it. It is governed by wisdom without allowing itself to be absurd. It has order without having measure. It is immolated without losing happiness. It is active without loss of tranquility; fruitful without failing to be pure; serene without excluding all holy emotions; devoted and prudent, sweet and strong, condescending and firm, immutable and movable, despoiled and enriched, fountain of all joys and of all sorrows. Oh, if all priests would love as Jesus loved! If all priestly souls would carry within them that infinite love!

CHAPTER 24

Love's Suffering

The interior of the Sacred Heart, an abyss of love and a sanctuary of purity, is also a prodigy of pain, and these three, as we have already mentioned, are intimately connected.

Love, which is a turning toward the good, is also a turning away from the evil contrary to the good which is loved. Therefore, all love bears hate within it. God, who loves Himself infinitely, hates sin infinitely. But in God, love and hate are joy and happiness. On earth, however, turning away from evil frequently means pain. Therefore, all earthly love has sorrow bound up with it. Sorrow is love in the presence of evil. If evil did not exist on earth, neither would suffering. Suffering did not exist before evil was introduced on earth by the defection of our first parents. Accordingly, the evils encountered by love are changed into sorrows. If evil is vast and indestructible, sorrow is hopeless and sterile; such is the sorrow of hell. There the entire capacity of the soul is filled with a comfortless and hopeless sorrow.

On earth all ills have a remedy or a consolation, and love reacts upon them according to its quality and conditions. Let us limit ourselves to the love of God. Some evils are obstacles to love and, in order to eliminate them, love is converted into purifying pain. Other evils are found in the very nature of love and can be reduced to one—absence of the beloved. Since the only evil for love is not to possess totally the beloved object, in the presence of that evil, love is changed into unifying sorrow. But when love has attained its perfection, its only sorrows are those of the beloved, and in opposition to them love becomes expiation and redemption.

SUCH WAS Jesus' sorrow, for He did not need to be purified, nor did He assume human nature without the full possession of God. It may be said that He had unifying sorrow in respect to souls, but this very sorrow is intimately united with redeeming pain.

The cause of all Jesus' suffering is sin, an evil in respect to God because it opposes His glory, an evil in respect to souls because it opposes their perfection and happiness. Upon reacting against this evil, which in a sense is infinite, the love of the Sacred Heart was changed into unutterable pain. That suffering has something of the divine, it is the infinite hatred that God has for sin, which in the bosom of the divinity cannot be pain. When reflected in the Heart of Jesus, it became an incomprehensible sorrow. In God this hatred is sanctity and justice; in the souls of the reprobate, it produces hell; in the Heart of Jesus it elicited those sorrows the Scripture dared to call the sorrows of Hell. Because of the divinity in Jesus' suffering, it surpasses all the sorrows of earth. Man can suffer deeply. The capacity of our soul for suffering is immense, but however numerous, however cruel, however deep our sorrows may be, they always have the narrowness of the human. In Jesus, the divinity placed in suffering something of the infinite, for in Jesus the Word suffers, and the cause, the intensity, and the manner of the suffering has something of the divine.

One cannot comprehend the suffering of Jesus because His love cannot be comprehended, because the divine cannot be comprehended. The maximum that we on this earth can understand and say of the divine is that it is above everything created, just as the most that can be said of the firmament is that its dimensions have nothing in common with the narrow dimensions of earthly things. Therefore, the most that can be said of Jesus' sorrow is that it is inexpressible, that it is above all known sorrows and that even the greatest sufferings on earth are as nothing in comparison with this immense suffering.

Gather together in thought and imagination all the sorrows suffered by men since the beginning of the world and all that they will suffer until the end of time. What a variety of martyrdoms! What intensity of pain! What an accumulation of suffering! The suffering of Jesus far surpasses this inconceivable mass of pain, as space surpasses our planet, as the light of the sun is a thousand times greater than all the little lights of earth, because that sorrow holds the infinite in its grasp, and this makes it bitter, intense, deep, unutterable.

In order that such sorrow might exist, a miracle was necessary, a mystery. It was necessary that the Word of God be united hypostatically with human nature, that the infinite and the wretched be intertwined so that eternal love could suffer and the infinite might fit into human pain. Of all the celestial elements that form the interior of Jesus' heart, the most understandable is sorrow. Who is not acquainted with it? Who has not felt it? To whom is suffering not more or less familiar? Love and purity are heavenly things, but suffering is earthly. It is our inseparable companion; it breeds in our innermost being; it is the fruit of our wretchedness; it is something of our own; it is something intimate. Nevertheless, with pain so well known to us, Jesus' suffering is as incomprehensible to us as His love and purity. Perhaps in some ways it is more difficult to understand, for we see only dimly how purity and love can be infinite, but how can we conceive that mysterious mixture of infinity and misery which comprises Jesus' suffering? We know earthly sorrow, but how shall we ever grasp the concept of divine sorrow?

All the sorrows of Jesus share in that divine character, as all the parts of a tree share in the nourishment of its sap. Even the sufferings of the most sacred body of Jesus, even His exterior ignominies have an immensity, an incomparability that makes them superior to ordinary ignominies and suffering. But just as the fragrance of a tree is concentrated in the chalice of its flowers, in the pulp of its mature fruit, so Jesus' sorrow is concentrated in an immense bitterness, in an incredible intensity, in an inexhaustible quantity in the precious flower and exquisite fruit, His Divine Heart. There suffering is most terrible, because there love is most divine. Like an aroma from heaven, this love saturates everything about Jesus. His words of life are love. His prodigies are love, His steps, full of majesty and grace, are love, His celestial smile is love, His fruitful benedictions are love. And because all these are embalmed with love, they are also impregnated with sorrow. Thus, the Sacred Heart, fountain of love's aroma, is itself a perpetual source of suffering.

If that ocean of bitterness were distributed throughout human hearts, it would cause their death, for who can withstand a superhuman sorrow? Let us acknowledge that the sorrow of Jesus is as incomprehensible as His love, and let us adore the mystery in silence.

O JESUS, how couldst Thou have lived thirty-three years, bearing in Thy heart that immense sorrow? How couldst Thou smile with Thy heart lacerated? How didst Thy serenity conceal Thy unspeakable interior martyrdom? However we contemplate Thee, Thou dost seem to us most beautiful, sublime, divine, but—permit me to say this to Thee—Thou art most beautiful when I catch a glimpse of Thy suffering. The summit of Thy life is Calvary, and the summit of Thy heart is pain; it is the interior cross that crowns Thee. Never do I appreciate Thy love more than when I envision the magnitude of Thy sufferings. When I consider them, I say with all the conviction of my soul: "Jesus loves me, since He suffered so greatly for me."

Thy greatness, Thy goodness, Thy sweetness, Thy serenity, the captivating harmony of Thy whole being are exalted as they shine before the eyes of my soul when I look at them permeated with Thy suffering. The other veils with which Thou dost cover Thy charms appear opaque—probably they are not suited to my smallness—but this veil of sorrow seems transparent and fine. It allows the infinite, the divine that Thou dost conceal, to shine through. Never art Thou greater, more divine, more beautiful than when Thou art suffering. Perhaps it is because suffering, a most familiar thing to us, accommodates itself better to our wretchedness. Perhaps its humanity makes us perceive Thy unique, incomparable charm more clearly by reason of the striking contrast.

BUT LET us presume to examine, as far as our smallness will permit, that mysterious suffering. Its origin is lofty and absolutely selfless because it is divine love. All our sufferings are mixed more or less with the fine dust of egoism, even the most noble and holy, and on this account they cannot be perfectly pure nor can they reach a high degree of intensity. But I suspect that the more selfless the pain, the more intense it becomes, as a perfume is more intense when less diluted, as gold is more valuable when it contains less dross, as the diamond shines more brightly when it is more pure.

In the suffering of Jesus all is divine love. Love is the only source of His suffering. One can suffer with love, on account of love, love being at the same time the support of suffering and the executioner. But love is not the executioner when it immolates; love immolates because it is a priest, as the Church sings: *"Amor sacerdos immolat."* The priest and the executioner, although they both immolate, are worlds apart.

In the charity of Jesus, love is the only thing that immolates; it is a priestly love. Its end is divine: the glory of the Father and the good of souls, for the suffering of Jesus is a glorifying and redeeming love. And so the fruit of that love is also divine; it is the purity of souls, which like clear mirrors reflect the glory of God. That sorrow in itself is divine; I have already asserted that. It is the earthly translation of the infinite hate which God has for sin. It is that divine hate which, by being reflected in the divine and human Heart of Jesus, is changed into unspeakable sorrow.

An incomprehensible mystery surrounds Jesus. During His entire mortal life He bore in His heart the joys of heaven and the sorrows of hell, since He always had the beatific vision in the superior part of His soul, while at the same time the lower part was plunged into an abyss of suffering. How to explain that strange combination? It is a mystery, no doubt, but if we may use conjecture, I would say that infinite love, which in God is infinite hate, is reflected in Jesus in a marvelous manner. Because it was love, it communicated to Him the joys of heaven, and because it was hate it filled Him with horrible pain. Is it not one same divine reality, is it not the love of God alone that causes the blessedness of the elect and the hell of the reprobate? Is not love like the column of fire that guided the Israelites in their wandering in the desert, a luminous column for the people of God and darkness for the forces of Satan?

Let this be as it may, it is certain that the sorrow of Jesus is intense, cruel, incomprehensible, unmitigated, not only on account of its source, because love alone caused it; not only on account of its fruit—the sinlessness of souls and the glory of God—but also because it is most pure in itself. It admits neither alleviation nor comfort. It is pure as the infinite is pure. It is pure as all that reflects the infinite is pure, even though it may be sorrow.

CHAPTER 25

‎֍‎

Burdened with Opprobrium

In the deep sorrows of the Heart of Jesus we may discern shades and degrees that convey to us a truer idea of the nature of those sorrows.

Without doubt, the most terrible impression produced in the Sacred Heart, so eager for the glory of God, was the oppressing knowledge that our sins were offenses against God and hindrances to His glory. The entire energy of love in Jesus' heart was concentrated upon the glory of God, the supreme good after the infinite good, who is God Himself. The love of Jesus recognizes but one good, God, and this good can be considered in Himself and in His reflection in creatures, which is the divine glory.

Jesus takes boundless complacency in God considered in Himself. In this good, which is above all, there is no shadow of evil nor can any evil oppose it; but that supreme good in its reflection in creatures—the glory of God—is opposed by offenses against God, which, as theologians teach, have a malice that is in a certain sense infinite. Jesus loves God's glory passionately as the sole object of His tremendous love, with all the strength with which His heart is capable. With that same passionate strength of love, He hates sin, which opposes the glory of God, and that hate is converted into sorrow within the interior of the Sacred Heart.

To understand this sorrow, it would be necessary to understand these incomprehensibles: the love of Jesus for the glory of God, the malice of sin and the number and varieties of all sins that have been committed and will be committed until the end of time. It would also be necessary to understand these profundities: the abyss of goodness in the glory of God, the abyss of love in the Heart of Jesus, the abyss of malice in sin, as well as the countless number of sins. These chasms form the abyss of sorrow in Jesus' heart.

Who knows God as Jesus knows Him? Who loves God as Jesus loves Him? Who knows and hates sin as Jesus does?

The panorama of all the world's sin before the eyes of Jesus weighed upon His heart. Who can comprehend the frightening profundity of these words of Scripture: "God laid on His shoulders our guilt, the guilt of us all" (Is. 53:6). Not only did Jesus see sin as a terrible spectacle, stretching out through the ages, offending His most pure gaze and wounding His loving heart, but He saw it as something for which He was responsible, because God placed upon Him the iniquities of us all.

Strange suffering! Purity itself to bear every filthiness! Boundless love to feel itself oppressed by all offenses against the Beloved! Supreme justice to feel itself responsible for all injustices! What a contrast! Who can tell the pain, the humiliation, the shame that those contrasts produced in the Heart of Jesus? We have already seen it to be beyond comprehension that the greatness of divine nature and the smallness of human nature are united in one Person. Who can grasp the idea that purity and sin, love and evil are united in the Sacred Heart, that in the abyss of all virtues God has placed the abyss of all iniquities? Who can tell the suffering that so strange a partnership must have produced? St. Paul expressed this mystery by saying: "Christ never knew sin, and God made Him into sin for us, so that in Him we might be turned into the holiness of God" (2 Cor. 5:21).

This unique suffering had diverse aspects or shades according to their relation to each one of the divine Persons. In respect to the Father, it was indignation upon seeing His majesty offended, deepest sorrow upon seeing the glory taken away from Him by sin, divine shame upon feeling Himself burdened with the sins of the world, and incomprehensible bitterness upon perceiving that, in a certain sense, He could not hinder the loss of the glory of love, though He was longing to give Himself without reserve.

In respect to the Word, that contrast is, in my judgment, pre-eminent, though in vain do I try to explain it. In Him are united the infinite whiteness of God and the blackness of sin—also infinite in a certain respect—the glory of love and the ignominy of sin. Those contradictions had to precipitate a catastrophe, and they did precipitate one, for the anguish of Jesus is a terrible catastrophe. Furthermore, Jesus saw and felt in the depths of His heart something like a frightening impotence to hinder the evil. It was evident that He would blot out many sins and that His merits sufficed to erase them all, but many, very many, would never be blotted out. Confirmed forever, made eternal and irreparable, the sins of the reprobate would never be blotted out, but would live on from century to century. They would be punished in justice, it is certain, giving glory to God in another form, but as an indestructible monument of human malice and inconceivable ingratitude. Perhaps, feeling this aspect of His immense grief, He cried out to the Father in Gethsemane, "My Father, if it is possible, let this chalice pass Me by" (Matt. 26:39).

In respect to the Holy Spirit, Jesus felt how sin saddens infinite Love, how it destroys or hinders the sanctifying work of the Holy Spirit, how this divine Perfecter fails in many souls, how He will never consummate His work except with the consummation of punishment and misfortune in hell. The Holy Spirit is purity, sin is filthiness; the Spirit is light, sin is darkness; the Paraclete is love, sin carries in its bosom the germs of hate; the Holy Spirit is fecundity, sin is sterility; the Sanctifier is harmony, beauty, perfection, but sin is dissonance, mutilation, ugliness, and monstrous malformation. Jesus desired that His Spirit be not saddened, but that His work be finished and His ideal idealized. Although it is true that by dint of suffering Jesus would blot out many sins, some would never be blotted out, but would sadden the Spirit eternally. These filled Jesus with a desolate anguish. But let us leave this mystery of pain to consider another aspect of Jesus' suffering, because it pertains to us.

By OPPOSING the glory of God, sin effects a momentous disaster, tearing away from souls their beauty—a reflection of God's glory— and thus depriving them of their life, a sharing in the divine glory. Sin robs them of happiness. It darkens the image of the Most Holy Trinity within them. It makes them sterile and, what is worse, it barters the fruits of life, which they ought to produce, for fruits of death. It impedes a series of graces which these souls ought to receive and a series of good deeds which they ought to perform. It snatches them from the bosom of God, from the Heart of Jesus, to place them under the ignominious tyranny of Satan. It would precipitate them into hell itself if Jesus did not snatch them back with the strength of His love and His suffering.

Jesus loves souls with an unspeakable tenderness, with a boundless intensity, as children, as spouses, as pieces of His own heart. If a mother feels within herself the ills of her offspring, if she would die of grief to know her children were to be condemned, what must Jesus have felt upon seeing the terrible evils which so many souls would suffer on account of sin? He bore us all in His heart and in it He felt all our misfortunes. Our ills are His ills and His heart suffered them all, only much more than we suffer, for He was a thousand times more alert and sensitive to them than we. As a mother plunges herself into any danger to save her child, Jesus cast Himself into the abyss of suffering to save us. But alas, many will be lost, and to my way of thinking, that was the most terrible of His sufferings. As a mother caresses her dying son for the last time, feeling the dreadful impotence of love before the mystery of death, so Jesus must have caressed the reprobate souls the last time—what a dreadful expression—with unutterable anguish. Feeling the frightful impotence of His love before the mystery of eternal death, He must tear pieces, as it were, from His heart—those souls which were to fall into disfavor forever.

O Jesus, our poor hearts are moved by looking from afar at Thy inconceivable anguish and we catch a glimpse of the gigantic struggle, the nameless agony of Thy heart, which is revealed to us a little, a very little, but nothing more. The rending echo of Thy heart reaches even to the depth of our soul: "My Father, if it be possible, let this chalice pass Me by" (Matt. 26:39). It had to be Thee, Jesus, who suffered that disconsolate anguish, and it had to be Thee who added to the words of Thy agony the cry of heroic love: "Only as Thy will is, not as Mine is" (Matt. 26:39).

But this immense sorrow was not the only one that souls caused Thee. We have all, except Thy incomparable Mother, given Thee the bitter chalice of ingratitude to drink. Truly, Thou hast experienced ingratitude. With Thy exquisite and unique sensitivity, with Thy delicate tenderness, how must that bitter chalice have tasted to Thee? To be indifferent to Thy love, to Thy delicacy, to Thy tenderness, to Thy solicitude, to Thy loving invitations, to Thy noble forgetfulness of our offenses, to Thy generous pardon, to Thy immense grief, to Thy nameless ignominies, to the Precious Blood of Thy body, to the ineffable blood of Thy heart, this is monstrous ingratitude.

We have all been indifferent, Lord; all of us have passed near Thy precious Cross, and seeing Thee agonizing on it, have given Thee the gall and vinegar of our inexplicable ingratitude to drink. Thou has tasted that most bitter draught and, sated with ingratitude, Thou hast responded to it by offering for the ingrates the bitterness of Thy soul. Thou hast accomplished the prodigy of changing into life and sweetness the gall and vinegar which our ingratitude gave Thee to drink.

Who is like to Thee, Jesus most sweet? Who loves as Thou dost love? Who suffers as Thou dost suffer? May Thou be praised forever and ever.

CHAPTER 26

✣

Our Response to Love

If we could only understand what we have cost Jesus! If we could dispose ourselves at least to think about what He suffered for each one of us! Our souls are enveloped in His tenderness and in His pain. We are the fruit of His love and His martyrdom. We unceasingly receive His gifts of all kinds. We receive them tranquilly, at times joyfully. But those gifts are marked with the blood of Jesus, the blood from His veins and from His heart. In order that we might taste the least of His heavenly consolations, Jesus had to taste the gall and vinegar of interior desolation. In order that our souls might remain spotless, Jesus had to shed His blood to purify them. Each degree of grace, which for us is a degree of glory, was for Jesus a degree of incomprehensible suffering, and each Communion we receive cost Jesus the sacrifice of Calvary and the interior sacrifice of His heart. Holy Communion is a banquet from heaven prepared with the blood of Jesus and the bitterness of His heart. It has all savors, because it was made with the condiment of all sufferings; it is the remembrance of His passion, but a living remembrance which brings us Christ's whole passion under the Eucharistic species.

We do not understand what one Communion is, nor the gift given to us in it, nor the tremendous suffering which that sublime gift cost Jesus.

We could discourse in a similar way upon all God's graces; all are dyed in His blood and saturated with bitterness. The light shining in our spirit, the love burning in our heart, the strength sustaining our soul, the virtues adorning it, the gifts of the Holy Spirit that deify it, the fruits of the Sanctifier, the grace that makes us sharers in the nature of God, the charisms, our present graces of preservation, graces of sanctification, all that form the world known as the spiritual life—all is the fruit of love and sorrow, all came forth from the Sacred Heart, and all conserve the heat of its flames and the bitterness of its martyrdom, although this bitterness is usually changed for us into sweetness.

If all the graces we receive were the fruit of love alone, there would be sufficient motive for us to die of gratitude and to make every sacrifice in order to correspond with that ineffable love. But if these graces are also the fruit of Christ's suffering, which lacerated the Divine Heart, causing it to bleed, how can there ever be gratitude sufficient to acknowledge them and love adequate to correspond with them? The contemplation of the interior of Jesus' heart would of itself suffice to sanctify us without measure. Why do we turn away our eyes and our heart from that Heart, the only object worthy of our life?

HOWEVER, WE ought to take into consideration that not all souls cost Jesus the same price, because all are not equally loved, as has been stated previously. Love has its hierarchy, and corresponding to this is the hierarchy of suffering. Upon a soul's place in these two hierarchies depend the quantity and quality of the grace she receives.

To these heaven-appointed hierarchies should correspond the hierarchy of reciprocating love in souls. I mean, the more Jesus loves

a soul, the more He suffered for her, the more graces He prepares
for her; and the more graces a soul receives, the more she cost Jesus.
The more a soul is loved, the more she ought to love.

Jesus said of Magdalen that she loved much because much was
forgiven her. This is the rule that I have just expressed, but it applies
not only to forgiven souls, but with even greater reason to those
preserved from serious sin. He who receives more should love more.

In the love of the Heart of Jesus there are two hierarchies, one
official and the other intimate. On the summit of the first are the
priests; on the summit of the second are the saints. Perhaps in the
designs of God these two hierarchies should correspond to each
other, that is, the holiest ought to be the priests. Is this not inferred
from what Jesus asked St. Peter and—keeping due proportion—
from what He asks each priest: "Dost thou care for Me more than
these others?" (John 21:15). To love more than others is to be holier
than they.

It seems to me that this parallelism of the hierarchies is unde-
niable if it is understood in a broader sense, namely, that the holiest
souls ought to be the priestly souls. Included in this category, of
course, are those who exercise a mystical priesthood. Be that as it
may, it is certain that we priests are favorites of Jesus. We receive
more graces than other souls; we occupy a place of honor in the
Divine Heart and consequently we cost Jesus more intense and
more cruel sufferings. Whatever is most excellent in the interior
cross of Jesus' heart is for us priests; it is our glory; it is the highest
stimulus to our love; it is our hope and it should almost be our
sorrow.

Because we cost Jesus so much, we must not be lost. Must those
choice graces, those interior sorrows of Jesus' heart be squandered?
Are we going to give Jesus, in addition to the griefs that we cost
Him, the unspeakable sorrow of casting us forth from His heart? If
the loss of a soul is so terrible for the Sacred Heart, how horrendous
must it be if a priest is lost? This consideration alone should suffice

to sanctify us. Because we cost Jesus so much, we should appreciate our dignity and preserve our priestly graces as a treasure, making them fruitful in their full plenitude. We ought to guard them as a most rich and valuable treasure. We cost so much; we are worth so much!

To protect ourselves is to protect Jesus, to protect His love, to protect His suffering, to protect the precious fruit of His tenderness and martyrdom. One understands, or at least glimpses dimly, that Jesus loves us so much, that we cost Him so much, that He desires our sanctification, working wonders to save us and to transform us into Him. How can we possibly want His intimate gifts to be sterile? His costly love complains of our ingratitude, for there is no ingratitude comparable to the ingratitude of a priest.

ON THE pinnacle of the second hierarchy are the saints, those souls who have received precious and abundant graces for arriving at a high degree of perfection. We have no idea of the graces a soul needs to be sanctified, graces of preservation that it may be kept from sin or, at least, be faithful in the midst of the innumerable dangers of this life. Souls are aware of some of these graces but not of others, for who can know all the dangers from which the Lord has preserved him?

A soul needs graces of purification, for even innocent souls, even those most richly endowed, have so many evil inclinations, so much dust of the earth, so many miseries and deficiencies. One does not know all the malice, even though it be germinal in nature, all the dust, all the wretchedness that there is in the best of souls, excepting of course, the ever Virgin Mary. Neither does one realize the complete selflessness that sanctity exacts and, consequently, the series of purifications which a soul needs to arrive at sanctity.

To arrive at union with God the soul needs torrents of choice graces: light to see God as the only ideal of her life; divine attraction, so that leaving everything, the heart may be drawn by invisible

things, thus overcoming the almost irresistible attraction of creatures. Then the heart may be fixed, as the Church says, where true
joys are to be found. Courage is needed to run the rough and sometimes bloody road along which one goes to God; strength to struggle, to resist, to conquer, to suffer.

OVER AND above the graces which prepare the soul for union, there
is the grace of union itself which is so remarkable. That God unites
Himself to the soul with singular love; that the Holy Spirit makes
her His temple and rules and guides her in almost all her move-
ments, making them divine; that the soul be transformed into Jesus
and live His life and share in His mysteries; that the Father regard
her complacently and complete her adoption; that the soul have
the very sentiments of Jesus and participate in His divine fecundity; that she be elevated to the contemplation of heavenly things
and receive divine kisses and caresses, until the moment arrives for
entering into the fullness of the joy of the Lord—all this is a stupendous grace. It is the grace of graces, fruit of the predilection of Jesus
and of His deepest sorrows.

Souls who have been raised to these heights have received and
continue to receive God's singular graces copiously. They are greatly
loved by Jesus and they cost Him much, very much. What should
be their love and their correspondence with grace?

PART FOUR

THE DIVINE REPOSE

CHAPTER 27

☩

Holy Abandonment

The Holy Gospel relates that after the apostles made a trial of their apostolic mission, Jesus said to them: "Come away into a quiet place by yourselves and rest a little" (Mark 6:31). The Gospel tells us nothing of how that rest was taken, but we can easily conjecture what peace, love and happiness that secret, intimate retreat with Jesus must have held for them.

There are occasions in life when God, approaching the soul, speaks similar words, inviting her with immense tenderness to rest sweetly within His Divine Heart and—dare I say it?—asking her to allow Him to rest in her.

Heaven is complete rest in the bosom of God, because earth is always a place of labor, of vicissitudes, of sorrow. The soul sighs to be freed from the anxieties of this life, as St. Paul desired: "I long to have done with it and be with Christ" (Phil. 1:23). But He, the divine friend, is pleased in granting to souls that love Him an experience of beatitude on this earth, in the heaven of His heart—is not that incomparable heart a heaven?—by inviting them to the repose of purity, love and peace within Himself.

Our poor heart longs for that rest because we are born for heaven. The work, the pain, the sufferings of this world do not constitute the definitive atmosphere of our soul. Our atmosphere is rest in God and it is formed by those divine elements of which I have spoken: light, purity, love, peace.

The divine oasis of the Sacred Heart, that secret and entrancing heaven, is opened up to the chosen soul who will find within an indescribable repose. Let the soul hasten to cast her cares and her worries into the flames of Christ's heart, there to be totally consumed. Trustful and happy, let her enter into the place of her repose to dwell in holy satiety, transported with light and with love. At the same time, the soul must be forgetful of earthly things in order to content herself with Jesus only, to bask in the splendor of the Heart that loves her so much, and to be filled with the holy fire, the celestial tenderness and the immortal life enclosed in that divine vessel.

Forgetfulness and surrender must be the dispositions of the soul that would rest in God. The forgetfulness of love! The surrender of love! Is it not love, possibly, that is forgotten and abandoned? In order to love, one must forget everything and center the gaze, the heart and the life upon the Beloved.

Therefore, Scripture speaks of such a soul as chosen "among ten thousand" (Cant. 5:10). Just as at dawn all the stars fade away so that the sun may shine in the sky, sovereign and alone, so also, in order that the mystery of love may be activated in souls, all creatures that scintillated in the night of our life must be obliterated, so that Jesus, a divine sun, may fill our souls with His victorious love.

At each stage of love and in each one of its unutterable mysteries, a new forgetfulness is necessary to let a new sun of love appear.

Yes, divine love demands a perfect forgetfulness of all earthly things. "Listen, my daughter," our Lord says to the soul, "and consider My words attentively. Thou art to forget henceforward thy own nation, and the house of thy fathers; thy beauty now is all for the king's delight" (Ps. 44:11–12). Like Moses, the soul ought to forget the things of Egypt, so that with bared feet and anointed with silence, she may penetrate into the desert of love and contemplate the divine vision in the burning bush. Joys and fears, anxieties and hopes, all must be forgotten. When creatures are silenced, Jesus will appear as the only one, the sovereign, the Sun of love which illuminates her whole being with light and life.

If love is oblivion, it is because it is abundance, plenitude of the Beloved, forgetfulness of all that is not He. Therefore, forgetfulness of all things should be accompanied by a new abandonment, new by reason of its complete fullness, new with the novelty of all that is final and eternal.

Even when the soul has always belonged to Jesus, because He has been her only love, because she has consecrated to Him every instant, perfuming Him with the fragrance of her sorrows, even then Jesus wishes that soul to surrender herself still more completely because He desires to possess her more intimately.

If we only knew how God longs to possess us! Love is possession, and as love is insatiable—because it is infinite or has the stamp of infinity—the lover is never sated with possessing the beloved. Even our poor hearts, so limited and miserable, have something of the infinite when love fills them, for they never tire of craving complete possession. If the human heart is never satisfied, how can the Heart of Jesus, both human and divine, be satiated with possessing the souls He loves so much?

At each new effusion of love, it seems to the soul that the love of Jesus has now spoken its final word; it seems to her that she cannot now conceive more perfect possession, more exquisite tenderness, deeper intimacy, holier fruitfulness. We forget that the love which prepares those delicious feats is infinite. Love has no final word and eternity itself will never hear it.

"Love has only one word, which it never repeats because it is forever speaking it," said Father Lacordaire. We heard this unique word in the far-off days of our childhood. That word, which we have never ceased hearing, whether in the fiery summer of youth, the autumn of life, or the placid winter of our existence, will continue to resound, majestic and solemn, in eternal life. It is ever new with the eternal, exhaustless, mysterious novelty of love.

But a new love, a new possession, demands a new surrender, more generous, more trustful, more tender than ever. And for such a surrender a new forgetfulness is necessary, one full and perfect.

To rest in the Heart of Christ is to submerge and lose oneself in Him. For these celestial attainments the soul must disappear in the ocean of oblivion, in the ocean of love.

But it does not suffice for the soul to prepare herself for that sweet, gentle repose within the Divine Heart. She must do something else more precious and sublime: offer her own heart to Jesus that He may come to rest there.

Holy Scripture mentions this rest of God: "God had come to an end of making, and rested on the seventh day, with His whole task accomplished" (Gen. 2:2).

God's rest is not the need that satisfies itself but the abundance that pours itself out. It is His work completed, His love taking eternal possession of the object of His love. His will fulfilled, His glory in brilliant splendor. Consequently, nothing enriches the soul more than God's repose within her, because this is the crowning of all her graces and the consummation of the divine mystery of love.

One secret and very appealing aspect of the divine repose merits our special consideration. Pure and perfect love makes the lover totally unmindful of his own welfare in favor of the good of the beloved. Our highest good is to repose in Jesus, because it is the satisfaction of our yearnings, the end of labor, perfect comfort in sorrow, the crown of virtue, the ineffable fruition of love. But there is something better than all this, more conducive to our happiness: it is the good of the beloved, the only thing that the true lover desires.

Willingly would the lover struggle perpetually with the vicissitudes
of life in order that the beloved might be contented and happy.

O wonderful effect of love! If the Beloved suffers, the lover
grieves unless she can suffer; if He rejoices, she rejoices, and the joy
of the Beloved is her perfect happiness. If He rests, she rests, nor can
she conceive of any other repose, for the only happiness of the one
who loves is the happiness of the Beloved.

If the place in which the Beloved rests is the very heart of the
lover, if He hears love's canticle calling to Him: "Into His garden,
then, let my true love come and taste His fruit" (Cant. 5:1), if He
comes and rests in the flowery garden of His spouse, the soul feels
a hidden happiness, indescribable and almost insupportable, for, if
we can scarcely support our own happiness, how can we support
that of the Beloved? What the soul experiences when it occurs to
her that Jesus is resting within her is not merely an ingenuous blush,
but a heavenly exaltation which transcends our natural capacity to
enjoy.

O most holy Virgin, what we least understand among all the
stupendous marvels of your soul is this: how were you able to sur-
vive, with Jesus abiding in you for thirty-three years, now resting
against your breast, again on your lap, and always in your heart,
your tenderness and your fidelity? To repose like John upon the
divine breast is something my mind conceives and seems to suit
our God-given capacity for happiness, but that Jesus may rest in
my heart! I can neither conceive it nor does it seem that any creature could support it, because it is to change the heart, the poor
creature's heart, into a replica of the Father's bosom, the everlasting
abode of Jesus' eternal repose.

Nevertheless, our souls sigh above all else for that insupportable
happiness, and meditating upon it, we experience an unspeakable
suffering, a divine paradox. We should like to flee and hide ourselves
within the earth so that Jesus might not rest in our heart, because we
think we could not support that happiness; and at the same time, we

should like to overturn the universe to have the happiness of Jesus resting in our heart, because that happiness, and only that, can fill the deep desire which love has hollowed in the very core of our being.

But let us not fear Jesus' rest in our heart. He demands so little in seeking His repose. He rested upon the manger straw; He rested upon the clumsy, swaying little boat on Lake Tiberias; He rested in the house of Bethany; He rested upon the rough, blood-drenched Cross. The one indispensable thing He needs in order to rest is love, a love that is constant, silent, tender and holy.

He needs humility also, very intense, very deep, but genuine and true, because such a humility does not close the door of the heart to Jesus, but opens it wide. Nor can the Beloved repose in anything but the most delicate humility that accommodates itself admirably to the demands of Jesus.

Everything upon which Jesus reposed in His mortal life has the stamp of humility: the manger, the boat, the Cross. In His mystical life He rests in tabernacles anointed with humility and in souls where humility has spread a soft couch inviting Him to rest.

The insignificance of the soul does not hinder Him, because He is enamored of smallness. Upon coming into this world, the Divine Word belittled Himself and He has remained pledged to smallness, because it is a remembrance of His passage through the earth, because it bears the perfume of His mortal life—idyll and tragedy of incomparable love. He loves smallness as the Israelites must have loved the manna of the desert, keeping it in the Ark of the Covenant; as St. Francis of Assisi in heaven must love the Umbria of his knightly adventures and the Portiuncula, his love's abode; as St. Thérèse must love the petals she used to throw at the statue of her Beloved; as all of us will surely love the steps of the earthly stairs that helped us ascend to love.

We seek greatness in order to rest. Jesus seeks smallness, because He knows very well that there is nothing so truly great upon earth as that which is insignificant in our poor human judgment.

Small is the manger, small is the boat, narrow is the Cross, and small are the tabernacles that Jesus chooses for His rest and His delight. He clothes the small with the immensity of His love, and to the little ones He entrusts the great missions of His providence.

239

Our miseries are no obstacle to Jesus' repose in our souls, for His merciful love He takes the sins of the world as He accepted the straw of the manger and the squalor of the rude boat. Our miseries, not because of their sinfulness but as a consequence of our nothingness and as signs of our abjection, are like the manger straw or the poor cloak that some apostle, no doubt, must have spread upon the boat so that Jesus might rest there.

Our miseries give a fragrance of earth to the place where Jesus rests. He loves this fragrance. At the same time these limitations guard the divinity in our souls while tempering its resplendence.

Let nothing deter the soul, then, from inviting the divine Spouse to rest within her. Let the Beloved come to His chosen one. The soft couch smoothed by humility, warmed by tenderness and perfumed with the fragrant myrrh of sacrifice is ready. Let the Beloved come to the manger, converted by love into a throne. Let Him come to His living cross and repose tranquilly in the refuge of a love, caressing and tender, delicate and strong, constant, faithful and holy.

CHAPTER 28

☙

The Soul's Repose in Jesus

A very trite, yet very exact, comparison is that of life with a river leaping turbulently and murmuring ceaselessly until precipitated into the ocean where it finds its rest. Life on this earth is in fact activity seeking rest, while life in eternity enjoys rest to the full. But just as the river in its long course settles into calm, silent pools, so our life has placid pools where the soul enjoys silence and peace. But whereas the calmness of the waves is transitory, the quietude of the soul can be lasting, although it has not as yet the immutability and majesty of eternity.

The ocean upon which the activity of our life embarks, the bottomless abyss of light and love in which the soul longs to be lost, is God. To be united to God, to be lost in Him, is rest for our spirit. "Our heart is restless until it rests in Thee," said St. Augustine, whose life until he was thirty years old was one continuous vexation. To rest is to possess God in fullness, security, tranquility, as far as this is possible on earth. It is to cast oneself into the infinite ocean of God to be completely lost in Him.

But God, being perfect unity and absolute simplicity, contains a measureless wealth of perfections. "God is light" (1 John 1:5),

"God is love" (1 John 4:16), said the beloved disciple who reposed on Jesus' breast.

And God is purity, fecundity and peace. Therefore, rest in God, although one entity, is marvelously multiplex; it has innumerable shades and most varied forms. To rest in God is to rest in light, in love, in purity, in fecundity, in peace. The Church asks for rest in light and peace for her departed souls: "*Requiem aeternam dona eis, Domine, et lux perpetua luceat eis. Requiescant in pace.*" We usually veil the sweetness of those words with the sad crepe of death, but they are words of freedom and of joy. They are a declaration of beatitude. To enjoy divine rest, one must die actually or mystically, because death is always the only door to true rest.

We have already stated this principle: in order to rest in Jesus, we need perfect forgetfulness, which is mystical death. St. John of the Cross thus describes perfect rest:

> Lost to myself I stayed
> My face upon my lover having laid
> From all endeavor ceasing:
> And all my cares releasing
> Threw them amongst the lilies there to fade.[1]

One must forget all, leave all, be "forgotten among the lilies," because perfect forgetfulness reaches into the realm of purity. Everything must cease. The majestic oblivion of death must descend upon the soul so that she may lean her face against the Beloved in the most delightful repose.

Not only during one particular stage of the spiritual life, but during our entire life we ought to leave all and forget all so that we may rest in Jesus. Creatures are disquieting. We disturb our own rest. To maintain divine tranquility in the soul, creatures must remain

---

1. *Poems of St. John of the Cross*, p. 13.

far away; the *I* must die so that only Jesus and the soul remain, permitting the latter to recline her face upon the Beloved. Hence, He implores all creatures not to awaken His love until she desires. She will never want to waken from this most happy slumber.

243

But one must not think that rest in God is idleness or inertia. There is no activity comparable to that of the soul when she is resting in Jesus, just as there is no earthly activity comparable to that of the blessed in heaven, and just as there is no comparison to the life of God, which is ineffable, eternal rest and infinite activity. The body rests when its activity ceases. The soul rests when its activity increases beyond all bounds, because it has found the goal of its desires and the substance of its happiness. To rest in light is to be submerged in infinite light, and to rest in peace is to be lost in unutterable peace. But when the soul has found that light and that peace, it is necessary that its activity become immense, that God increase the soul's strength so that it can contain the divine treasures.

But if rest in God presupposes death, that rest is true life because it is full of activity. St. Paul describes rest in God when he says: "You have undergone death and your life is hidden away now with Christ in God" (Col. 3:3). To rest in God is to die and to live. To rest in God is to die to all creatures and to live in Jesus, or rather, to have Jesus as the full and only life of the soul.

To rest in God is to feel that everything created has disappeared, as Moses and Elias disappeared from the gaze of the apostles on Tabor's height, and like them, to see no one but Jesus. When the soul has reached the height of transformation and sees nothing but Jesus—the only light of her spirit, the only love of her heart, the only fruitfulness of her life, the only reason for her existence, the only satisfaction of her desires—that soul has found the most delightful rest in Jesus.

Rest in Jesus, then, is loftiest perfection, consummate love and perfect happiness. Blessed are those who rest in Jesus!

Repose in Light

Let us consider one by one the principal forms of divine rest, and let us commence with rest in light, of which the Church speaks.

As those little nocturnal moths, greedy for light, keep flying around a lamp with tireless tenacity, so does the human spirit seek light. Souls do not always realize that desire for light, and ordinarily they understand better the natural desire for love; but the two desires are brothers. They are intimately connected and in the lofty realms of the spirit they seem to be blended. St. Augustine speaks of light as if it were the object and the end of love. "*Caritas veritatis*," he says, that is, "the charity of truth," the love of light. According to the doctrine of St. Thomas, although love brings us to the possession of God, this possession is fully realized by the intellect. The essence of heaven is the beatific vision—marvel of light—and beatific love is only a joyful consequence of divine contemplation. The blessed souls love without measure; they rest without fear and enjoy in plenitude, because they see God face to face, because they are bathed in unfailing light, because they live eternally in light.

We can rest in the light even in this world, because faith is "that which gives substance to our hopes" (Heb. 11:1), because Jesus, as He said in the Cenacle, has given us to know all He heard from the Father. Living faith that "finds its expression in love" (Gal. 5:7), when purged of its deficiencies by the gifts of the Holy Spirit and made clearer and sweeter through their influence, attains that rest in light even here in the soul's exile.

In the language and teaching of the Fathers, the active life is labor, struggle, the rough road that the soul travels painfully, whereas contemplation—fruit of faith and of the Holy Spirit's gifts, marvel of light, most pure light of those who love—is leisure, repose and peace. To rest in light is, consequently, to immerse the soul in infinite light, in the treasures of light eternal, in the unfathomable abyss of the divinity.

Although we may regard creatures with a very clear vision, our

spirit is not at rest, because each encounter, if it is a satisfaction to
the soul, is also an incitement to new efforts, to higher knowledge.
Each step of that stairway of light invites us to climb the next step.
The life of science is a constant investigation; it is an endless change
in which joys and triumphs are an oasis offering transient rest to the
spirit so that it may continue its laborious pilgrimage through the
limitless desert.

When the soul contemplates God in the divine light, she finds
her rest, because contemplation is the end of the road, the summit
of the ascent. It is not like the knowledge of creatures, a step in a
flight of stairs, a link of a chain. It is the royal dwelling to which all
stairs lead. It is the infinite and eternal ring from which hang the
multiple links of created things.

Eternity does not suffice to exhaust that divine contemplation, but the copious light that it emits, activating the blessed soul
eternally, is not the ray of any other light, nor a scintillation from
some other source, but it is the eternal outpouring of all light, the
supreme origin of all brilliance.

Therefore Jesus said: "Eternal life is knowing Thee, who art
the only true God, and Jesus Christ, whom Thou hast sent" (John
17:3).

Creatures, too, are contemplated in that divine light, but in
serenity, harmony and peace, as one from a mountain peak gazes
upon the shadowy slopes and the surrounding peaceful valleys. The
traveler, scouting through those valleys and clambering up those
mountain flanks, wearily surveys the terrain at each level, but in
fragments. From the summit he views it as a serene and harmonious whole. His spirit is not fatigued; on the contrary, it rests as it
expands under the spell of the limitless horizon.

To rest in light is to contemplate God and to see everything—
creatures and events, time and eternity from His luminous being
and through His deep, penetrating gaze.

Happy the souls that God introduces into the royal dwelling of divine contemplation! Happy those who look upon the world and life only from those lofty heights!

To behold God, His perfection, His love, His beauty, His secrets, His life; to see the light that has neither source nor beginning; to look upon the light engendered by the Father in the splendor of His holiness; to behold "that most happy light" which is eternal love, the kiss of fire between the Father and the Son; to be immersed in that light, triune and one to be bathed in those divine splendors, to be lost in that abyss of light—that is to rest in light.

The soul elevated to that indescribable repose contemplates in astonishment the spectacle of God's inner life and wonders at the marvelous facets of that light. Jesus reveals to her what He heard from the Father: the unity and trinity of God, the Incarnation of the Word, the mystery of the Cross, the Holy Eucharist, the Church, the priesthood, and souls. She sees all things from the eminence of Jesus' heart; she contemplates all through the divine eyes of her Beloved.

Then the souls rest in the silence and peace of those lucid contemplations. She enjoys that divine rest without anxiety, fear or constraint, and she knows through one sweet experience that conversation with wisdom has no bitterness and that intimate communication with God never produces tediousness.

BUT IT is necessary that the soul live in that light which God has poured out upon her in torrents. How beautiful a thing it must be to live in light! Thus souls will live in heaven. Thus they ought to begin to live on earth. Light is the habitat of souls, the food with which they are nourished, the air they breathe. Transparent crystals fashioned by a divine breath, souls are an immense reservoir for light. Their destiny is to be impregnated with light, their glory and their happiness to become luminous, to become light, according to St. Paul's audacious expression: "Once you were all darkness; now, in the Lord, you are all daylight" (Eph. 5:8).

To live in light is to live in closest contact with God through contemplation. It is to hold intimate relations with the Father, the Son and the Holy Spirit. It is to fill the mind with the clarity of heavenly things, and afterwards to transfigure the world with the gleam of that divine light, to idealize everything with the resplendent tint of heavenly effulgence, as the earth is transfigured and idealized when soaked with the mystic gold of the evening sun.

Light possesses the prerogative of transforming everything: it embellishes muddy spots and even makes unclean pools of water glisten. Even more, the light of God transforms exile, changing it into a copy of the Fatherland.

Viewed in that light, everything is good, as the Creator saw all things when they came from His hands. Although it is true that the imperfection of creatures and the terrible power of human liberty has stained the world with ugliness and uncleanness, the light of God, which Christ brought us and which for twenty centuries has been shining in the center of the Cross, suffices to purify the world and restore its pristine beauty, because that light shines in shadows and puts gleams of grandeur even into what is most abject.

In the brightness of that light, lepers are our brothers, as St. Francis saw them; smallness is transformed into greatness, as St. Thérèse of Lisieux showed us; miseries are precious, as Benigna Consolata discovered; suffering is a treasure from heaven, the Cross veils exquisite happiness, and we men are members of the mystical body of Jesus and living temples of the Holy Ghost, as St. Paul preached. The very uncleanness of sin, seen in the dazzling light of God, can neither obscure the divine image impressed upon the sinner's soul nor break the admirable harmony of the universe. Rather, through the wonderful strength of contrast, it makes the glory of God shine more brightly and more splendidly.

To live in light, to rest in light, means these three celestial things: to enter totally, to plunge oneself boldly into the secrets of divine contemplation; to impregnate, to flood the interior life of the soul with that heavenly brightness; and to transform the active life, to transfigure the world, exalting it with the light of God. Jesus desires that the soul invited to repose should perfect these three things in her life.

In the first place, the soul must not stop, either through timidity or lowly opinion of self, when Jesus invites her to penetrate the secrets of the divinity. Humility is not, nor can it be, an obstacle to the attainment of the most profound contemplation, but rather, a firm ladder for reaching it. Humility is light, the first rays of dawn that prepare for the outburst of light in the resplendent day of the spiritual life. Precisely because humility reveals to us our own smallness, it gives us a claim to the revelation of light, for it is written: "I give Thee praise that Thou hast hidden all this from the wise and the prudent and revealed it to little children" (Matt. 11:25). One does not enter the royal castle of light on his own feet, but in the divine arms, and to be carried in arms, we need to be small.

True spiritual modesty does not hinder divine communications but prepares for them and makes them more appealing. That delicate sentiment of the soul arises from her glimpse of the greatness of the Beloved, the sweetness of love and the immensity of happiness. Therefore if at first, modesty holds the soul back, making her concentrate upon herself, afterwards, by increasing desire and inflaming deep love, it casts her impetuously into the arms of the Beloved, into the bosom of love, into the ocean of happiness. One would say that the soul's momentary delay through diffidence, like relaxing moments before great enterprises, reconcentrates her energies so that she may dart into the unknown.

Is it not true that those glimmers of divinity reaching the spirit stop and attract at the same time? They stop, because the infinite is sensed, and they attract through the irresistible force that the divine has for our soul, which was formed for the divine. Let the soul be detained in due time, but let that detention be momentary, and let it prepare the soul for intense activity. Let the soul retire within

herself and gather up her energy in order to strike out with the
strength of God into the ocean of light.

THE SECOND requirement that Jesus makes of the soul preparatory
to rest in light, is that she live the interior life with the celestial
clarity of divine communication. Her interior life ought to consist
of some very intimate, luminous and sweet relations with the three
Divine Persons so that the words of St. Paul may be realized: "We
find our true home in heaven" (Phil. 3:20), and those other words
of St. John: "What is it, this fellowship of ours? Fellowship with the
Father and with His Son Jesus Christ" (1 John 1:3).

The soul needs to live interiorly in a constant, deep intimacy
with the three Divine Persons. Her interior life ought to be with the
Trinity, through the Trinity, in the Trinity. The triune and one God
should be her inseparable companion, her divine ideal, her repose
and her peace.

United to the Incarnate Word by the closest bonds of unspeakable
love and transformed into Jesus, the soul ought to love through the
Holy Spirit, perfectly surrendered to His action. Under the impulse
of the same Divine Spirit and united to Jesus, she should live and rest
in the bosom of the Father and glorify Him ceaselessly through the
loving, living offering of Jesus for souls, especially priestly souls.

As St. Paul advised Timothy to meditate upon these things and
to live in them (1 Tim. 4:16), so I advise. Let the soul enter fully
into the abyss of the divinity and share in the intimate life of God,
as far as the designs of God upon her demand. Dead to all earthly
things, let her be hidden with Jesus Christ in God.

THIRDLY, LET us note that not only the interior life of this soul
should be tinged with this celestial color, but even her active life,
which should be nothing but the overflow of her interior life. It
must be illuminated with the light of God, with the light of the
Trinity, which elevates and inspires lofty ideals.

Hence it is necessary that the soul see persons, events, creatures, everything, from light's elevation through the clear and penetrating eyes of the Beloved. Let us illustrate with an example. We receive a visitor; exteriorly, we conduct ourselves with the naturalness and courtesy proper to well-mannered persons. That visit will not differ externally from any other visit among persons the same rank. But this is nothing more than the veil. In reality, that visit ought to be a hidden but true extension of the soul's inner life, which should look at the visitor as Jesus sees him, a soul bearing the image of God, redeemed by the blood of Jesus, the living temple of God, and destined for eternal felicity. One must love him as Jesus loves him, endure him as Jesus endures him, sacrifice oneself for him as Jesus did, and do him good in the measure marked out by the designs of God. If we do this, the person who visits us will receive, perhaps without realizing it, a divine influx. Although that person might receive nothing, such a visit will, at any rate, be for that soul something meritorious, sweet, holy, a true prayer and intimate communication with God, for God yearns to communicate Himself always and by means of all creatures and all events. He desires the soul to come to Him for rest through all paths and at every instant.

When the active life is lived in this way, it is a form and extension of the contemplative life. The distinction between the two has no meaning, for there is in the soul only one life, celestial and divine.

Living the active life in this way is not an impediment to contemplation and to love. Neither is it so prosaic as it usually seems. The light of heaven embellishes it and makes of it a ladder by which the soul ascends to God.

It is evident that the divine light does not take away the repugnance and sorrow so common in the active life, but it does make even those distressing burdens brilliant and beautiful, just as the sunlight embellishes the mire of stagnant pools.

Let our neighbors be as incompatible as possible, and as

troublesome as we may fancy, the light of God will reveal to us in
the depths of each soul and through its folly and defects something
godlike which the Lord placed there. We cannot help but love them
sincerely and endure them sweetly, because there is something of
Jesus within, and Jesus deserves all our love and sacrifice.

However sad, painful or terrible an event may be, the light of
heaven transfigures it and in its reality, discovers to us the hidden
designs of a loving God. Through the coarse wrapping of that event,
we read the divine message of love hidden within it.

Yes, he who lives in light rests in it, because he finds God everywhere and in everything, and God is the perfect repose of our souls.

Repose in Love

The soul's rest in God may assume a multiplicity of forms and
yet it seems to me they all integrate into the same reality but with
something proper to each one belonging to the whole. Thus, light
is the term of rest, love the strength that leads to rest and, in a certain sense, it is rest itself, because love is also complacency in light.
Purity is the necessary condition of rest, the atmosphere breathed
by the soul that enjoys the divine calm, while peace and fecundity
are the celestial fruits of repose.

One can scarcely conceive that the soul rests in love, because we
think love is mobile, unquiet as a subtle flame. Love is never satisfied nor does it ever rest; if it eats, it becomes famished; if it drinks,
it thirsts more; when it has realized all its designs, when it has suffered all martyrdoms and enjoyed all happiness, it judges itself a
useless servant. Then it embarks upon a new course. Will it find rest
upon the unsteady waves of this agitated sea? Love is precisely like
the ocean whose surface is agitated, but whose depths are always
unchanged, always tranquil. True love is like that, a rest for the
heart in spite of the activity demanded and the sacrifices imposed.

Love is unquiet when it seeks, struggles and doubts, but it is delightful repose when, filling the soul completely and sure of itself, it possesses the Beloved intimately.

In the first stages of the spiritual life the soul loves God sincerely, but she suffers and groans, because other affections dispute the absolute sovereignty of divine love in her heart. Creatures still fascinate her, and although she longs to belong entirely to the God she loves, she still sadly perceives that there are fibers in her heart that respond to the attractive vanities of the world. Divine love will conquer, no doubt, but since the soul is struggling, inquietude follows. When holy despoilment wrenches from the heart the last earthly affection, triumphant love will rest in victorious peace.

BUT VICTORIOUS love still finds within itself a new source of restlessness and martyrdom. With heroic effort it expelled all intruders from the citadel of the soul, but after the victory, the place conquered by love remained covered with ruins and desolation. Creatures no longer fascinate the soul with their vanities, but the divine Beloved has not yet come to change the dismal, uncultivated plot of the enamored heart into paradise. The soul suffers from an intense, desert-like solitude, for no longer experiencing an attraction for creatures, she inclines toward the absent Beloved with all the ardor of her loving desire. Like the spouse of the Canticles, she goes out through the streets and marketplaces seeking the Beloved and asking everyone she meets if they, perchance, have seen Him whom her heart loves. Throughout that torturing search can the soul repose in love?

One day, on some flowery path, in some happy moment, by some divine mystery, the Beloved appears magnificent in beauty and love. The soul faints before the divine apparition, and in silent happiness she realizes love's mystery. "I found Him, so tenderly loved, and now that He is mine I will never leave Him, never let Him go" (Cant. 3:4), exclaims the lover in her heavenly rapture. "His left hand pillows my head; His right hand, even now, is ready to embrace me" (Cant. 2:6).

Is this not divine rest? No doubt it is, but as with human love the uncertainty of fidelity, the fear that happiness may pass away, that love may depart, tortures souls and injects anxiety into the delightful rest. Will it be the same with divine love? Will Jesus, to whom I have surrendered my heart, continue loving me eternally? Will I keep on loving forever the one who has always loved me? Will not the inconstancy of my heart make me forget divine love?

As long as love doubts, rest is impossible. Certainly, the surety of mutual love is necessary if the soul is to rest in affectionate tranquility. Is not that security the essential prerogative of deep, true love? Frustrated is the love not sure of itself; unhappy the love not sure of the Beloved. Even human love experiences that sweet security. Alas, how often security is put to flight by forgetfulness and betrayal! It is the glory of love to believe itself immortal, and to me it seems nobler and more beautiful that love be deceived in thinking itself immortal than that it judge aright in doubting itself, for then it would die at birth.

In the case of divine love, that security is not an exceedingly noble illusion but a happy reality. In Scripture Jesus is called faithful and true (Rev. 19:11), and there, too, we read that the gifts of God are without repentance (Rom. 11:20). The first gift of God, St. Thomas teaches, is love. The Scripture, the Eucharist and the Cross are three immortal monuments assuring us that God's love is unfailing and eternal. Neither our miseries nor our ingratitudes can cool in the least the love of Jesus for us, because this incomprehensible love is not founded upon what is ephemeral and vacillating in our nature but upon the immutable and eternal kindness of God. We should not doubt even our own love, a love that the Holy Spirit, who is given to us, pours out into our hearts. When this love has taken possession of the soul, it is in itself inalienable and immortal. Therefore St. Paul exclaimed: "Of this I am fully persuaded; neither death nor life, no angels or principalities or powers, neither what is present nor what is to come, no force whatever, neither the height above us nor the depth beneath us, nor any other creature, will be able to separate us from the love of God, which comes to us in Christ Jesus our Lord" (Rom. 8:38).

These words are not the cry of a man, they are the cry of love, of the love that bears within itself the germ of immortality.

O HOW sweet and delightful it is to rest in love! In a certain way, rest in love is more perfect than rest in light, because the latter attains its plenitude only in heaven, whereas love procures plenitude in exile. Here below one never sees as in heaven, but one does indeed love as in the everlasting abode. Light on earth is always a dawn, never a noonday. In this life love can become an ocean as in eternity. The only difference is that here below the waters of love have the bitterness of grief, whereas those above are an indescribable honey of blessedness.

Earthly love has no shores. Free and powerful it spreads out and invades everything without anything or anyone's being able to say: "You shall come thus far and you shall not pass beyond; here your proud waves shall be broken."

When that love which expands without hindrance in the immensity of our soul has the ineffable unity which is its glory, when it enjoys the intimate possession of the Beloved without anxiety or fear in the tranquility of security, in the silence of happiness, what can be compared to that divine rest? You, blessed in heaven, surpass souls on earth in light and in happiness, but you do not surpass them in love, because here one loves as much as one loves in heaven, and here one rests in peace, like Jesus in the Tiberian bark, though shadows fall, though the tempest rages and turbulent waves arise, pushed by the winds of struggle and sorrow.

Rest usually corresponds to the road traveled, efforts made, and desires that have buffeted the soul. The paths of love are long and rough. Heroic the efforts that lead to its possession, and vehement the longing that love sinks deep in souls. Therefore, rest in love is deep and very sweet, proportioned to life's sorrows, to the torture of waiting, to the fatigue of the combat, to the vastness of the solitude endured, to the might of love, which is strong as death and terrible as hell.

Happy the souls that rest in love! They forget their anxieties and afflictions as the Israelites forgot the vicissitudes of the desert when, seated beneath the fig tree and in the vineyard, they ate in peace the delicious fruits of the promised land. "Not that I count these present sufferings as the measure of that glory which is to be revealed in us," said St. Paul (Rom. 8:18). I dare to parody those words to fit the soul's rest in love. No, there is no proportion between the fatiguing efforts of the spiritual life, its titanic combats, its desolate nights, its interior tortures, its boundless deserts, its bitter griefs, and the flood of happiness, the delight of repose, the security of union, the glory of possession of the Beloved and the mystery of transformation into Him that is attained upon this earth when the soul rests in the arms of her God, when she can say in the intoxication of her happiness: "Close my love is to my heart" (Cant. 1:12), and when He conjures the daughters of Jerusalem not to waken His loved one until she desires (Cant. 2:7).

To rest in love to our heart's content, to the extent of the soul's capacity, this is to satisfy our soul in an inexhaustible ocean. It is to expand our desires to immensity, even to satiety. It is to embrace the Beloved until His life blends with our life. It is to feel ourselves loved as we did not know how to dream of love. It is to enjoy the happiness of knowing that the Beloved takes complacency in our love; it is to forget ourselves, not through heroic abnegation, but through the intoxication of our happiness. It is to be lost in the abyss of love and to be transformed mysteriously into the one we love. It is satiety; it is joy; it is peace; it is heaven!

REPOSE IN PURITY

A type of rest in Jesus is that very touching scene in the Cenacle. John, the disciple whom Jesus loved dearly, reclined upon the Master's breast. The virgin disciple rests upon infinite purity in the purest virginal tranquility. The repose of Jesus is ever thus. Earthly purity, through a miracle of purity, reposes upon heavenly purity.

If there is anything difficult to understand perfectly, it is purity. We understand love more readily, because both in heaven and on earth it has the same name, the same essence, the same law. But purity is something heavenly; we define it precisely by eliminating the terrestrial. Yet this negative concept does not really reveal the celestial substance remaining when we have drained off the coarse dregs of earth. Purity is simplicity, it is life, it is a divine scintillation, the aroma of heaven, a copy of the infinite essence. The soul born for heaven and made for God is the fruit of a most pure breath from the mouth of the Most High. It finds its repose only when it finds its center, when it returns to its origin, when it enters the immaculate bosom whence it issued forth.

St. Thomas teaches that things attain their intrinsic perfection when they reach the principle of their being. Therefore, souls reach their perfection when they possess God. Only in the infinite bosom can they attain their rest and their beatitude.

Souls cannot rest on earth; they need to ascend to find tranquility and peace. The Psalmist, longing for peace, exclaimed: "Had I but wings, I cry, as a dove has wings, to fly away, and find rest" (Ps. 54:7). Souls need wings of purity to rise to the divine region of purity where rest and peace dwell.

Precisely in order that souls might rest while in this exile. Infinite Purity, the center and origin of souls, descended to this world and clothed Himself with human substance. This human substance was changed into the substance of purity and light through intimate contact with the divinity. Since Jesus appeared upon the earth, souls find rest without leaving the world. It suffices to recline upon Jesus' breast, for in Him we see with our eyes and touch with our hands the Word of life.

That immaculate breast, sanctuary of purity, flowery field of celestial lilies in which souls find their repose, because they touch divine purity at its source, is not something inaccessible or something reserved for the seraphim of heaven or the exalted souls on earth. It is not a flower of an enclosed garden that only privileged hands may cut, but it is the flower of the fields, which all may approach to inhale its aroma and enjoy its heavenly sweetness. That breast is ours; it is mine; it belongs to everyone. The poor and lowly can recline upon it, revel in its purity, rest in its sweetness and listen to the divine, mysterious palpitations of love.

Souls can rest only in purity, and purity is God whose "dwelling is in unapproachable light" (1 Tim. 6:16) in heaven. But being inaccessible through our efforts, He made Himself approachable through His gifts, as St. Anselm says, in order that souls on earth might rest on the immaculate breast of Jesus, who became for us "our wisdom, our justification, our sanctification and our atonement" (1 Cor. 1:30).

In order to rest on that divine breast, one thing suffices: purity. The sinner carries within himself the inexhaustible well-spring of uneasiness. "For the rebellious, the Lord says, there is no peace" (Is. 48:22). The just, on the other hand, live in peace. Into clean hearts the Lord pours "a flowing stream of peace" (Is. 48:18), according to the expression of the prophet Isaiah.

Repose and peace are found only in unity. When the spirit germinates a multitude of discordant thoughts, when the heart is agitated by sundry affections, the soul, like a bark upon the fluctuating waves, is tossed about in perpetual unrest. In order to rest, the soul needs purity of spirit to concentrate all its thoughts in one gaze of light, and purity of heart to establish all its affections in one single divine love.

Only light can be fused with light; only purity can comprehend purity. Therefore, to hear the pure throbbings of the Sacred Heart, to find in the immaculate breast of the Master the divine effusion that gives souls abundant peace and unutterable repose, to understand the Divine Heart formed of purity and light, it is necessary to have the luminous insight and the spotless soul of the chosen disciple.

STILL MORE, the soul's rest in Jesus is itself a mystery of purity; who can penetrate it? To attain a faint understanding of the mystery, it is fitting to consider another reason why the soul cannot rest in creatures. Rest connotes plenitude and surrender. Hence, anxiety, restriction and reserve hinder calmness. In order to rest, it is necessary to surrender oneself to that which constitutes rest. The soul must be alert to bask in the light it longs for, to love as much as the heart craves, and to permit the spirit to expand with desire, as a sea without shores. As for creatures, one may not regard them without caution nor give free rein to desires regarding them. If the soul were to act thus, she would forsake the confines of truth, of harmony and of order, for all that is directed to creatures has its own measure, whereas love and true rest admit of no measure.

Full rest requires that the object of our repose be such that it can be desired without limit, possessed without reserve, and loved without excess. Only the divine can be so desired, possessed and loved, because the divine is most pure; so much so that the soul may desire it without fear, love it without stain, and possess it without loss of her celestial luster. Therefore, the Church places on the lips of St. Agnes these precious words referring to Jesus: "When I love Him, I am chaste; when I touch Him, I am spotless; when I receive Him, I am a virgin." The soul is a bird from heaven and to rest she needs a world of purity that will neither stain her whiteness nor darken her fairness.

The divine mystery still remains unexplained. Not only can the soul rest in God without fear of staining her purity, but she also enhances her beauty and increases it through that rest. As the bird

resting in a fragrant nest becomes perfumed itself, so the soul resting in God becomes impregnated with purity, not only because to
be pure is to approach God and to receive His reflection, but also
because God's embrace and His happy possession are mysteries of
the divine life in the spotless splendors of sanctity.

For the soul to rest in purity is to fulfill her desires without
fear of defilement; it is to love the pure to the point where she
is permeated with purity; it is to renew her own purity in eternal
purity through an ineffable prodigy of purity. The soul was born for
purity and only there does she find her repose and happiness. For
this precious rest it is necessary that the soul be light, and through
a mystery of light be immersed in the eternal light, as the innocent
disciple reclined upon the most pure Heart of Jesus in virginal tranquility.

GOD HAS placed in souls a profound intuition for appreciating the
value and the beauty of purity as well as an insatiable desire to possess and increase it. But those fortunate souls should not forget that
in order to obtain purity, the principal means, or rather the only
way, is to be united to Jesus and to rest in Him.

Let them purify themselves by repentance, sacrifice and suffering. All that pertains to Jesus purifies our souls, especially the
Holy Eucharist, the sacrament of purity and of virginity. Let them
not forget that Jesus is the source of purity, and in order to increase
it, the soul must be intimately united with Him and enter fully
into His divinity. The glance of Jesus purifies. His divine contact
cleanses, His caresses beautify souls and His possession is a mystery
of purity that divinizes the soul.

To repose in Jesus is, I repeat, to rest in purity and to be impregnated with it. To love Jesus, to receive His divine caresses, to possess
Him intimately with unspeakable love, to recline upon His divine
breast, to penetrate His most pure heart, to bathe oneself in His
light, to be burned in His fire, and to live His life is to renew the

soul's purity and increase it without measure, because He is the
260 whiteness of eternal light, the spotless mirror of God's majesty and
the image of His kindness.

Repose in Fruitfulness

Rest in Jesus produces two fruits: peace and fecundity; the former for the soul itself, the latter for others.

The Psalmist establishes a mysterious relation between rest and
fecundity: "Is not sleep His gift to the men He loves? Fatherhood
itself is the Lord's gift" (Ps. 126:3).

Fruitfulness is proper to perfection; when maturity is reached,
productivity is possible. God, who is infinite perfection, is also
infinite fecundity.

Fruitfulness is supreme joy in heaven and on earth. The eternal
happiness of God is His ineffable fecundity in the august mystery
of the Trinity. The supreme happiness of earth is the immaculate
fruitfulness of Mary who gave Jesus to us. In the Old Testament it
was joy and benediction to be the ancestor of Jesus according to the
flesh; in the New Dispensation it is joy and benediction to form
Jesus in our own soul and in the souls of others.

Therefore, St. Paul called his spiritual children "all my delight
and prize" (Phil. 4:1). And St. Jerome makes a pertinent comment upon that Gospel passage wherein a woman acclaimed the
mother of Jesus as blessed and Jesus answered: "Blessed are those
who fear the word of God and keep it" (Luke 11:28). The Saint
writes: "Beautifully did the Savior acquiesce in the woman's testimony by declaring that not only is she happy who merited to bear
corporally the Word of God, but all those who conceive the same
Word spiritually by faith, giving birth to Him by good works, since
they nurture Him in their own hearts and in the hearts of others.
The Mother of God herself was certainly happy on account of the
temporal mystery which she shared in the Incarnation of the Word,

but she was much happier because eternally she would remain His
guardian, as it were, to love Him.

Truly, the supreme perfection and complete happiness of souls
consists in this spotless and ineffable fecundity that has Jesus as its
end, for perfection as well as happiness does not consist in something selfish, but in something generous. It consists not in concentration within oneself, but in the giving of one's abundance. When
souls are so enriched that life runs out from their abundance, they
have attained their perfection and their happiness.

Therefore, all generations have called and will call the ever
Virgin Mary blessed, as she prophesied in her immortal canticle,
because God wrought in her such great and wonderful things that
her most pure soul is a copy of the Father's perfection and happiness, for, like Him, Mary could say to Jesus, "Thou art my Son. I
have begotten Thee this day" (Ps. 2:7).

It pleased the Lord to communicate to souls a sparkle of His
perfection and His happiness, since Jesus said: "But you are to be
perfect, as your heavenly Father is perfect" (Matt. 5:48). St. John
wrote: "But we know that when He comes, we shall be like Him"
(1 John 3:2). In order that we might bear in our soul that divine
sparkle, the Father communicated to us in Jesus and through the
Holy Spirit a germ of divine fecundity. He made it our glory and
our happiness to conceive Jesus in our hearts and in other hearts,
and to give birth to Him by a divine mystery, and, in a sense, to
nurture Him in an inexpressible manner.

This hidden mystery of our fecundity, which is likewise the
mystery of our happiness and our perfection, is vividly expressed
in this incomparable passage from the Apostle: "With this in mind,
I fall on my knees to the Father of our Lord Jesus Christ, that
Father from whom all fatherhood in heaven and on earth takes its
title. May He, out of the rich treasury of His glory, strengthen you
through His spirit with a power that reaches your innermost being.
May Christ find a dwelling-place, through faith, in your hearts;

may your lives be rooted in love, founded in love. May you and all the saints be enabled to measure, in all its breadth and length and height and depth, the love of Christ, to know what passes knowledge. May you be filled with all the completion God has to give" (Eph. 3:14–20).

In these words is contained the whole doctrine of Christian perfection, and this perfection is a mystery of fruitfulness. It originates in the paternity of the Father, which it resembles. The divine fruit of that fecundity is Jesus, who is born by faith in our heart and strengthened by the Holy Spirit to attain the excellence of the interior man. Jesus grows in our souls, filling them with charity, in which we are rooted and founded. When souls become filled with God in ineffable plenitude, the life of Jesus fills souls with His treasures and increases in them through a wonderful fecundity.

To become a saint is to become Jesus; it is to conceive Jesus in our soul and to cause Him to grow therein. But Jesus cannot be enclosed in the narrow confines of a human heart. When He dwells there, He diffuses Himself, like a resplendent light, a delicate perfume, a penetrating sound, thus reaching even the limits of the world.

When a soul becomes Jesus, she in her turn conceives Him in other souls, and infuses Him into other hearts. Her glory is to disseminate the light of heaven, the glory of the Father, as the sun in the midst of the firmament sheds the glory of its light in all directions.

One realizes from all that has been said that the supreme rest of souls is this divine productiveness. The mighty desires God placed in souls, the powerful and inexhaustible activity, the boundless aspirations, the irrepressible development of their lives, all these sources of divine unrest cannot be calmed except by the appearance of Jesus, fruit of heaven and earth through a divine mystery. The most sweet Jesus, blessed term of all holy, virginal fertility, when born in our souls, fulfills all our desires, realizes all our aspirations, satisfies our mighty activity and makes our life expand in joy and peace.

For the soul to rest is to produce Jesus mystically in herself; it is to diffuse Him and multiply Him in unity, so to speak, in innumerable souls that are His joy and His crown. This fructifying power is evident in all holy souls, but it appears in an extraordinary manner in those whose spirit and mission are characterized by fecundity. Thus, though all saints have become like little children, St. Thérèse of the Child Jesus exemplifies pre-eminently the simplicity of spiritual infancy. All saints practiced detachment, but it is St. Francis of Assisi who betrothed himself to poverty. All saints possess gentleness, but this heavenly prerogative is the distinctive glory of St. Francis de Sales. So, although all holy souls participate in the divine fecundity, it is in a singular degree the heritage of souls favored with this mission.

For each soul has its own mission: St. Thomas Aquinas to develop clarity of mind; St. John of the Cross and St. Teresa to point out the paths of perfection; St. Vincent de Paul to recall to men the new commandment of Jesus; and so with the others. The mission of a soul that has received the grace of spiritual fecundity is to conceive and engender Jesus mystically and to diffuse Him around like a radiant light, like a delicate perfume.

Such a soul is a soul-mother, and by an ineffable mystery has a new name, a new love and a new mission in regard to Jesus.

In this holy and most excellent fruitfulness are concentrated and fused all the spiritual prerogatives of that soul: her clarity, her purity, her love, her sacrifice. All these heavenly things have as center and crown that virginal pregnancy whose fruit is Jesus.

Therefore, for those souls fecundity is the greatest repose. As the ancient patriarchs rested in their desires and their hopes when they received the promise of the Lord that their descendants would be multiplied as the stars of heaven; as the blessed Mary rested in a heavenly peace when she clasped to her breast her precious Son, and when she saw in Him, more numerous than the stars of heaven, the souls redeemed by His blood and incorporated with Him by faith and love; so souls that have received from God spiritual maternity as a special gift, find their rest in clasping Jesus to themselves and in Him all the souls to whom, according to the divine designs, their vivifying influence should be extended.

What a magnificent mission! What sublime repose! But it is not only holy admiration of God's marvels or heartfelt gratitude for His benefits that such fecundity should produce in the soul destined by God to bear spiritual offspring. The greater knowledge of the graces intertwined with that productiveness must be a powerful stimulus to enter fully into God's plans and to arouse in that soul the holy dispositions which fecundity demands.

> Fecundity on earth is always a mystery of pain....
>
> When the Divine Word descended to earth, He embraced the Cross, united Himself to suffering and deposited in it the germ of the fecundity that He had brought from heaven. Since that time nothing germinates except in sacrifice, and the works of God do not prosper except in the shadow of the Cross, bedewed by tears and blood....
>
> All the work of Christ was born from His sacrifice, and no one can continue it except "by completing what is lacking to the passion of Christ in His members," except by forming an integral part of that infinite Cross whereon the "whole Christ"—Jesus and the members of His mystical body—continue immolating themselves.

From that Cross gushes forth a copious torrent of blood—the body's blood and the heart's blood—which is transformed into another flood of graces to purify the world and save souls.

We must not forget that not only is it suffering that gives life to souls, but suffering must arise out of an ocean of purity and of love. Still more, that purity and that love have their celestial origin and marvelous efficacy in the divine that lives in the soul, in the divinity that one must contemplate and in whose secrets of light, of love and of life the soul must be completely engrossed.

Repose in Peace

Another excellent fruit of the soul's rest in Jesus is peace. At first sight, peace and rest seem to be one and the same thing, but one can rest without peace, for rest is something earthly, whereas peace is something heavenly. Therefore the Church begs for her departed children the rest of peace.

Jesus brought us the divine gift of peace from heaven. The angels announced it in Bethlehem as a sweet promise, and when Jesus, His mission accomplished, arose from the tomb, He gave peace to His apostles as the fruit of His sacrifice. *Pax vobis!*

Peace is not only something negative, a lack of struggle and anxiety, but it is also something positive, a close resemblance to heaven, a ray from God's tranquility and happiness.

Peace is the result of harmony. It is "the tranquility of order," said St. Augustine, so exact and profound in his statements. When all in the soul is in accord, when all her activities are harmonized in a divine unity, when her life is an echo of God's life, she enjoys peace, realizing within herself two Scriptural expressions that have a deep parallelism: "Peace on earth to men that are God's friends" (Luke 2:14). "Every day is a feast day to a contented heart" (Prov. 15:15).

Nothing else of earth approximates beatitude so much as peace. Jesus teaches in the Sermon on the Mount that peace is supreme blessedness: "Blessed are the peacemakers, for they shall be counted the children of God" (Matt. 5:7).

St. Paul gave us an excellent directive for understanding peace when, referring to Jesus, he said: "He is our bond of peace" (Eph. 2:14). God is peace, and our peace is Jesus, for through Him infinite peace became visible to our eyes and attainable to our desires. To give peace is to give Jesus, to possess peace is to possess Jesus, and to rest in peace is to rest in Jesus.

When the soul is in perfect possession of Jesus, who is light, purity, fecundity and love, when the soul is transformed into Him, when Jesus has full possession of the soul and the soul penetrates the profundities of Jesus, then the soul finds her rest in peace.

The entire spiritual life is a constant ascent toward peace. It is the long and painful pilgrimage through the desert of this world to the promised land of peace. Like the Israelites at the foot of the vine and the fig tree, in order to relish its fruits, one must leave the Egypt of the world far behind and pass over the Red Sea of suffering, traverse the boundless sands of desolation, conquer all enemies and shatter the walls of egoism with the victorious canticle of love. Happy the souls that rest in peace, because they have found Jesus and possess that celestial treasure in an ineffable plenitude.

One possesses Jesus when all the yearnings of the soul are concentrated in Him, when all activities have Him as the sole object, when He is the only light of the spirit and the only love of the heart, when He is one's life, fecundity, and joy. To possess Jesus in this way is to rest in peace.

St. Thomas teaches a very profound and fruitful doctrine about peace. Peace has three causes: the virtues of the active life prepare for it, placing in the soul the divine order that results from the subjection of the lower faculties to the higher. Hence, there are no antagonistic tendencies in our being, and the struggles that exhaust the soul and hinder its flight toward God cease. The second cause of peace is love, the divine charity that blends all the soul's affections and desires into a unique love, vigorous and inviolable—the unparalleled, conquering love of God.

But peace itself is light and wisdom. It is the reflection in the creature of eternal wisdom. It is a created wisdom but also an image of the infinite. In a word, peace is the image of Jesus in the soul, a bright, celestial image that transforms the soul into Jesus. It is

Jesus Himself living in her, encompassing her with light, harmony, beauty and happiness.

So then the stock that produces this fruit is divine grace with its cortège of virtues. The flower that evolves and supports this fruit is love, but the fruit itself is light and wisdom, because it is the image of Him who is the Light of light and the Wisdom of the Father, the image of Jesus that transforms the soul into Him.

It is clear from this that rest in peace is the fruit of all other types of rest and the supreme rest in Jesus.

This peaceful repose is not something ephemeral, which like a flash of glory shines in the soul in the midst of the night, but it is something enduring and immortal, like a day without sunset. The soul that rests in peace never loses its interior calm. It rests always, whether in contemplation or in action, in grief or in joy, in comfort or in desolation. Neither anything nor anyone can deprive the soul of peace, because neither anything nor anyone can take away the inner light and deep love, because neither anything nor anyone can steal the soul away from Jesus or Jesus away from the soul.

Introduced into the mysteries of Jesus, which are the profundities of the divinity, the soul feels herself very far from every disturbing element. A new love, lofty and exceedingly pure, arises in her heart. The splendors of God envelop her, heightening the bright image of her adorable Jesus, transforming her into Him in a most perfect manner.

PEACE IS silent.

The firmament on serene nights is a marvel of peace. The stars run their mysterious course in sacred silence and their splendid scintillations sing the glory of God without words and without sound. The blossoming field displays its flowers and scatters their perfume in a silence that fills the soul with sweetness and peace. So it is with everything that possesses and diffuses peace.

But the silence of peace is not the barren stillness of the desert nor the dead muteness of the tomb; it is the quiet of the contemplating soul, of the loving heart, of the spirit ecstatic before beauty.

The silence of God is exceedingly rich as He Himself is rich. It contains treasures of truth and harmony, and it is called silence, not because it lacks divine words and divine concepts, but because when the soul penetrates that divine silence, everything around her becomes quiet, and because what the soul contemplates in the depths of God does not fit into the pettiness of our lowly thoughts, but finds a place only in the expressive majesty of a silence of admiration and love.

REPOSE IN SUFFERING

Can one repose in suffering?

At first sight one thinks it impossible to rest in suffering; rather, one would banish all sorrow in order to rest.

Rest requires that our longings be fulfilled, our aspirations satisfied, and that our faculties find the object of their activity and desires. Suffering comes precisely from what would oppose our desires and our aspirations, from the fact that our activity does not find what it seeks and desires. By what strange paradox could the soul rest in suffering?

Nevertheless, Christ rested on the Cross. Did He not say that He desired eagerly to drain the chalice of His passion (Luke 12:50)? And when He drank the dregs of that chalice, did He not send forth a cry of rest and of peace saying: "It is achieved" (John 19:30)? Souls that love Him also find in His Cross an exquisite rest, the deepest rest to be found on earth.

St. Teresa of Avila desired only two kinds of repose: that of death to unite her with God in an ocean of light and love, or the repose of suffering to satisfy the ardor of her heart: "*Aut pati aut mori.*"

St John of the Cross desired as a recompense "to suffer and

to be despised for Jesus"; and is not rest the recompense for life's struggles and sacrifices?

St. Thérèse of the Child Jesus said: "I found happiness and joy in the world, but only in suffering."

The fact is that Jesus with His divine contact transformed the Cross. He converted it from a gibbet into a throne; He changed it from a martyrdom into heaven. He turned what was impotent and defeated into the power and the wisdom of God (1 Cor. 1:24) and a supreme victory over death and hell. Therefore, the Apostle said: "Where then, death, is thy victory?" (1 Cor. 15:55).

This is the height of the power, the wisdom, the love of God: to draw life out of death, to change sorrow into joy, and to make the Cross a rest for the soul.

IN ORDER to plumb this heavenly mystery of the Cross, it is necessary to penetrate another divine mystery: love.

Love being the mutual surrender of those who love each other, a complete gift of the one to the other, love is not satisfied and consummated except when that mutual surrender is total and complete. Inasmuch as that consummation is not realized, love does not rest. Just as the symbol of love, fire, does not rest but extends its flames in all directions, so love seeks to kindle what it loves with its unquenchable fire. "It is fire that I have come to spread over the earth, and what better wish can I have than that it should be kindled?" (Luke 12:49). Do not these words of Jesus mean that His heart burns with an immense love for us?

The repose of love consists in this, that the Lover give Himself without measure and also that He obtain the full possession of His beloved. The first is heaven; the second is the Cross.

Heaven is the entire, ineffable, eternal gift of the Beloved to the soul that loves Him; it is infinite light penetrating the depths of the understanding, divine fire permeating all the fibers of the heart with beatific burning, life and happiness completely filling the soul.

The gate of heaven is death; therefore, the saints covet death with holy ardor.

In this life there are reflections of eternal happiness, there are resemblances to the indescribable gift of heaven, there are delicious drops of the blessedness that surpasses all the joys of earth. Is not that most delightful intimacy with God to which Jesus invites the chosen soul a replica of eternal life, a silent and joyous introduction into the secrets of the august Trinity?

But love has another earthly path to travel in completing the mystery of its life; it consists in the soul's giving to the Beloved the full, supreme donation of herself. This donation is affected only on Calvary between the arms of the Cross and under the august majesty of pain. Thus, Jesus completed His boundless love on earth before consummating it in the everlasting abode.

Can it be that suffering hides among its folds an imitation—shall I dare to say it?—of infinite weakness and wretchedness, our own infinity, so to speak, which has the audacity to compete with the immensity of divine love? Can it be that pain amplifies our gift, making it unlimited, because we are giving all we are to the Lord, because it is offered, not as a calm oblation passing from our hands to the divine without change or destruction, but as burning incense consumed and changed into fragrant clouds, an oblation that alters and destroys the gift in perfect holocaust, an oblation in which life and death are mingled by a divine art, a gift in which the lover is overwhelmed in the immensity of wretchedness in order to chant the praise of the infinity of plenitude?

Who can comprehend the mystery of suffering? It is certain that all deep, generous love seeks pain as its most cherished gift and its most sublime canticle. The new love that Jesus came to kindle on the earth finds its rest only when it climbs Calvary, stretches itself upon Christ's Cross and, transported with sorrow and with love, unites its life and its death with the life and the death of Jesus. Wherefore, it will be understood that the soul's rest in Jesus, far from suppressing her sorrows at their source, increases them, making them divine.

271

What would the soul in love with Jesus do if they took her treasure away from her, that is to say, if they removed from her life suffering, her inseparable companion, her faithful friend, her crest of honor, the symbol of her happiness, the key of her life? Would she be able to live without it? Without it, could she enjoy the happiness of repose? Without it, would she be the living cross upon which Jesus continues the loving mystery of His immolation?

But the Lord will not take away from her this precious inheritance. Her repose in light, in purity, in love, in fecundity, in peace, would be incomplete without rest in pain, for the soul can rest only in Jesus. If Jesus is light, purity, fecundity and love, pain also is boundless, inexpressible, divine. He rested upon the bed of pain, the Cross, and He bears in the interior of His heart another cross which is the mystical rest of some privileged souls.

These souls ought to seek their repose upon Christ's interior cross more than upon the Cross raised upon Calvary's height, for the inner cross is the most cruel, the most sweet, the most beautiful, the most loving. If Jesus should ask these souls what He asked Thomas Aquinas and John of the Cross: "What reward do you desire?" they ought to tell Him: "Nothing else, Lord, than the cross within Thy heart." That cross must be the rest, the happiness, the precious treasure and the greatest recompense of souls dedicated to the Cross.

Once again, repose in Jesus, far from mitigating suffering, increases it, because all these heavenly realities upon which the soul must rest are all different forms of the only reality upon which souls repose—Jesus. All those celestial things which in eternity are fountains of purest joy, on earth are copious torrents of sorrows.

Light, love, purity, fecundity, conceal beneath their heavenly beauty the loveliness of pain, for Jesus is hidden in them all. Jesus is formed of two elements: one of heaven and the other of earth, one of infinite love and the other of immense suffering.

CHAPTER 29

✹

Repose of Jesus in the Soul

In the preceding chapters we saw how the soul should prepare herself—by light, love, purity, fecundity, peace and pain—to rest in God, and thus to satisfy her most imperious and urgent desires. But as we pointed out from the beginning, when the soul has attained repose in God, all is not finished; something more delicate and sublime remains for her to do, namely, to offer her heart to Jesus for His resting place. Wonderful it is that the soul attain repose in God, but it is a more profound mystery and a deeper secret for the soul to become God's resting place.

Jesus passes near all souls; He stops at some and waits at the door; in others He remains; in very few does He rest. For Jesus to rest in a soul means to choose her as a dwelling, to occupy this abode entirely and to be content therein.

Jesus pours out in the soul in which He rests the fullness of His light, His love, His fecundity, His purity and His peace, not in an absolute sense, it is evident, but according to the divine designs upon that soul, as St. Paul says: "Each of us has received his own special grace, dealt out to him by Christ's gift" (Eph. 4:7).

But in order that Jesus endow souls with His plenitude, it is necessary that He be sure of their love, fidelity and generosity.

It would suffice to say that Jesus needs to be sure of the soul's love, for fidelity is love that watches, and generosity is love that gives itself. When Jesus rests in a soul, He asks her beforehand, as He asked St. Peter: "Dost thou care for Me more than these others?" (John 21:15). When Jesus hears the sincere and generous confession of love, He entrusts Himself to the soul and rests in her, as He entrusted souls to the apostle and rested in his fidelity.

In no soul has Jesus rested as in Mary's, because the heart of the Virgin and Mother recalled to Jesus (speaking in our language) the most loving bosom of the Father, who is the supreme, the eternal, the most blessed repose of Jesus.

The kind of rest that Jesus takes in souls is implied in what I have just said: the rest proper to Jesus is the Father in heaven and Mary most holy on earth, because she is an image of the heavenly Father. Jesus reposes in souls in proportion to their resemblance to the Father and Mary.

Jesus' rest in souls has various forms similar to the soul's rest in Him. It is fitting to study these aspects of Jesus' repose.

THE REPOSE OF LIGHT

Jesus rests in souls that understand Him.

Here on earth, when a person knows us well, comprehends our ideas, surmises our desires and endeavors to please us, that person is said to understand us and we repose in him, confident that he will always act in conformity with our ideas and desires. Jesus also rests in souls that understand Him. He reveals His secrets to all souls that He loves, as He said to His apostles: "I have made known to you all that My Father has told Me" (John 15:15). But He discloses His secrets more clearly and profoundly to His intimate friends, as to those three chosen apostles, Peter, James and John. He revealed

to them the secret of His glory on Tabor and the secret of His grief
in Gethsemane.   *275*

It is not an easy thing to know Jesus intimately and to delve
into the divine intimacies. The apostles who lived with Him more
than three years in holy familiarity did not know Him fully until
the Holy Spirit descended upon them. He said to them one day:
"Here am I, who have been all this while in your company; hast
thou not learned to recognize Me as yet?" (John 14:9). Truly, they
neither understood His teachings nor penetrated His spirit nor realized His way of thinking and feeling. Their intimacy with Jesus,
which the hiddenness of Christ's mysteries permitted, did not make
them more penetrating men.

We have the same experience. Dom Delatte[1] observes that
what happened to those with whom Jesus dealt in His mortal life
happens to souls. Many times they do not recognize Jesus. "It is
a ghost," said the apostles when they saw Jesus walking upon the
waters of Tiberias. "He is a pilgrim," said the disciples or the road
to Emmaus. And when Jesus appeared to Mary near the sepulcher,
the former sinner believed that He was a gardener. When, after His
resurrection, He showed Himself to His apostles on the shores of
Lake Genesareth as they were approaching the shore in a boat, they
did not know Him; the only one who recognized Him was John,
who said: "It is the Lord" (John 21:7).

I want to emphasize that the same thing happens to souls; on
very many occasions they do not know Jesus. Still less do they understand His designs, discern His wishes, or understand His divine
teachings. A few, a very few souls do know Jesus thoroughly and
understand Him, and in these He takes rest. It eases Him so much
to rest in souls! But those who give Him this comfort are few indeed.

Souls in whom Jesus rests recognize Him, although He may
come in disguise. Some secret instinct, some loving presentiment,

---

1.   Cf. *L'Evangile de Notre-Seigneur Jésus-Christ, le Fils de Dieu.*

some intuition of the heart whispers to them: "It is the Lord!" Souls in whom Jesus rests know how to receive His divine communications, penetrate His teachings, surmise His thoughts and desires. They are enlightened souls, "souls of light," in whom the divine light is reflected sharply and perfectly as a tranquil lake reflects the sky in its crystal surface.

MARY'S SOUL was flooded with light. She kept all the mysteries in her heart, meditated upon every word she heard, and she understood Jesus as no one else on this earth has ever understood Him. The Gospel passage on the wedding at Cana suffices as an example of this perfect understanding. When Mary said to Jesus: "They have no wine," Jesus answered her in a way that still disconcerts commentators; one might say it was a repulse. Yet Mary discerned His innermost designs, and sure of the miracle, said to those concerned: "Do what He tells you."

Joseph, the just man, so silent and selfless, was an enlightened soul. In the midst of profound mysteries he understood the divine will clearly and executed it with marvelous fidelity.

What celestial prerogatives do light-gifted souls possess that our Lord reposes in them?

They are pure souls; the brightness and clarity of the sun's light is directly proportional to the lucidity of the atmosphere through which it passes, and the purer the soul, the better God's light penetrates it. Jesus declared: "Blessed are the clean of heart; they shall see God" (Matt. 5:8). To this purity of soul, St. John, no doubt, owed his profound intuitions.

Enlightened souls are simple souls, for it is written: "Knavery the Lord hates, and keeps for honest men His familiar friendship" (Prov. 3:32). Simplicity, like poverty, seems like stupidity; but it is very far from being such, for it is a reflection of God who in His wealth and His wisdom is most simple. There is a close relation between God and guileless souls, between wisdom and simplicity.

Enlightened souls are humble, for Jesus said: "Father...I give Thee praise that Thou hast hidden all this from the wise and prudent and revealed it to little children" (Matt. 11:25). Humility, which is truth, is the supreme disposition for receiving the light of God, who is truth. On the other hand, when the Word came to earth, He clothed Himself with the mantle of humility. In order to know Jesus, one must know by intimate experience this lowly covering, which He changed into royal purple.

But above all else, enlightened souls have love. Someone has said that the heart has reasons that the intellect does not understand. Who doubts the deep intuitions of love? Divine love, especially, which springs from light and produces fruits of light. It teaches better than any other light or gift what the Beloved is: His innermost thoughts, His secret desires and His hidden designs. The soul that loves sees through the eyes of the Beloved and feels the holy throbbings of the Sacred Heart.

ONE EARTHLY love is especially characterized by deep intuitions and a capacity of unsurpassed comprehension—maternal love. In it are accumulated all the qualities that form souls of light: the maternal heart is pure and loving, simple in dealing with children, and forgetful of herself, in order to give herself to her children and sacrifice herself for them.

Souls whose supernatural love has these characteristics are souls of light in whom Jesus rests, because their love is a reflection of the infinite love of the Father and the maternal love of Mary. One might say that there are three classes of light-flooded souls: virginal souls through their purity, souls that have become as children, following the way of spiritual infancy through their simplicity, and maternal souls through the intuitions of an intense, sacrificial love. Surpassing these three classes in excellence are those souls who royally combine these three aspects and who, like Mary, are pure as virgins, simple as children, selfless as mothers. In these souls Christ finds His perfect repose in light. Therefore, He is reflected in them like a sun of love that reflects its superb splendor in the pure, tranquil mirror of a serene lake.

The Repose of Love

The repose of love can be understood in two ways: Jesus rests in a soul because He is sure of her love; rather, Jesus takes His repose in a soul because that soul lets herself love perfectly.

In a certain sense, only in love can Jesus rest; if He were not certain of the love of a soul, how could He rest in her? We can rest only in what is our own; in order to repose in a heart, it is necessary that this heart belong to us in some manner. Therefore, we rest completely in the heart of our mother, because we know that her heart belongs to us as no other on earth.

Jesus dwells in every heart that loves Him, but He rests only in the heart that belongs entirely to Him, that He possesses perfectly, that is His own in the complete extension of the term.

To repose in a heart is not to distrust it; it is not to fear that the heart may forget or betray. It is to have the assurance that the heart will love us as much as we desire, and give us what we ask without hesitation or qualification.

What peace, what satisfaction, what sweetness, what strength we feel when we are sure of a heart, when we know that it belongs to us completely, when we have the certainty that the whole love of the heart is ours and that we find there all the love we can desire. Therefore, we repose sweetly in the Heart of Jesus, because His heart is entirely ours and there we find all the treasures of love the soul can dream of.

Jesus longs to have such hearts that they may be His completely, that they may beat only for Him, that they may give Him all the love that He desires, because although the hearts of creatures are essentially limited, He Himself can pour into them torrents of love to satisfy the desires of His heart. When Jesus finds such a heart, He rests there.

There are very few hearts in which Jesus rests, because there are very few that He possesses entirely and that are disposed for every sacrifice in order to show Him love.

Jesus reposes in the infinite heart of His Father and in the Immaculate Heart of Mary. No rest of love is comparable to Jesus' repose in those hearts ineffably His own. Hearts similar to theirs, in which there is a reflection of the Father's love and ray of Mary's tenderness, are the hearts in which Jesus finds His repose of love. To these hearts He entrusts Himself, to them He abandons Himself, and in them He gratifies His insatiable longing to be loved.

Happy the heart that has never betrayed or forgotten Jesus, the heart whose beatings are all for Him! Happy the heart in which there is no trace of love that is not for Jesus! Happy the heart that always gives Him all the love He wants, regardless of the sacrifice! That heart and its love belong completely to Jesus, absolutely and forever, even though, poor creature that it is, it is burdened with deficiencies and miseries.

Jesus rests easily in that heart, abandoning Himself to its solicitude and surrendering Himself to its tenderness. Is there happiness comparable to this? I do not know of a sweetness on earth more perfect, nor a happiness more complete, than that of knowing that Jesus is sure of our love and that He reposes trustfully in our heart.

This rest becomes sweeter and more perfect the more the soul penetrates the divine, because then love increases, becomes more refined, and participates more deeply in the integrity and immutability of God. The abyss of light that the soul then contemplates in the divinity opens up a new torrent of sorrow within her, and at the same time carves out a new source of love. Jesus is more certain of the love of that soul, because upon introducing her into the heavenly dwellings, there has been reflected upon her, more intense and abundant, the tenderness of the heavenly Father.

BUT, AS I have already said, Jesus' repose of love in souls has another meaning; the one just explained is the rest that Jesus finds on account of being loved; the other of which I am going to speak is the repose that He finds because He loves.

Love is divine restlessness until it is satisfied by pouring itself lavishly into the beloved. One might think that it is an easy thing for love to find one who will receive the weight of its fullness, but this is not so. We are so tiny and limited, not only in our loving, but also in allowing ourselves to be loved! The plenitude of Jesus' love is something divinely overwhelming for souls; it is a colossal weight of happiness, and at the same time an immense weight of pain.

The love of the Father rests in Jesus, and in that Divine Son He satisfies the infinite burden of His tenderness. Jesus, letting Himself be loved by the Father, admitted into His heart inexpressible joy and sorrow. The joy which that love effects is heaven; the sorrow that it brings is the passion, the whole passion, exterior and interior. Two crosses are symbolic of this twofold passion: the one upon which Jesus was nailed, the other that surmounts His heart. Therefore, in Jesus' soul the delights of heaven and the "sorrows of hell" are intertwined by a divine paradox, by an overpowering mystery.

Such is love, light and cloud, joy and grief, like the pillar that guided the Israelites. When the infinite love of the Father fell like a divine invasion into the soul of Jesus, this soul, allowing itself to be loved as no other could do, experienced all the sweetness of eternal happiness and all the martyrdom of the utmost suffering.

All souls that permit themselves to be loved by divine love also receive, in the degree marked out for them by the divine plan, this tremendous double weight of joy and sorrow. I do not know which of these burdens is the more overwhelming, because I do not know which our weakness can withstand more successfully, happiness or martyrdom. Therefore, there are few souls that allow themselves to be loved, because there are few, very few, that know how to support joy, and few, very few, that know how to endure sorrow.

To allow oneself to be loved, many rare things are necessary. One needs a gigantic strength to keep from collapsing under the vastness of heaven or the heaviness of hell. One needs a love strong as death and gentle as a breath of happiness. One needs purity because this celestial prerogative expands the soul so that it can receive what is divine. One needs a deep humility to hollow out in the soul a vacancy so large that the divine plenitude can fill within. It needs an indescribable simplicity so that the soul may not wonder at the prodigies of divine love and may permit herself to be guided through unknown regions and be caught up into the mysterious demands of eternal love. It is necessary that God Himself place in souls unpredictable sacred gifts and heavenly charisms so that they can receive the full, ineffable, mysterious gift of God.

With immense love and tender solicitude, Jesus Himself prepares the soul in which He is going to establish His ineffable repose of love. He prepares her with a long and constant martyrdom, with divine communications, with loving caresses, with a whole interminable, magnificent chain of graces. And as the crowning of that long, delicate preparation, He makes her the singular gift of sublime love that consists in more than loving, in letting herself be loved with childlike ingenuousness, with artless simplicity, with ardent audacity, with sweet mildness, with irresistible strength.

Then Jesus drops upon the soul the weight of His incomparable love. The shadow of the Cross envelops her and a ray from heaven illumines her; she reaches the climax of happiness and of martyrdom.

Blessed the soul that allows herself to be loved completely so that Jesus may repose in her, pouring forth in that chosen heart the boundless ocean of His love!

THE REPOSE OF PURITY

There is in Scripture a charming phrase that the Church applies to the Virgin Mary: "He who fashioned me, He, my own Creator, has taken up His abode with me" (Eccles. 24:12). If the dignity of the creature is measured by its approximation to God, what must be the dignity of that woman blessed among all women, who was chosen that the Creator might repose in her womb and in her heart? If to possess God is the happiness of souls, what beatitude must that soul enjoy in whom infinite happiness rests? If sanctity is the reflection of God in souls, what holiness is comparable to that of her who is the resting place of the divinity?

For God, to rest is to inundate with His plenitude the one in whom He rests, to remain there in a definitive manner, to give Himself without measure, to communicate Himself without reserve, to hand Himself over forever. Who can tell or imagine what is contained in that unfathomable phrase: "He who fashioned me, He, my own Creator, has taken up His abode with me" (Eccles. 24:12)?

In order that the Word of God, infinite purity, might rest upon earth, the Lord formed an incomparable purity unequaled for all time. God formed it by treasuring up in Mary the purity of a divine fecundity. The divine Sun of love needed a heaven of purity so that it might shine there. Jesus rests also in souls like Mary's, though not in the same degree or plenitude.

The Canticle of Canticles sings that "ever He would choose the lilies for His pasture ground" (Cant. 6:2). Jesus passes by what is not pure just as He passed near sinners to cleanse them, just as He passed near the human race to redeem it. He goes everywhere, even through muddy places, and He does not become soiled, just as the sun touching the mire is not stained. But in order to rest, He needs a field of lilies; only in purity does He rest.

A field of lilies attracts the Divine Beloved and enraptures Him with the virginal fragrance of its flowers and, holding Him captive, it makes Him repose there. What does purity have, that it attracts Jesus, captivating Him and alluring Him to rest?

Just as it might be said that a mirror has a capacity for reflecting light, so purity in a soul has a capacity for reflecting God. Glass, because it is transparent, permits the light to penetrate it; purity, because it contains nothing carnal, can be impregnated with God, who is light. The purer the soul, the better it contains the divine. Scripture states that purity brings us nearer to God. Therefore, virginity, which is a sublime purity, gives souls possessing it the right to follow the Lamb wherever He goes and to sing a new song that only virgins know.

Since for Jesus, to repose in a soul is to pour into her His plenitude, that sweet rest presupposes an immense capacity in the soul for the heavenly, and consequently, a high degree of purity.

Between Jesus and purity there exists a profound harmony. Everything in Him is purity: His eternal origin because He was engendered by the Eternal Father in the glory of sanctity; His temporal origin because He was born of the most pure Virgin Mary; His celestial expression, His living words, His most holy deeds. Purity is His native atmosphere, His dwelling place, the perfume in His wake. His doctrine is holy; His morality is most chaste; His Cross is a torrent of purity; His Church, a field of lilies; His sacraments, wellsprings of purity; and His Eucharist, the sacrament of purity, the bread that nourishes souls with celestial innocence, the wine that engenders virgins.

As purity harmonizes only with purity, Jesus seeks innocent souls in order to unite Himself with them, or He purifies souls, making them heavenly, to accomplish in them the mystery of His love. Therefore, the Spouse who feeds among the lilies reposes in purity. As the dove returned to the Ark because there was no place to alight on the flooded earth, so when Jesus encounters souls deluged in sin, He does not find a place for His virginal foot and He returns, so to speak, to the bosom of His Father, waiting for the souls to be purified.

All that pleases and delights Jesus, all that retains Him in souls is related to purity: the love that enraptures Him, the sacrifice that anoints His heart with the perfume of myrrh, the humility that attracts Him, the simplicity that captivates Him. All virtues produce purity—crown and splendor of them all. A pure soul is for Jesus an enclosed garden where the flowers of all the virtues bloom and whose air is perfumed with emanations from paradise. To this most delightful garden the Beloved comes; in it He dwells and in it He finds His repose.

In a pure soul nothing disturbs the calm of Jesus, and everything attracts Him. A sinless soul is for Him a close imitation of Mary's heart, a reminder of the most pure bosom of the heavenly Father. Jesus works prodigies in order to impregnate with purity the soul where His rest is being prepared: He pours out His graces upon that chosen one in torrents; He cultivates in her the flowers of all the virtues, watering them from the heavenly springs—the gifts of the Holy Spirit. Each word of Jesus resounds within the soul, each glance of His divine eyes brings a new increase of purity, while the divine purification of suffering fills her life, cleanses her and imparts to her a celestial luster. Therefore, the soul feels the imperious necessity of increasing in purity so that Jesus' repose within her may be more delightful each day.

The Virgin Mary has no equal, but she can have and should have many imitators. One way of imitating her—and not the least charming—is by offering Jesus the repose of purity. Then the soul, like a weak but exact echo of Mary's voice, can repeat this heavenly phrase: "He who fashioned me, He, my own Creator, has taken up His abode with me" (Eccles. 24:12).

The Repose of Fruitfulness

Jesus grants a divine intimacy to the souls He loves. He makes them instruments of His action and in them He continues His sacrifice. To each one of these gifts corresponds a special kind of repose for Jesus. Those already considered—repose of light, of love and of purity—are forms of the repose of intimacy; the one I am going to discuss now is the repose of fecundity and action.

Jesus is sufficient for Himself to accomplish His marvels, but He desired to use us as His instruments, as much to honor us and give us an occasion of merit, as to establish intimate, spiritual relations among souls, like those of which St. Paul speaks when he says: "Yes, you may have ten thousand schoolmasters in Christ, but not more than one father; it was I that begot you in Jesus Christ when I preached the gospel to you" (1 Cor. 4:15).

Not all the instruments that Jesus employs are equally docile, equally productive; some hinder the efficacy of the divine action, others diminish it. How few are those who faithfully promote the designs of Jesus!

Souls that are always disposed to serve Jesus as He wishes, without measuring their strength, without counting the sacrifices, those that forget themselves to follow the divine impulses with docility, souls who are faithful in fulfilling the mission that Jesus has pointed out to them and who accomplish the divine work lovingly and faultlessly, are a delightful repose for Jesus.

Jesus rested in St. Peter. After receiving three times his impressive profession of love, He placed souls and the Church in St. Peter's hands, and for nineteen centuries he has been accomplishing the God-given work with exemplary love, heroic abnegation and perfect fidelity.

A perfect type of this repose is Mary most holy. Jesus desired her to be the universal instrument of the works that He accomplishes for souls, not by an exterior mystery, as in the case of St. Peter, but by a fecundity that was interior yet efficacious. He desired that she be the Co-redemptrix of the human race by her love and her sacrifice, the Mediatrix of all graces who, in Jesus and for Jesus, has a universal and most gracious maternity in regard to souls.

Jesus enjoyed all His modes of rest in Mary in an admirable manner, with singular plenitude and with perfect peace. In the course of the centuries, Jesus selects souls who in a greater or lesser degree participate in St. Peter's mission, such as priests. Other souls participate in Mary's mission in various degrees.

Happy the apostolic souls who, following Peter in his humble love and selfless fidelity, provide rest for Jesus. Happy are those who, sharing in Mary's mission by an interior fecundity, offer to Jesus the repose of Mary's maternal heart.

To offer Jesus this kind of rest, one needs virtues that are neither few nor ordinary. A comparison will be helpful. Let us consider one of the instruments that we employ in our everyday tasks. A pen, for example, must have certain qualities in order to be useful. It must not be self-moving; if it were, it would upset the push we give it and instead of writing what we want, we would write something else. The soul that serves God as an instrument should have neither initiative nor movement so that our Lord may write what He wishes. In order to be God's instrument, complete self-forgetfulness is needed: renunciation in selecting our work or employment, so that we do what our Lord has marked out for us rather than what attracts or pleases us; abnegation in accomplishing the divine work without seeking our own honor or profit, but only the glory of God and the pleasure of His heart; selflessness in arranging everything relative to that work without reference to ourselves, thinking only about God and His holy will.

The pen needs to be held in my hand, otherwise it would not write my thoughts. Likewise, in order that a soul do God's work, it needs to be united to Him. The more intimate and binding this union, the better instrument this soul will be and Jesus will rest in her with greater happiness. So it was that before giving St. Peter charge of souls, Christ wanted to be sure of his love, for love, by uniting us to Him, makes us perfect instruments of His action. Love, a self-denying love, ardent, docile, blind, surrendering self, giving self without reserve—this is the great virtue of an apostle, the indispensable requisite so that Jesus may find this delightful repose in our souls. When a soul forsakes the divine will in her apostolate, doing some work other than that which Jesus marked out for her, the union of that soul with Jesus is imperfect; her love does not have the ardor, the fidelity and the purity of true apostolic love.

The pen must follow the movement of my hand with docility; if it lacks flexibility, it will not write what I want, and it will cost me a great deal of effort to write. Similarly the soul that Jesus uses as an instrument must be docile and flexible under the divine action, must accommodate herself to all the demands of God's will, and must accomplish even in the least details the divinely appointed task.

When the work ends, the pen is laid down; it returns to an inactive state, without being affected either by the success or the failure of its performance. If what the pen wrote merits praise, the honor redounds to the writer, not to the pen. This should be the attitude of the soul that God has used as the instrument of His marvelous work. It returns to silence and tranquility without admiring itself or glorying in what God wrought through it means. The Evangelist points out that the faithful servant, after having served his master devotedly, should say sincerely and simply: "We are servants, and worthless; it was our duty to do what we have done" (Luke 17:10).

What perfect self-forgetfulness, what loving surrender, what heroic abnegation, what gentle pliability, and what extreme fidelity the soul must have to serve Jesus as the instrument of His action in such a way that He may rest in her!

GREAT VIRTUES are necessary in souls so that in a mystical and obscure manner they may possess a divine fruitfulness similar to that possessed by Mary—greater virtues, perhaps, than in souls that God chooses for an external mystery.

That heavenly Lady and Mistress, who helped Jesus in a universal and perfect way in the magnificent work of the redemption of the human race, possessed a humility so deep that God, the Omnipotent, whose name is holy, wrought great things in her. She has a fidelity so perfect that the Church calls her "Virgin most faithful"; she had a maternal love, pure, disinterested and tender to the degree that she loved Jesus as no one else has ever loved Him, not even the seraphim, and that love is the best imitation of the Father's love. She shared as no one else the suffering of Jesus, whence she is justly called Queen of Martyrs. Therefore Jesus reposed in her, communicating to her a universal and perpetual fecundity so that she might be the mother of all souls and all might receive from her the torrents of grace flowing from the divine plenitude of Jesus.

In this respect, sacerdotal souls and those whom Jesus has willed to share in Mary's spiritual fecundity ought to imitate this most holy Mother so that Jesus may find in them the repose of fruitfulness. To this end they need to be humble even to the point of forgetfulness; docile and yielding even to having no initiative, will or taste of their own; loving and tender as a mother and selfless even to heroism; faithful and careful even to the stage of denying nothing to Jesus and not hesitating before anything in order to do His work and to share in His fruitfulness. These souls should serve as an instrument in all that pleases Him, without ever stopping under the pretext of humility or through a false idea of reverence.

Productiveness increases in souls in proportion to their nearness to the heavenly Father from whom comes all fecundity in heaven and on earth. Therefore, the desire to offer Jesus this kind of repose must characterize their spiritual life by a most binding union with the Father. In Him, Jesus and souls find their supreme rest. In order to offer perfect rest to Jesus, it is necessary to enter into the bosom of the Father and there to be immersed in His tenderness and to participate most copiously in His fecundity.

WHEN FRUITFULNESS increases in souls, the virtues and dispositions that such souls need, to offer repose to Jesus, must also increase. Self-forgetfulness must be more perfect to destroy their restraint before God's designs and to promote those divine plans with simplicity and audacity, however lofty and other-worldly they may seem. They must permit themselves to be directed with perfect flexibility by the Holy Spirit so that there is nothing in them, as far as possible, that is not arranged and moderated by the Spirit of God.

These souls ought to increase their love to limitless lengths, if this be possible to a creature, and with love should grow the qualities inherent in it—purity, tenderness, zeal, delicacy, disinterestedness. They should enlarge their heart so that Jesus may repose more sweetly, and so that all the souls engendered for God by that divinely prolific heart may fit into it. The repose of fruitfulness has this prerogative, that instead of offering Jesus only one heart, it offers Him thousands of hearts mystically united to His fruitful heart.

Even suffering, however plentiful it may have been during life, must be augmented, if not in extent, then certainly in intensity, in sensitivity, in courage, in merit. It must be a suffering more interior, more pure, more Godlike both in its origin and in its end.

And when death comes to put an end to exile, Jesus will repose in the fecund heart with the intimacies of heaven, with the eternal feast of beatific love. This repose of fruitfulness will be continued for the soul by offering the souls on earth that it engendered for God. Those souls are the fruit of its fecundity, inheritors of its purity, of its love, of its pain, mystical prolongations of its being. And the resting-place that they offer to Jesus will have for Him the same warmth, the same fragrance, the same softness as that upon which He reclined during so many years in this world.

The Repose of Suffering

That it pleased Jesus to repose in suffering is beyond dispute, for He rested on the Cross. A heart is at rest when its ardent desires are satisfied, for rest is nothing else than the satisfaction of our desires. One of the most burning desires of the Heart of Jesus was to suffer, to plunge into that ocean of sorrow: His passion.

"There is a baptism I must needs be baptized with," He said on one occasion, "and how impatient am I for its accomplishment" (Luke 12:50). That baptism, without doubt, was His passion; when He accomplished it even to the crucifixion, His heart was in repose because His desires were fulfilled.

It is not necessary to discourse at length to understand how suffering could bring rest to Jesus, since the sacrifice of Calvary satisfied the yearning of His soul, the love of His heart. Before all else, Jesus longed to glorify His celestial Father, to render Him the supreme glory that was the purpose of the Incarnation and the Divine Word.

St. Ignatius Loyola urges us to seek the greater glory of God in all things. This motto is the motto of love, since love seeks the good of the beloved, and the only good that we can give to God is to glorify Him. But the greater glory that we seek to give to God is something relative, proportioned to our capacity. Jesus, however, rendered to His heavenly Father the greatest absolute glory, for the supreme height of glorification is doubtless a God who suffers and dies to glorify God. Therefore, the Word of God became flesh in order to offer infinite glory to the Father. The divinely chosen form for this supreme glorification was sacrifice, which is the death of the victim to expiate sins, repair offenses against God and acknowledge the supreme and absolute dominion of God over all things.

Therefore St. Paul says that Jesus, "to win His prize of blessedness, endured the cross and made light of its shame" (Heb. 12:2). The same Apostle teaches us that the will of the Father, which Christ came to fulfill and to which He referred when He said upon entering the world: "I am coming to fulfill what is written of Me" (Ps. 39:8), is precisely the sacrifice of the Cross. With this sacrifice Jesus gave to His Father the highest glorification and, consequently, fulfilled the deepest desire of His heart. His highest love. His supreme passion. How contentedly Jesus must have rested upon His most painful Cross!

After the Father, Jesus loves souls. These two loves are fused into a divine unity in the Most Sacred Heart of Jesus, since the good of souls is the glory of God. Impelled by this tremendous love for souls, Jesus longed to give them a supreme proof of His love and to do them the greatest good consonant with the loving designs of God. This supreme proof and this greater good are realized in the sacrifice of Calvary, because, as He Himself said: "This is the greatest love a man can show, that he should lay down his life for his friends" (John 15:13), and because the sacrifice of the Cross had as its divine fruits our redemption, our sanctification and our glorification.

It can be said, therefore, that the boundless desires of Jesus' heart were satisfied on Calvary, and hence that this Heart found rest on the Cross. This repose was so complete that the sacrifice of Jesus satisfied His desires, glorified His Father and wrought good to souls. Jesus wanted that sacrifice to be immortal, and in His wisdom, omnipotence and love He found the mystical way in which His sacrifice might continue in the Eucharist and in souls. Since the sacrifice of Jesus is eternal in those two forms, the Sacred Heart reposes constantly in the Eucharist and in souls.

Upon the Eucharistic altars, Christ's sacrifice is ever perpetuated. The Father, appeased, accepts the fragrance of honor arising to Him from the earth at every moment. The words of the prophet are realized: "No corner of the world, from sun's rise to sun's setting, where the renown of Me is not heard among the Gentiles, where sacrifice is not done, and pure offering made in My honor" (Mal. 1:11). How joyously Jesus rests in that everlasting sacrifice offered at each instant upon our altars!

The sacrifice of Jesus is also continued in the souls in which He lives and suffers mystically. Those souls are crosses and altars for Jesus, and in them He continues His triumphal sacrifice. Therefore, souls who thus immolate themselves are the repose of Jesus, the continuation of His rest upon the Cross, the complement of His repose upon the altars.

Although all holy suffering pleases Jesus, He rests only in perfect suffering, only in those souls who resemble Calvary's Cross, only in those who are like the altars upon which the Eucharistic sacrifice is offered.

On the cross and on the altars, sacrifice is not something accidental; the cross and altars are especially destined for sacrifice. So are the souls in whom Jesus finds His repose of pain, souls destined for sacrifice, true victims united to the great Victim, Jesus. For them, suffering is a portion of their inheritance, the gift that they have received from God, the character of their love, the seal of their mission. For them the mystery of love and of life, which they must contemplate, cherish and imitate, is the mystery of Calvary. They are myrrh trees living in the garden of the Church, scattering their fragrance whenever they are cut or bruised.

Souls that resemble the Eucharistic altars are sinless souls, just as the altars of sacrifice are spotless. With what solicitude and with what an array of ceremonies the Church purifies the altars that she consecrates! With what love and with what care the Lord cleanses the souls that He consecrates for suffering! Not every sorrow offers rest to Jesus. Only that sorrow which arises from a clean soul, a sorrow pure in origin, one that like the fragrant smoke of rarest incense proceeds from an unworldly heart, from a heaven-gifted soul, offers rest to Jesus.

To resemble the Cross and the altars, souls need to be united to Jesus and transformed into Him, because not only were the Cross and the altars destined for a very intimate contact with Jesus, but they are also the emblems of Christ. Therefore, so that Jesus may repose in souls, souls must be intimately united with Him. What is closer to us than the bed upon which we seek our rest? Jesus and His Cross are in closest contact. Before His most holy body rested upon it, He carried it in His heart. Joined together, they have illumined the world and spread upon it the fires of love; together they live in our churches and in our souls through all centuries, and on the last day, when Jesus will come, full of glory, to judge the living and the dead, the Cross will shine gloriously in the sky as a sign of love for the elect, as an emblem of eternal justice for the reprobate.

Jesus and the souls in whom He rests must also be united—nailed together like living crosses. The Cross is a symbol; it expresses the boundless sorrow with which eternal love espoused it when He came to earth to form with those two precious elements—appeased justice, that caused mercy and love to descend upon the earth, that knit together in one tender, mighty embrace the majesty of God and the misery of man. In the mystical sacrifice, in the perpetuation of Calvary that is accomplished in souls, Jesus is love, souls are suffering, and again the mystical nuptials are brought about, or rather, that unique espousal of love and of suffering is continued, so that sacrifice may continue always on earth, so that between heaven and earth the Son of Man may always be raised upon the perpetual Cross, and the victim of glory and of peace always joins God with man. What a penetrating union must exist between Jesus and the souls who serve Him as crosses and altars! Only eternal love can repose upon earth's pain, purified and sanctified by contact with Jesus.

The suffering in which Jesus rests must be the purest of the pure, because not every pain can receive, like a cross between its arms, the sweet burden of Him who is infinite purity. The suffering in which Jesus finds His repose must be pure in its origin, pure in its essence and pure in its purpose. Such a sorrow must come from a selfless soul; it must be exempt from smallness and egoism; it must be destined to scatter purity upon the earth. In a word, the suffering in which Jesus rests is not simply human suffering, but His very own, participated in by the creature and perpetuated in its soul-life.

Only the love of Jesus consecrated the Cross; no other sacrifice is offered on the altars than that of Jesus. Souls that serve as a resting place for Jesus because they are crosses and altars should not harbor in their heart any other sorrow than Jesus' sorrow because the suffering that they bear must have the same heaven-born origin, the same sublime characteristics, the same lofty ends as the sorrow of Jesus. The supreme victim, the only victim, is the one that is immolated in that soul, there continuing its loving, fruitful, ineffable sacrifice.

One should think that since the cross and sacrifice are such human things, they must terminate on earth and not enter deeply into the secrets of God. But it is not so. In order to accomplish Calvary's sacrifice, Love descended from heaven, clothed itself with our flesh, while pain, although the fruit of earth before its divine outpouring upon the Cross, ascended to heaven from the Heart of Christ. When that Sacred Heart was lanced, suffering intertwined with love produced the divine fountain of water and of blood that sanctifies the world.

Something similar happens with living crosses and their mystical sacrifice. First, love descends into the soul through the grace of the transforming union, and through the extraordinary efficacy of that remarkable grace of the soul's suffering, a poor creature's suffering ascends to the heaven of Jesus' heart and becomes pure, holy and fecund.

With Jesus, through Jesus, the soul ascends to the heaven of the divinity, and upon entering that divine dwelling, love and suffering bind themselves more strongly with the soul; love becomes more intense, and suffering more refined. Then Jesus, more closely united with His living cross, offers a perfect and more fruitful sacrifice.

Rejoice, blessed soul, who dost offer Jesus the mystical repose of suffering, the most precious heritage that has fallen to thy lot. Thou shalt never tire of offering to the Divine Victim thy body and soul to perpetuate that fruitful sacrifice upon the earth for the glory of the Father and the salvation of the world.

The Repose of Peace

Peace is the plenitude and the culmination of repose; it is perfect rest, rest without fear, rest with joy, changeless rest. To rest in peace, three things are necessary: all desires must be fulfilled, one must be in full possession of the desired object, and there must be certainty that this possession will never be lost. When Jesus' desires regarding a soul are all satisfied, when He possesses that soul totally, and when that satisfaction and possession are definitive and everlasting, Jesus rests in peace in that happy soul.

St. Thérèse of the Child Jesus wrote that Jesus had fulfilled her wishes. Could not Jesus say as well that little Thérèse had fulfilled all His wishes? She herself affirmed that she had never denied Him anything. Certainly He rested in peace in that heavenly soul.

How few souls gratify all the desires of Jesus! How many times we deny Him what He asks of us! How often we hamper His plans! At times we do gratify some of the wishes of Jesus, but again we ignore them. He keeps standing at the door of our heart, begging for what He wants. We leave Him there, for we do not intend to give in to Him.

Because Jesus is sensitive and refined, He respects our liberty, awaits our consent, so that He may carry out His designs in us. But many times through our lack of generosity He remains there with His graces in His hands, His projects in His soul, and His unfilled desires in His heart. Happy the souls who surrender to Jesus without reserve, who deny Him nothing, who accommodate themselves to His will, who give pleasure to Him in everything and who do not fail to fulfill lovingly all His desires; happy a thousand times because in them the Divine Beloved rests in peace.

Peace is like the essence extracted from all spiritual flowers, a fruit containing the honey and substance of all fruit. Perfect peace buds from the virtues and gifts with which Jesus has endowed the soul; it emanates from all the sacrifices and gifts that the soul makes to Jesus. Therefore, supreme blessedness for the soul is peace. Jesus greeted the apostles after the Resurrection by saying to them: "Peace be to you," because peace is the fruit of all the teachings of Jesus, of all the effusions of His love, of all the exhalations of His purity, of all the irradiations of His fecundity, of all the martyrdoms of His sufferings.

The peace that the soul offers to Jesus so that He may rest in her must be the synthesis of all kinds of rest, emanations from paradise formed with the aromas of all flowers. Light, love, fecundity, purity and pain must combine their fragrance harmoniously, in order to perfume the garden in which Jesus rests, so that He may find perfect repose in the soul.

IN ORDER that Jesus repose in the soul with the repose of peace, it is necessary that she interpret His intimacies with a clarity from heaven, that she give Him love, all the love He asks her for, and that she accept the great burden of tenderness that Jesus gives her, allowing herself to love perfectly. It is necessary that she be for Jesus a flowery field of lilies, offering to Him a couch of white petals with virginal fragrance. It is necessary that by an extraordinary fertility she give Him souls, many souls, spotless, faithful and loving, and that she mingle with the fragrance of lilies of purity, roses of love and the myrrh of suffering, the holy emanations from the altar, incense and the cross.

When all these celestial forms of repose are intertwined harmoniously, when they are reduced to a divine unity, each one occupying its proper place in this beautiful whole, then the mystical King of peace (Heb. 7:2) will be formed, "of Lebanon wood; a golden frame it must have, on silver props, with cushions of purple; within are pictured tales of love" (Cant. 3:9). There Jesus will rest in peace; there He will rest forever.

In order that Jesus repose in the soul, it does not suffice that all His desires be fulfilled. Each one of those desires must be satisfied entirely; Jesus must possess that soul totally. It is not sufficient that all flowers grow in that garden, they must all be brilliant and perfume the atmosphere profusely, so that the soul will disperse "the fragrance of the earth when the Lord's blessing is on it," as Scripture says (Gen. 27:27). Intense light, supreme love, heavenly purity, perfect fecundity and great suffering are prerequisites to offering Jesus the repose of peace. Souls in whom Jesus rests are those in whom the heavenly seed sown lavishly by the divine Sower bears a hundredfold.

Mary realized as no one else the ideal of the soul in whom Jesus finds peace. All virtues attained supreme perfection in her such a manner that one cannot say which virtue dominated her soul. Since it appears that all were equally dominant, what surprises us is the harmony that knits them together, and one does not know which to admire more: the perfect unity of the whole or the exceedingly rich variety of the elements composing it. Her purity casts angelic whiteness into the shade. Her love would suffice to inflame the universe. Her light is surpassed only by the Divine Sun, Jesus. Her fecundity has as its fruit the blessed fruit of the Father's fecundity, and her sorrow approximates Christ's sorrow in its immensity, for the dolorous Virgin stood at the foot of the glorious Cross. Souls in whom Jesus rests must resemble Mary.

THE SUMMIT of peace consists in the flight of all fear; still more, it consists in communicating the unspeakable joy of a blessed security. Peace does not exist when one fears to lose His possession. Heaven would not be the plenitude of happiness if it were not inamissible and everlasting. On earth, therefore, peace is rare and imperfect. Rather, peace does not exist upon this earth unless Jesus gives it, because on earth there is nothing inamissible and immortal; so our Lord said that the world cannot give peace.

How many sinless souls, loving, deluged with light, has Jesus possessed only to lose them eventually? He was forced to tear them away from Himself, like pieces of His own heart. Jesus rests in souls that are His forever, in those that exclaim with the Apostle:

"Neither death nor life…nor any other creature will be able to separate us from the love of God which comes to us in Christ Jesus" (Rom. 8:38).

In the souls in which Jesus peacefully reposes, there can be no passing eclipses of waning love, momentary wilting of fading roses, no fleeting separations of imperfect souls, not to speak of final and everlasting divorce.

True peace is the sure and perpetual fruition of what is loved. Peace always has the savor of eternity, and its heavenly delight consists precisely in this: that each drop of it contains an abundance and into each moment fits the fullness of eternity. When Jesus and a soul love and possess each other in time with that savor of eternity, when Jesus knows that the kiss of love which He imprints on the soul is eternal, and when the soul feels that the love she offers Jesus knows eternal life and that in each one of these caresses there is a touch of perpetuity, when both feel joyful because their mutual love is a never-setting sun, they live and rest in peace because immortal souls can repose only in the imperishable and immortal.

What a sweet paradise to be with Jesus! His divine kisses are drops from heaven. If we were to think that He might go away and those divine drops be lost forever, love would lose its indescribable delight; perfect love would not exist because "love drives out fear when it is perfect love" (1 John 4:18).

I dream of such a love, one that cannot be lost, a love that is never exhausted, a love that, although subject to the vicissitudes of exile, hides within itself the brightness of eternity, a love in which each kiss contains heaven, and each caress hides happiness, a love in which each look brings with it the light of glory, and in which each word is the only one, the supreme, eternal word of love.

If our poor heart cannot rest in a love that is amissible and finite, how could Jesus rest in any kind of love?

The repose of peace for Jesus, therefore, can be realized only in souls that have surrendered themselves completely, souls that give

Him at each moment all He asks, even at the cost of any sacrifice, and in souls whose love and possession know Jesus to be eternal life, because each look brings a glow of divine light, and each caress holds heaven, and each of His words is the unique, ineffable, eternal word of love!

CLUNY MEDIA

Designed by Fiona Cecile Clarke, the CLUNY MEDIA *logo
depicts a monk at work in the scriptorium,
with a cat sitting at his feet.*

*The monk represents our mission to emulate
the invaluable contributions of the monks
of Cluny in preserving the libraries of the West,
our strivings to know and love the truth.*

*The cat at the monk's feet is Pangur Bán, from the
eponymous Irish poem of the 9th century.
The anonymous poet compares his scholarly
pursuit of truth with the cat's happy hunting of mice.
The depiction of Pangur Bán is an homage to the work
of the monks of Irish monasteries and a sign
of the joy we at Cluny take in our trade.*

"Messe ocus Pangur Bán,
cechtar nathar fria saindan:
bíth a menmasam fri seilgg,
mu memna céin im saincheirdd."

Printed in the USA
CPSIA information can be obtained
at www.ICGtesting.com
LVHW092110260424
778412LV00006B/111/J

9 781950 970780